The Ministry of Children's Education

Foundations, Contexts, and Practices

Introduction by Margaret A. Krych

Fortress Press
Minneapolis

THE MINISTRY OF CHILDREN'S EDUCATION
Foundations, Contexts, and Practices

All Scripture quotations are from New Revised Standard Version Bible, copyright © 1989 Division of Christian Education of the National Council of Churches. Used by permission.

Editors: Barbara S. Wilson, Mark Gardner, and James Satter
Cover design: David Meyer
Cover photo: Getty Images

The paper used in this publication meets the minimum requirements of American National Standard for Information Sciences—Permanence of Paper for Printed Library Materials, ANSI Z329.48-1984.

Manufactured in the U.S.A.

08   07   06   05   04   1   2   3   4   5   6   7   8   9   10

CONTENTS

INTRODUCTION

T his is the fourth book written by the Christian education professors in Lutheran seminaries. The first, *Education for Christian Living* (edited by Marvin Roloff in 1987), focused on the whole educational enterprise in the congregation. The second, *Lifelong Learning* (edited by Rebecca Grothe in 1997), turned to adult education, while the third dealt with confirmation and youth, *Confirmation: Engaging Lutheran Foundations and Practices* (1999). The various issues covered in the three previous books cross denominational lines, but that is especially evident here. This book on educational ministry with children will be used widely by Christians of all persuasions who seek to fulfill the church's responsibility to its young members.

The Ministry of Children's Education: Foundations, Contexts, and Practices is exactly what the title suggests. This book gives a theological rationale for educational ministry with children, as well as very practical guidance for designing and implementing specific programs within that ministry. The authors are all passionate about their subject matter, and the chapters reflect their deep commitment to educational ministry with children and their desire to help the church find ever deepening ways to exercise that ministry today.

This comprehensive book covers a great deal of theoretical and practical ground. Each chapter introduces the main subject matter with a scenario from childhood, followed by the main content of the chapter. All of the chapters provide specific tools, such as discussion questions or teaching suggestions, to help readers process the information. The authors have designed the book for easy reading and engagement by those in congregational leadership with children, but they nevertheless draw on a vast array of scholarly resources and research that generally lie behind the scenes. Readers with little formal background in the field will find the material easy to follow.

We know more about child development and the needs of children today than at any time in the past. Yet problems and gaps in meeting children's needs in our society are clearly apparent—lack of funding for intervention programs, variable quality of education at the preschool and elementary school levels, inequitable distribution of medical and psychological services for children, unstable and hurried families that pressure children in an increasingly complex world, media that have both good and detrimental effects on children, the treatment of children as commodities in a capitalist society . . . The list goes on. At such a time, there is urgent need for the church's faithful and caring educational ministry with children and their families. This book highlights the importance of such ministry and is a welcome addition for equipping the people of God in their service of children. Grouped into three parts, this book deals with foundational issues, contexts, and practical guidance.

Part I is foundational, with two chapters on theological issues and a third on children's development. Chapter 1 develops a theological foundation for why, what, and how we teach children in the church. It helps congregations build a solid and articulate basis in the faith for developing and continuing a quality ministry of education with children. The chapter explores several doctrines for ways they call us to teach and also implications for what and how we teach. The chapter explores the work of Christ in justification, Baptism, ministry in "two kingdoms," the Word, and the church, and considers not only the basis they give for educational ministry with children but also their implications for content and methodology of children's educational ministry.

In chapter 2, Diane J. Hymans explores the psychological and intellectual development of children from birth to the beginning of adolescence and examines the question of how those dynamics relate to the growth of children in their lives of faith. Hymans first examines the theories of Erik Erikson and Jean Piaget for understanding children's development, then goes on to explore John Westerhoff's categories of *experienced faith* and *affiliative faith* as she traces the child from infancy through toddlerhood, preschool, elementary school, and into early adolescence. She includes an examination of Howard Gardner's multiple intelligences, and Kieran Egan's role of imagination in relation to faith.

In chapter 3, Norma Cook Everist examines the child in our society, viewed variously as problem, protégé, possession, in need of protection, and then as voiceless, victim, hero, and immature person. She notes that children are symbols and signs of an affluent society, of success and celebration, symbols of the holy and of the future, signs of security, yet signs of unsolved issues in our society. She finds in the Apostles' Creed the creating, providing, preserving, protecting, and empowering God. An examination of passages of Scripture elucidates the biblical understanding of the child. Everist then explores Martin Luther's views of children and education, and concludes with some brief verbal snapshots of children at various age levels.

Part II examines the various contexts for children's educational ministry, including home, media cultures, and the world at large. In chapter 4, Mary E. Hughes opens the section with the child in the home and family, broadly defined to include the many configurations of family. She defines family ministry as the church's efforts to strengthen families as they seek to live faithfully, which involves living together as family members, creating homes that are sacred spaces, and strengthening the home-church partnership. Hughes gives helpful resources, practical guidance for effective parenting, and comments on four special challenges for parenting: violence, disabilities, death, and sexual abuse. She also suggests ways to develop homes as sacred spaces and gives specific strategies for strengthening the home-church relationship.

Mary E. Hess focuses on the media culture as the primary context in which children's ministry takes place, and argues that communities of faith must understand children's ministry as a deliberate cultural intervention. She points to *cognitive*, *affective*, and *psychomotor* aspects of learning, discusses the importance of the incidental learning, and argues that the vast majority of learning takes place relationally. In the media culture, representations of relationality are fairly narrow and limited, so Hess suggests that we need to provide *confirmation*, *contradiction*, and *continuity* around issues of relationality for children and the adults who nurture them. Children's ministry is about creating a learning environment with adequate and appropriate support for learning with and from children.

Nelson T. Strobert deals with the topic of raising faithful children in the world. He explores the global perspective that is a part of everyday living in the United States and ways that Christian education must prepare our children for living, working, and thriving as children of God in the context of the global village. Strobert explores the biblical understanding of the global dimension of the gospel, and calls for religious education that will help children develop an international, intercultural, and global perspective yet preserve particularity. His chapter includes practical guidance for incorporating a global dimension in the classroom with children.

Part III covers five practical topics for congregational life: building an overall comprehensive children's ministry program; connecting children and the Bible; teaching in engaging ways; supporting families, and energizing congregations to learn together.

Chapter 7 seeks to enlarge our vision of an overall program for children's ministry in the congregation by first developing appropriate congregational objectives for educational ministry with children and then training teachers and leaders. These steps are followed by the developing of settings that will fulfill the congregation's goals for educational ministry with children. The author explores 13 settings for educational ministry with children, a number of which will be viable in most congregations. They include independent learning, overnight events, opportunities in the children's free time, weekly classes, one-on-one learning, family learning, children's interest groups, worship services, community groups, church-sponsored schools, choirs and music programs, and public and local media. Guidance is given for starting the overall program and for keeping it going.

In chapter 8, Carol R. Jacobson deals with how the Bible can be used with children in appropriate and life-giving ways. She brings to the chapter her own love of the Bible and her experience of teaching it to children. Some of the questions that Jacobson pursues are: What does it mean to understand the Bible, and what do we wish to accomplish in engaging children with the Bible? Are young children capable of understanding the Bible stories? Are they ready for the complexities and questions they will encounter in the biblical narratives? Can children engage the Bible in ways that don't just confuse them at best, or cause them harm at worst? She argues persuasively that children can engage and experience the Bible and are often skilled interpreters of it from their own perspectives.

In chapter 9, Susan Wilds McArver discusses teaching methods that engage children. She builds on the premise that children learn best when they are most directly involved as active participants in their own learning. McArver explores six themes found in the writings of Martin Luther that relate to teaching children and that have application for today. Then she recommends 10 core principles to keep in mind while preparing active, engaging, learning activities for children. The chapter concludes with a number of useful pedagogical techniques for experiential learning through storytelling, crafts, multimedia, field trips, guests, games, and music.

In the final chapter, Nathan C. P. Frambach deals with the congregation's ministry to children, which is the birthright of the baptized and is the privilege and responsibility of all adults. He points out the importance of all ages together in the community of God, and of relationships in an intergenerational environment that nurtures the faith of the young, helps them discover and exercise their gifts, and aids them to live into their calling as sons and daughters of God. The best approach, Frambach believes, is to provide apprenticeship in Christian leadership, and thus integrate, equip, and empower children to be agents of the faith and bearers of the Christian gospel.

All in all, *The Ministry of Children's Education: Foundations, Contexts, and Practices* is a resource that will help congregational leaders, teachers, and pastors think more deeply about the importance of educational ministry with children and also grapple with new and practical ways of engaging that ministry. The authors profoundly hope that their contributions will be of benefit to the church, and that their own joy and delight in ministries with children will be communicated through these pages in a way that will ignite in the readers a passion for children's educational ministries in the congregations to which they belong.

Margaret A. Krych

PART I

Foundations

CHAPTER I

Theology of Christian Education for Children

Margaret A. Krych

Overheard (on bicycles)

"Boy, WILL I BE GLAD to get into junior high and stop going to Sunday school."

"Why? Don't you like it? I think Mr. Samford is neat."

"Oh, he's okay for a teacher. But I mean, you don't see adults going to Sunday school, do you? Or high school kids. I'm not going once I get out of sixth grade. There's no point in it anyway. You hear the same stuff over and over again. We know it already. Anyway, my parents said I could drop it."

Heard (in committee meeting)

"I THINK WE WASTE too much time and effort on children's education. For centuries the church put its efforts into teaching adults. I think we should get back to that."

"I'm really glad to hear you say that. A church our size can't afford to have learning for all age levels, and we've focused on kids for too long. I think we should put all the kids together in one class with one teacher, and then we'd have enough volunteers to teach teenagers and adults."

"Yes. That way we would teach the parents, and they could teach the kids. Isn't that what Luther wanted when he wrote the Catechism?"

"Wait a minute, you two—you aren't suggesting we just stop Sunday school for children, are you? I don't think our parents would be able to handle it—certainly not for years. Besides, you can't put all ages of children in one class with one teacher. It won't work."

I s Sunday school a waste of the child's time—a hearing over and over of the "same stuff that they already know"? Is children's learning itself a waste of the church's valuable person and time resources? Should we put all children together and spend our efforts teaching youth and adults?

Martin Luther would answer a resounding no to the second of these three questions, which is a good place to start on the issue of the church's responsibility to teach the young. (We will get to the other questions as we go along.) Luther was passionate about education for all age levels, children as well as youth and adults. In his preface to the Small Catechism, he begged the pastors and preachers "to help us bring the catechism to the people, especially to the young."[1] Luther's concern for teaching children and adults was grounded in the gospel: the desire that all might hear the good news of forgiveness of sins through the mercy of Christ alone. In this chapter we will consider the theological foundations of educational ministry with children and some implications that arise from those foundations for the way we teach in the church.

Historical background

It is true that the focus in the early church was on the teaching of adults. Adults (including those we now call teenagers) were those who were being converted and baptized. So if households included children, then the children would have been taught as part of the household's learning about the faith.

When Christianity became an approved religion under Constantine, more and more children needed instruction in the faith following baptism. The home was the locus of catechization in the Middle Ages.[2] Luther appreciated the practice of domestic education, which was reflected when he wrote the Small Catechism:

> [Luther] calls upon a coalition of three groups—government officials, pastors, and parents—to take responsibility for the teaching and training of the young in the faith. . . . Of these three groups, Luther placed the greatest emphasis on the family. From the very beginning of the evangelical movement, parents were enlisted as valued allies in the formation of holy households.[3]

In the preface to the Large Catechism, Luther adjures the heads of households to examine the children weekly in the knowledge of the catechism.[4] Unfortunately, many parents were unable or unwilling to fulfill their teaching responsibilities, and the reformers increasingly turned to pastors, schoolteachers, and secular authorities to help in instructing children in the faith. However, their role remained supplemental to that of the family.[5]

Eventually in Europe, with the establishment of schools that seemed to do a much better job of teaching, parents began to assume less responsibility for the Christian education of their offspring. Catechetical instruction became more and more the prerogative of the schools.

The Sunday school movement in England, which began as a means to educate poor children to read and write, gradually became solely a religious institution as public education became the norm for all children. The Sunday school movement spread to North America at the end of the 18th century and into the 19th century. Parents increasingly began to delegate the religious education of children to the institutional church. Today, even the role of godparents or sponsors has often turned into simply the giving of gifts on birthdays and baptismal anniversaries.

More recently, we have begun to recover the role of the whole community of faith in learning and teaching, including that of children.[6] Within the faith community, good education in class settings is indeed a tried and true way for the Word of God to be communicated in age-appropriate ways to children, and is often one of the options in a comprehensive congregational program of education for children. See the chapter "Building a Children's Ministry Program." In the classroom, the teacher should endeavor to incorporate experiences of communal friendship and fellowship, and seek to provide a wide variety of learning procedures, so that the good news of Jesus Christ is engaging and exciting for children. Of course, it is appropriate and desirable that the children will also be incorporated into the wider life of the community in the many group experiences (other than classes) that abound in congregations for worship, social events, service, and just plain fun for all ages. Such experiences also are likely to become both teaching and learning opportunities.

Theology as foundation

Theology gives a foundation for why, what, and how we teach in the church. First, it gives a reason for teaching. It answers the question, "Why is it necessary for the church to teach children?" Second, it also gives the content that we teach, acting as an anchor and corrective to our own whims and fancies, and keeping the teaching of all age levels, including children, grounded in Scripture. It guides the curriculum and deals with the question, "What does the church teach children?" Third, theology is the norm for our methods. It gives a criterion in the gospel for how we operate in the classroom, what we do, the objectives we set, and the way we relate to children. It also serves to warn us about procedures we need to avoid if our actions are to be consistent with our spoken message. Thus, theology deals also with the question, "How does the church teach children?"

In other words, we can't talk about our beliefs without also asking how those beliefs affect what we teach children and the way we teach them. It is all part of a package. The next sections look at several doctrines and not only say why they call us to teach but also some implications of what this means for what and how we teach.

The gospel

The Augsburg Confession of 1530 (Article VII) declares that "we cannot obtain forgiveness of sin and righteousness before God through our own merit, work, or satisfactions, but that we receive forgiveness of sin and become righteous before God out of grace for Christ's sake through faith when we believe that Christ has suffered for us and that for his sake our sin is forgiven and righteousness and eternal life are given to us."[7]

This article points us to the amazing reality of God's work for us in Jesus Christ to bring us back, to reconcile us, to God's own self. Separated from God by sin, we have no way of helping ourselves, of working upward to earn God's acceptance of us. We stand under the judgment of God for the rebellion and disobedience that permeates us "in thought, word, and deed," as the prayer of confession has it. But God in mercy and unbounded love came to our rescue in Jesus Christ and brought us back to God through Christ's death on the cross. God's gracious activity in Christ was not the result of anything we did or could do but was totally undeserved, purely out of divine love that accepts the unacceptable in spite of the fact that we are unacceptable.[8] The gospel is this good news of God's generous love and forgiveness in Jesus Christ for all who believe. Our appropriate response is faith—trust in God's promises and mercy in Jesus Christ. Such faith is a gift of the Holy Spirit, called forth through the Word which judges and condemns and reveals our sin (law) and yet proclaims God's gracious merciful forgiveness (gospel). So we say that the Word kills and makes alive as the Holy Spirit works daily in the life of the Christian. God's gracious love is good news for every age level, even when the child is so young that she cannot grasp ideas such as *gracious* or *sinful*. And so, in the church we look for ways to communicate the good news from the earliest years on through the whole life span in ways that learners can grasp and appropriate and, most of all, experience at the heart of their existence. We teach so that they may rejoice and delight in God's free gift.

Some argue that the gospel is basically communicated through preaching in the gathered assembly,[9] and therefore that Christian education can be nothing more than reflecting on preaching or preparing for it.[10] However, other theologians such as Paul Tillich believe that the God's word is communicated through teaching situations as well as through preaching. Therefore, teachers are those who proclaim the gospel in educational settings, especially to the young.[11] In this chapter, we will follow Tillich's lead.

An important issue is where to start teaching content, that is, teaching the good news of Jesus. Martin Luther reversed the order of medieval catechisms that began with faith and moved to contrition to satisfaction. He replaced this order with a new one—the Commandments (law) that drive us to Christ and then to the prayer that turns us to God for help.[12] Luther knew that we do not fulfill the Commandments. Instead they show us who we are, the law-breakers. This drives us to the "medicine" of Christ's work for the forgiveness of sins. "The ordering reflected the heart of Luther's theology of the cross, namely, that God kills in order to make alive. Theology begins with the recognition that humankind stands under the evaluating eye of God."[13] It then moves to the work of Christ for salvation.

Tillich followed Luther's law-gospel pattern in teaching. He saw that the Word of God does two things in our daily lives through the work of the Holy Spirit: it judges (kills, condemns) us, and it proclaims God's merciful forgiveness (makes us alive). Tillich believed that this pattern is essential for the content as well as the methodology of teaching. He always started with the human situation, our need and our inability to do anything to help ourselves get back to God, and then he correlated God's good news with that need. In other words, by following the Reformation tradition he sought to make clear to the learner that God's work in Jesus is exactly what we need, and the most important thing that we need. Tillich's way of putting it was that we all have deep questions to which the gospel is the answer. This answer is a gift from God, spoken to our existence from beyond it.

Such a question-answer pattern is indeed helpful in teaching children (although the phrase "law and gospel" itself will be beyond their comprehension). As a teaching tool, the pattern reminds us that we need to consider in what ways those deep questions emerge for children and how the answer of the gospel meets just those questions and needs. Sometimes people think that children are basically happy and innocent, unaware of negative things in themselves or in the world. In fact, psychologists tell us that children have experiences of alienation, self-centeredness, hostility, and guilt. The deep questions that emerge from such experiences need the answer of the gospel, and this will be the case long before the child will use the term *sin*. Specific stories of God's love and mercy, of Jesus' kindness and helpfulness, of Jesus' concern for children, will help children to identify Jesus as the answer to their deepest needs.

The basic source for Christian learning about the gospel is the Bible. Therefore, the Bible will always have the primary role in the content that we teach children in the church. We will also want to instruct children in the story of God's people led by the Spirit of God through the centuries since the point when the Bible story ends.[14] In all teaching, the gospel message must come alive for children—it must affect their very existence. We must relate the Bible story to the life experiences of the child.

The gospel at various age levels

Why teach different age levels separately? Why not put them all together? This is an issue with which many congregations wrestle, especially those with limited resources. The answer to grouping children must be informed by the gospel. We want each age level to hear the gospel in ways that are relevant and understandable to them. This is not a simple task because children think in qualitatively different ways than adults and actually develop through different stages of thinking as they move through childhood. Therefore, grouping will need to take account of these different stages of thinking if we wish to communicate the gospel in appropriate ways for children.

Children's brains develop to maturity over roughly the same number of years as the rest of the body. That is, they do not reach the adult stage of thinking until at least age 12. From birth to age 2, the child's thinking moves through three stages that often are grouped together as the *sensorimotor* stage. Then the child enters the *preoperational* stage (usually lasting from around ages 2 to 7), followed by the *concrete-thinking* stage (roughly ages 7 to 12). Finally, the child develops the ability to think the way teenagers and adults do, somewhere around age 12 or beyond. Given individual differences in genetic timetables, some children will develop faster or more slowly than others; it is usually safe to assume that the vast majority of children will have completed this process by age 15.[15]

In the *preoperational* stage children are not yet able to reason logically. They see things only from their own point of view, reason from particular to particular, cannot relate parts to the whole, and cannot reverse their thinking to check the accuracy of reasoning. Nor can they distinguish between fact and fantasy. Therefore, their thinking may appear to adults to be distorted or amusing. While absolutely appropriate for their age level, their mode of thinking makes it tricky for teachers to communicate theologically with preschoolers. Sometimes teachers become impatient because they are anxious to pass on all of the faith at once to the young believer. As teachers, we need to relax. Most of us would laugh at or reject out of hand the thought that someone would try to teach algebra or calculus to a 3-year-old. Yet we sometimes forget that the theological reasoning in the Bible is just as complex as algebra. That is, it requires the same kinds of reasoning ability. Just as in math we look for simpler concepts and link them to age levels, so we must do the same when teaching the Bible. We are delighted when the 4-year-old begins to count, rejoice when the 5-year-old recognizes some written numbers, and begin to introduce addition to the child around 7 years of age. Then follows subtraction and eventually multiplication and division. So it is with the theological development of children. We can rejoice all along the way as their learning about God's love in Jesus Christ develops from the simpler ideas in early childhood to the more complex ones as they move into adolescence.

In the *concrete-thinking* stage from approximately 7 to 12 years, children progressively develop concepts of space, time, causality, and speed, the ability to generalize, to distinguish between fact and fantasy, to see the viewpoint of others, and to grasp simple concrete similes (characteristics that can be perceived through the senses). At about 9 or 10 years of age, children begin to take intentionality into account when judging right and wrong; they develop more mature moral concepts and grasp forgiveness in a new way. Whereas around ages 6 or 7 children understand death as universal, by 10 years or older they begin to grasp the irrevocability of death and the cessation of bodily functions.

With these new ways of thinking, concrete thinkers are clearly able to grasp a great deal more of the Bible and traditional Christian teaching than they were able to do as preschoolers. However, the *concrete-thinking* child is still limited to thinking about those things that, in principle, are perceivable through the senses. They will give sensory referents to those things that are not perceivable through the senses simply because there is no other way they can think about these subjects.

In all parts of the world, usually somewhere around 12-plus years of age, children's brains mature to the point where they are able to use *formal operations* (abstract thinking). Now children can reason from general principles to specific actions, posit hypotheses and draw logical conclusions, consider alternatives, identify all possible combinations, and analyze their own thinking.[16] They can grasp universal generalizations and use metaphor. They can reason about something that, in principle, cannot be perceived through the senses, can imagine ideals and perfection they have never encountered, and can reason about that which is actually contrary to fact. All of these new skills are critical to mature theological thinking and are typical of the thinking presupposed by biblical writers who themselves were adults and who used such thinking in their daily lives and in their writings.

It should be clear at least that we cannot lump all ages of children together and communicate the same content to them. If we do, we either will shortchange the older children or teach over the heads of the younger children. The tragedy is that some child will not hear the gospel in ways that make sense for his or her deepest needs at that point in life. Since young children's comprehension is at a different stage from that of elementary children, at the very least we need to group children so that God's good news is presented appropriately at each cognitive stage. Further, since the social and emotional experiences and needs of the preschooler are different from those at the early elementary and later elementary years, pastorally and educationally it makes sense to group children so that the gospel may be related to all aspects of their life, not just the cognitive level.

The gospel in content

The youngest children need to know that God loves them all the time, even when other children, siblings, parents, or other adults are mean or angry or irritated. Because their experience is so limited, young children need reassurance over and over that God loves them. Because they are so tied to the particular, children need to hear their own name at the end of the sentence "God loves you, _____ ."[17]

For this reassurance to be meaningful, the child already needs to know existentially, even if unable to express in words, the experiences of love, trust, security, and safety. Parents or other caregivers usually meet these deep needs from the moment of birth. Without such experiences, it is difficult for the child to understand what "God loves you" means. A daughter who has been sexually abused will understand something very different from what you mean when you say, "God loves us just like a father." Therefore, theologically and pastorally, the first teachers of Christian education for children are their parents, whether they recognize it or not. Throughout this chapter, the term *parents* means the primary caregivers of the child, whether they are biological parents, adoptive parents, foster parents, grandparents, group-home caregivers, or other guardians. However, the parental role as teacher should not merely be by default. Christian parents should understand their calling from God to be the Christian educators of their children from birth. Pastors have an important role in delivering this message when preparing parents for the baptism of their children.

With the youngest children you need to move quickly to gospel. The law is meant to drive us to the gospel, but how can it do so unless we first know something of God's love for us in Jesus? Very young children have not heard enough of Jesus to have an ongoing awareness of the good news. They need constant reassurance and reminders. Don't overemphasize God's wrath and judgment; these can be frightening concepts for a preschooler. On the other hand, we do not want to imply that sin does not matter or is trivial. Children can understand that there is something wrong between ourselves and God, ourselves and others, and ourselves and the people God intends us to be. Just be sure to reiterate the amazing love of God for the child.

With older children, you can emphasize the gracious gift quality of the gospel. Jesus Christ came to reveal God's love for all and to bring forgiveness, which we could not earn, on our own. He did this before we even knew about it. As children develop an understanding of time during the *concrete-thinking* stage, they will appreciate that God loved them even before they were born and every moment since. God will always love them as far ahead as they can imagine, all their lives and beyond.

Older children still need to hear that God loves them when other people are angry or cruel. They need to know that they can count on God's love even when other children taunt them, as often happens during the elementary years. When children experience alienation and rejection, as they do at times in even the best of families, they must know that God's love continues whether or not they are popular, earn wonderful report cards, or are chosen for the team.[18] Knowing God's acceptance, care, and forgiveness can fulfill the child's need at the deepest level.

Around age 10, when children develop a more mature moral understanding and grasp forgiveness in a new way, you can provide opportunities for class members to confess sin and speak the word of forgiveness to one another. For this to happen, you need to have a high level of trust in the classroom between teacher and students as well as between the class members themselves.

Even though children may not understand the full import of sin and salvation, you will want to avoid using phrases that are antithetical to the gospel and that can interfere with later learning about the gracious nature of God's free gift that we can never earn. For example, avoid saying, "God loves you just the way you are." That is not gospel! If God were content with us "just the way we are" there would have been no need for the cross. Rather, God accepts us as we are—broken, sinful—in spite of the way we are. Children are not fools. They know they aren't the spotless creatures that God asks them to be. Similarly, it should go without saying that we should avoid any implication that we can be as good as God wants if we would just try harder. Likewise, never say, "God loves good boys and girls and doesn't like bad boys and girls." It is precisely because we are *all* sinful that Christ was crucified.

Children's experiences of estrangement are most likely to be in the realm of personal relationships with friends, family, teachers, and other people important in their lives. Much of our teaching about God's acceptance and love will be focused in this area, on the answer of God's love in Jesus that brings us forgiveness and acceptance. But we should look for children's deep questions in other places too. Sometimes they will experience the limitations of their reason, to which the answer is God's wonderful presence in Jesus who told and showed us what God is like. Especially after age 7, children will experience the question in terms of death, to which the answer is that God who never dies will care for us forever, even after we die. Children also experience difficulties and loneliness in their daily lives at school, in families, and in communities, to which the answer is the ever-present Spirit of God always with us to comfort and help us. Finally, older children may have fears of war and planet pollution and natural catastrophes, to which the answer is God's promise one day to do away with everything that makes us sad and fearful.[19]

It takes wisdom and patience to try to engage the children's world and see things from their point of view. This is necessary if we are to communicate the gospel in ways that make sense to children. Our adult relationships and ways of thinking are very different from those of children. We often forget the world of our own childhood (which may be different from the world of children today). It will be helpful to spend time with children of various age levels, listening to their descriptions of their life and experiences, and then to reflect: How can the gospel relate to the questions these children are experiencing today?[20]

The gospel in action and attitude

It is not only through content and words that teachers communicate the gospel. At all ages of childhood, your own unconditional love for the child will reinforce the words you speak. The kind of love to which we are called is reflected in the Greek word *agape*. This is the quality of love that God has for us, that seeks the lost and accepts the unacceptable. Teachers in the church are called to accept children in spite of what they do and say. Children often feel rejected and judged by teachers, and teachers in turn feel frustrated and attacked by students. But "the educator who is filled with agape accepts the child and gives it the certainty that it is accepted in spite of its dislikes and doubts and protest and loveless actions."[21] Such agape love is not something we can develop on our own. It too is a gift of the Spirit.

Tillich reminds us that one of the problems in education is that teachers and students treat one another as objects to be manipulated and controlled. This happens in all of education, but in the church we have hope that secular educators do not have. We have the Holy Spirit, God's spiritual presence, who can transcend the split between teacher and student. In the grasp of the Spirit, "the attitude of superiority and the will to control the other one (for his [her] good) is replaced by the acknowledgment that the educator or the guide is in the same predicament as the one he [she] tries to help."[22] So we teach prayerfully, asking the Spirit to give us humility and to stand before God even as the child, begging for God's help and comfort in our deepest needs.

In teaching, we will not treat children as innocent nor expect them to be perfect. Nor will we act surprised when children are mean to one another. All of us are sinners in need of God's forgiveness, and we need God's good gift of law to keep society running with civility (the first use of the law). Therefore, it is appropriate to set rules that will keep peace and order in the classroom, preferably with input from the children who usually know from school the rules that will contribute to the smooth running of the group.

Your own faith is an important factor in teaching the gospel to children by the power of the Spirit. Faith involves us totally—our will, our emotions, our cognition, all that we are. Believing teachers, grounded in the Scriptures, are called to point to Jesus. Your own prayer, worship, joy in the gospel and desire to share it with others, bear witness to what you teach. However, we also need to remember that the gospel is not primarily about the teacher's experience but rather about God's own activity on our behalf in Jesus Christ. Therefore, the teacher is called to be transparent. The children need to see through and beyond the teacher to the Christ himself, who calls them to faith.

Baptism

While justification is the center of our theology and of teaching, many congregations also express the foundation of their educational ministry in terms of baptism. This is an excellent plan if most of the children in the congregation and in the neighborhood are baptized. Baptism indeed has far-reaching implications concerning why, what, and how we exercise educational ministry. Baptism is the sacrament in which the Word of promise is connected with the element of water. Because of justification by grace through faith, we proclaim the good news to all who will hear. [23] Therefore, we baptize young children and infants of believers, since it is the families' and the congregation's intention to bring up the children the fellowship of believers surrounded by the good news of God's love and mercy. The education of young children and infants follows baptism. We also baptize older children, youth, and adults who respond in faith to God's word of promise, the proclamation of forgiveness of sins for the believer. Both pre-baptismal and post-baptismal instruction are appropriate for older children, youth, and adults; they will have instruction that prepares for baptism as well as ongoing Christian education throughout their lives.

In baptism, God encounters the person, imparts God's Spirit to the person, and claims the person as God's own child. The person is incorporated into Christ's death and resurrection and receives forgiveness of sin and eternal life, becoming a child of God and an heir of salvation. He or she becomes a member of the church with its attendant blessings and responsibilities. Every day is a return to baptism, a repenting and cleansing, a dying and rising to new life by the power of the Spirit. Baptism leads to sacrificial service in this world and looks forward to the life to come, when the work of the Spirit will be completed once for all. In both baptism of infants and baptism of older persons, it is incumbent on the church to provide education for the baptized so that he or she will grow up or continue in the faith, and learn about the God who loves us so much and has done so much for us. This is why, in the baptismal service, parents make the following promise:

> . . . to faithfully bring *them* to the services of God's house, and teach *them* the Lord's Prayer, the Creed, and the Ten Commandments. . . . place in *their* hands the Holy Scriptures and provide for *their* instruction in the Christian faith, that, living in the covenant of *their* Baptism and in communion with the Church, *they* may lead *godly lives* until the day of Jesus Christ. [24]

Sponsors of older children and adults similarly promise to help and support them in every way so they may bear witness to the faith and lead godly lives. This implies that the baptized person will receive sufficient instruction in the faith and the Scriptures to bear witness and to grasp what leading a godly life is about. But parents and godparents cannot do all the instruction by themselves. They need the church to provide instruction beyond what the family can give. Baptism calls the church to provide learning opportunities in a variety of ways for all who are baptized. Each community of believers needs to plan carefully for such lifelong instruction in the faith, to meet the age levels and particular needs of the members in their care.

Baptism, content, and method

Baptism also has implications for content and method in religious education. By the early elementary years, children are ready to learn simple understandings of baptism. For example, baptism is a time when God's love is expressed in a new way for the person, and in baptism a person becomes a member of the church.[25]

By age 10, the child develops a new thinking ability that grasps intentionality as an integral part of right and wrong. Once intentionality is taken into account, children realize that it is not just the amount of damage done or the fact that they were caught, but rather that their very thoughts and innermost desires can themselves be in need of forgiveness. They begin to understand that forgiveness involves restoration of relationships, which can be destroyed by attitudes, that no one but they and God are aware of. Forgiveness takes on a whole new dimension and can be linked to baptism. Moreover, the baptized have a vocation, a calling, in baptism to speak God's word and pray and serve the needs of the neighbor in their daily lives. (This calling for children will be dealt with in the section on "Two Kingdoms.")

The full importance of baptism probably will not be grasped until the early teenage years when the child develops the capacity for abstract thinking. Christian education of children presupposes that youth and adult education will follow and build on the learning received through the elementary years. It takes a lifetime to search the depths of these topics: the great gifts of God; Christ's life, death, and resurrection; repentance and forgiveness; the church's worship, witness, and service; the continued work of the Holy Spirit in our lives; the Word and Sacraments; and the relation of baptism to daily living. All of these learning areas and more arise from baptism and provide a life-long journey in learning for the believer.

We must use wisdom and compassion in teaching groups of children so that we do not give the impression that non-baptized children have no place in the church or are inferior to the baptized. Yet at the same time we must be careful not to imply that baptism isn't important. It very clearly is important, and we need to invite parents to have children baptized, and promise children whose parents refuse that the invitation to baptism will always remain open, and that some day they will be able to decide for themselves if they wish to be baptized.

Our treatment of children either reinforces or negates the message we speak. If each learner is God's own precious child—of value because God loves him or her—then we will want to respect each one and treat him or her as deeply valued by us also. Before insisting that children do things our way, consider whether their own ways may be as good or better; respecting the learners' own ways of doing things lets them know that you value them. There are many individualized techniques in teaching that help the children express themselves in their own ways and help develop the individual's potential.

We also should respect each age level, including the youngest. Jesus had a soft spot for children who wanted to get near him. So should we. It is never appropriate to use teenagers as the only or primary teachers of preschoolers on the assumption that "they can't do much harm to such little kids." Actually, teaching preschoolers is more difficult than teaching older age levels because of the unique cognitive and social-emotional needs of young children. Mature teachers are more appropriately assigned to the younger children (although teenagers may assist them).

When dealing with God's own children, we will choose teachers carefully. Teaching God's children is a great honor and deserves adequate preparation and discernment of gifts. Never is it a good idea to beg from the pulpit, "If there's anyone who could just give an hour, please let the superintendent know. It doesn't take much effort or preparation, and anyone can do it." Would we be pleased if the local school superintendent raised staff by these means? Why should we expect careful selection and training of teachers of reading and math, but put up with halfhearted efforts and poor preparation when it comes to communicating the most important message of all? Of course, it is not only important to choose teachers carefully, it is also essential to train them well in Bible, theology, church history, developmental theory, teaching methods, curriculum, prayer, and worship. See the section on "training leaders and teachers" in the chapter "Building a Children's Ministry Program."

Baptism is a great equalizer. In baptism, teachers and students alike stand before God, equally recipients of God's gracious work, as fellow learners of the gospel. This fact calls teachers and students to give each other mutual respect and joy in learning, and to avoid suggestions of superiority on the part of the teacher.

Finally, and importantly, education of the baptized includes education of those whose special learning needs are often neglected in congregations. Baptism calls us to teach the baptized children of God who have disabilities and those who are specially gifted, and to do so in ways that are challenging and paced according to individual needs. Learn what you can about the needs of children in your class; parents will be able to tell you of ways the school is meeting their child's needs during the week. In many cases, the child will be mainstreamed in regular groupings and any adaptations in class routine can be made fairly easily. Other children in the class often will have learned in school how to give assistance when it is required. Sometimes an adult may be added to the teaching team to help with special needs. Be sure to ask about special needs material—for example, materials in Braille are often available from publishers even when they are not advertised. For gifted children, a list of available enrichment resources in the library may be sufficient in many cases.

Two Kingdoms

Luther firmly related education to the Two Realms in which God is sovereign and in which we live. God rules both realms—the realm of creation (in which God has given the law to restrain wickedness and vice and to help ensure justice and peace) and the realm of redemption and grace (in which God rules through the gospel). We live in both realms or kingdoms, and therefore need education to live in both realms. We need to learn of God's good gifts of law and government that help us live in the world. We also need to learn the Word of law and gospel so we recognize our human condition before God yet also rejoice in God's forgiveness of our sin. Children live in the Two Realms and therefore need education at their own level to help them live faithfully in the present as well as to prepare them for serving God throughout their lives.

When Luther wrote "To the Councilmen of All Cities in Germany that They Establish and Maintain Christian Schools" [26] and "A Sermon on Keeping Children in School," [27] he emphasized education in the gospel to serve the spiritual estate and also education that would prepare children to serve in society. He advocated education in the Bible so that children could grow up to serve in church offices, such as pastors, preachers, teachers, sacristans, and so on. [28] Such education is necessary to serve Word and Sacraments, which impart the Spirit and salvation. Luther advocated instruction in the biblical languages, Hebrew and Greek, so that the biblical texts would be available to the people to preserve the gospel in its purity. [29]

Luther also reminded his readers that temporal government is a divinely ordained estate and therefore called for education that would prepare people to serve in the worldly realm in positions such as jurists, writers, physicians, and schoolmasters. For this purpose, he wanted children to study many subjects, including Latin, German, history, music, mathematics, and poetry. He even argued that teaching should be done in enjoyable ways. [30] Far ahead of his time, Luther called for education for both boys and girls, special education for gifted children, and the establishment of libraries.

In Melanchthon's "Instructions for the Visitors of Parish Pastors," [31] preachers are told to exhort the people to send their children to school to be educated for competent service in both church and state. The "Instructions" even include an entire syllabus of study for schools that includes creeds and prayers and one day set aside for Christian education, especially study of the Bible. The rest of the week was devoted to other subjects, including reading, grammar, writing letters and poems, and studying Latin and Aesop's fables. The children were divided into groups so that instruction would be suited to age levels.

In using the Two Kingdoms as a basis for education in the church, we realize immediately that one-half of the education is usually done today in public or private schools. Churches usually concentrate on the specific biblical component, but Luther would encourage us to maintain vigilance as to the quality and value of the education that will lead to good citizenship as well.

First, education for the sake of trusting in God's promises and telling the good news. This is where congregations usually put their energies with children. In baptism, all Christians have a calling, a vocation, to speak the Word, pray, and serve the needs of the neighbor. This vocation is exercised in a variety of settings in daily life—family, work, congregation, community, volunteer organizations, and leisure opportunities. That is, it is exercised in church and in the world.

Children are able in their own ways to exercise this baptismal vocation. They are often more eager and less self-conscious in speaking the Word than are adults. There are no more sincere evangelists than children, who will share the good news they have learned with family members, friends, and relatives. Children, of course, can be taught to pray in increasingly rich ways as they mature, and they can serve the needs of the neighbor. Young children will help loved ones they know. Older children will have a wider circle of people whose needs they can meet.

For all of these purposes, children need learning. As Luther recognized, they need to learn the gospel message and study the Scriptures, both for the sake of their own faith and so that they can share the good news with others at their own level. Children need to learn to pray privately whenever they wish and in public as they share in the church liturgy. They will learn prayers by memory (such as the Lord's Prayer) so that they can join with all the gathered community in worship, and they will learn to create prayers that can be said in class devotions. In some congregations, children may learn to create prayers that become part of the prayers of the church in worship services, and children can learn to serve others. Preschoolers may have difficulty seeing how they can meet the needs of others because they see things from their own point of view and are inclined to do what makes them happy. Once the children reach the *concrete-thinking* stage, however, they develop the capacity to see things from another's point of view. At first you need to help them with this new-found capacity, but by fourth or fifth grade they usually can explain why they think a particular action or task will be helpful to someone or meet the person's needs.

Second, education for the sake of citizenship and service in the worldly realm, which is as much God's realm as the spiritual estate. A number of congregations sponsor church-related nursery schools or kindergartens. Some also sponsor elementary schools, and some even continue with junior and senior high school. In these cases, Luther's concerns are met through a full curriculum that includes religious instruction as well as the usual school subjects of math, science, languages, social studies, and so on.

Most congregations cannot sponsor such schools for older children, but they can take up Luther's theological concern by making sure that the congregation is actively involved in monitoring the quality of public education for children in the community. Sometimes pastors and other church leaders are invited to advise the district on character education. In other cases, congregation members attend school-board meetings and take an active role to ensure funding and volunteer support for schools. Congregation members may become tutors or classroom aides as well. All congregations can pray for teachers and administrators, and encourage members who serve in educational institutions. Luther makes clear that good education for children is a theological issue. For service in the temporal sphere, which God has ordained, children need the best education possible so they may serve society throughout their lives.

The issue of vocation arises in connection with children's daily lives now, not just in connection with future service. Children need to learn how to engage their current vocation of being a child—as student, family member, participant in the congregation, sports team member, band member, one who plays and enjoys the world, and so on. Help children see their opportunities to serve God and others in their daily lives.

Children may need help in reflecting on the vocation of student. In our society, children spend much of their time in school, but rarely do they perceive school studies as a calling from God. School, however, is in fact one of the daily settings where they exercise their baptismal calling. Fruitful discussion on school experience can make a world of difference to the child's attitude to peers and teachers, and can encourage exploration of new interests and projects to pursue.

In teaching about vocation, balance talk of church with talk of world. Never give the impression that being an acolyte or a greeter is much more important or a better way to serve God than doing homework, practicing the piano, or helping with family chores. In fact, our vocation in baptism would lead us to understand that all those everyday activities are precisely the locus of speaking the Word and serving our neighbors. They also prepare the child for future service to people and to the community. These daily activities of childhood are indeed a delight to God.

You may start some sessions with the children's everyday lives and then move to the Bible. You also might begin others with the human situation in the Bible narrative and then help the children see clearly how that narrative relates to the child's everyday world today. In either case, Bible and daily living need to be kept in close relation to each other.

Choose methods that will reflect your content. Children need to be able to envision what faith looks like in daily life situations. Preschoolers find it difficult to imagine situations they have never experienced. But 4- and 5-year-olds can handle daily routines such as, "Let's pretend you are the mother and you are the father and you are my brother." Older children can manage to role-play everyday situations fairly readily, even those in which they have not actually participated but may have observed. Such role plays can lead to sharing ideas about living as God's people in the family, at school, in the playground, in community service opportunities, and in sports teams, clubs, bands, choirs, camps, and all of the other activities and groups in which they participate.

The Word of God

In developing a theological basis for education, one must include the Word of God. Jesus Christ is properly called the Word of God, as John 1:14 reminds us. Jesus is the primary way that God has spoken to us, telling us who God is and showing us how much God loves us. Because Jesus is the Word Incarnate, we refer to the gospel, the message of God's good news for us in Jesus Christ, as the Word of God. In fact, we refer to the Word as both law and gospel because the Word rebukes and judges us, but also proclaims God's promise, the news of God's forgiveness of sin. In Jesus we see and hear both law and gospel. The cross is the ultimate word of judgment and redemption, of condemnation and salvation.

The Bible is centered in the gospel—every text within it can be for us at various times both law and gospel, can judge or can comfort, and the same text may at one time condemn and at another reassure us of God's mercy. Therefore, we call the Bible the Word of God. Since it is the definitive written witness from the early church, the Bible is the most important source for what we believe. It is the criterion by which we measure all other expressions of Christian truth, such as creeds, hymns, or catechisms. No other book or tradition is equal as source for theology. Therefore, the Old and New Testaments have a unique place in the teaching and learning of the church.

The Bible was written by adults for adults. Therefore, much of the language and concepts are difficult or beyond children. Fortunately, there are plenty of passages suitable for children, and the entire Bible does not have to be covered in childhood—most will be studied during youth and adulthood. The important point is that children learn that the Bible tells us about God's love and Jesus. As they move through childhood, children can look to the Bible to tell them who they are in the eyes of God and how much God has lovingly done for them and all people.

We believe that the Word comes to us today through preaching and through the sacraments. While young children will probably not respond to sermons, older ones may grasp some of what is read and proclaimed in public worship. They may watch baptisms and come forward to receive a blessing or receive the elements in Holy Communion, depending on the age of the child and the practices of the congregation.

In teaching children, we will want content that witnesses to Jesus Christ first and foremost. The gospel must be at the heart of all Christian education. We will want content that respects the Scriptures and makes them central. We will approach the Bible with the same law-gospel interpretation we have mentioned above. That means, we always want to teach children in such a way that the Bible speaks to their deepest needs, revealing to them who they are in God's sight, and speaking clearly to them of God's promises of love and mercy. We will teach the Bible so that the message of Jesus the Christ is paramount. That is, we will teach the Word rather than focusing on words.

With children of all ages, avoid statements that give the impression that the Bible is literally true. In this way, there will be no need to un-teach such ideas when in the later *concrete-thinking* stage children ask what happened literally and what did not. Also, avoid giving the impression that the physical printed book itself is holy. The very name on the cover (Holy Bible) may give that impression to children who can read. Some children even think the book itself has magical powers. In fact, the physical book is just that—it has margins where we can write notes and pages that we can highlight. It is good for children to make their Bibles their own in this way. The Lord of the Bible is holy and should be worshiped. The fact that the Lord is the central message of the Scriptures is what makes the Bible holy.

In teaching, it is important to use the Bible in class even with the youngest age levels who cannot yet read. You can hold the Bible open to the page and tell them that the story is written there and that some day they will be able to read it for themselves. Encourage parents to read from the Bible to children at home. Since children often follow the examples set by others, encourage parents to read the Bible for themselves and to let their children see that they enjoy doing this.

By all means, give Bibles to children once they can read sufficiently well—usually around third grade is a good time to do this. Give them a good translation but preferably a text printed in paragraphs not columns, because that makes for easier reading. Be sure that the children's section of the church library has a variety of Bible storybooks that retell Bible stories with words and quality art suitable for different age levels. The library should also have a selection of Bible atlases, concordances, and Bible dictionaries suitable for older children so they have the tools they need to explore the Scriptures. Always teach in the knowledge that it is the Holy Spirit who makes the Word effective. Pray that each child will respond in faith as you communicate the gospel in teaching.

The church

Children belong to the body of Christ, the one holy, catholic, and apostolic church. We affirm that the church is one because it has one Lord and has its unity in the Word. We affirm also that the church is holy, because the Lord is holy, and the Holy Spirit lives and works within the church. We further affirm that the church is *catholic* (that is, *universal*) because the work of Christ has universal significance and because the oneness of the church stretches backward and forward through time and across all geographical boundaries, uniting all believers in Christ. We affirm that the church is apostolic, that is, it has the apostolic message of salvation as well as the apostolic task of spreading that message throughout the world.

In the Augsburg Confession, the church is defined as "the assembly of all believers among whom the gospel is purely preached and the holy sacraments are administered according to the gospel."[32] This means that the church is essentially the people gathered around the forgiveness of sins through Christ, because this Word is the center of all preaching and of the sacraments. The Augsburg Confession goes on to state that the unity of the church depends on the gospel being preached in conformity with a pure understanding of it and the sacraments administered according to God's word. Nothing more is necessary. This gives the church a great deal of freedom in adopting rites and ceremonies, since such human traditions are not necessary either for salvation or for the unity of the church.

We call the church the *communion of saints*—a community in which we share the gospel, Christ forgives sins, and the Spirit calls, gathers, enlightens, and sanctifies, as Luther's Small Catechism reminds us. "Daily in this Christian church the Holy Spirit abundantly forgives all sins—mine and those of all believers."[33]

The church worships, witnesses, and serves the neighbors' needs. Members of all ages need education to prepare for these functions and to appreciate the blessings and responsibilities of membership. The members of the community possess various gifts that are used in the service of the church and the world, and need discernment and learning so that the gifts can be used to the greatest advantage of all. The members are bound together in all their diversity because of their faith in one Lord, and the fact that there is one baptism and one message of the forgiveness of sins. The church is a microcosm of that final gathering around God's throne, when all nations and races of people will worship their creator and redeemer together.

Children experience the church as a community long before they can talk about it. In fact, their conceptions of the church are usually fuzzy in the preschool years, and the term *church* for them may simply mean a building. *Preoperational* children cannot form class inclusion, so identifying Lutherans as a subset of Christians or or larger Church is beyond them. It is wise, therefore, to simply talk about the people who love God.

David Elkind's research shows that even 5-to-7-year-olds have only a general notion of religious identity and may confuse denominational terms such as *Catholic* and *Protestant* with national and racial designations.[34] From ages 7 to 9, children identify religious denominations in terms of particular actions, such as a Protestant going to a Protestant church building. (In this stage, children begin to appreciate that cats and dogs do not belong to the church!) It is not until ages 9 to 12 that the children understand that religious differences are a matter of beliefs.

However, children can focus on the story of the church. They can learn about the apostles telling the good news of Jesus and the wonderful stories of faith and heroism in the lives of believers throughout the centuries. Don't forget to include stories of child believers. Check the children's section of the library for attractive books on church history, including the lives of saints and church heroes.

Children will enjoy learning about the traditions of their own congregation, and they can early learn to join in the practices of worship and the social events. They will enjoy being present for baptismal ceremonies and communion services. The great music of the church and the drama of the liturgy inspire children as well as youth and adults. Young children do not need long explanations of what they are doing, simply enough learning so they can join in as part of God's people of all ages who do and say and sing these things.

Be aware of ways that children may genuinely serve the congregation—by singing in a choir, serving as an acolyte, assisting with greeting or ushering, helping set out napkins for coffee hour, drawing bulletin covers, and a host of other possibilities. Such experiences remind both children and adults that the youngsters have a place in the congregational activities.

In the *concrete-thinking* stage, children develop an understanding of space and geography, so third grade through six grade are excellent years for dealing with the church throughout the world in all its diversity and yet its trust in one Lord Jesus Christ. In addition to stories of missionaries, be sure to include stories from indigenous churches so that children learn to appreciate the strength and vitality of congregations far away.

Because baptism incorporates children into the life of the church, we need to provide experiences that foster community. Unlike adults who have many social experiences available to them in the congregation, the child often has the whole cognitive, emotional, social, and spiritual experience of the people of God right in the Sunday school classroom, or in a one-on-one mentoring situation, or however else your congregation structures children's learning. See the chapter "Building a Children's Ministry Program." Therefore, we need to pay attention all the more to ensure that *koinonia* (fellowship) is experienced within the class group itself. Such fellowship experiences are enhanced by classroom methods that encourage interaction and working together on projects or other tasks.

Celebrate the diversity of the church in your classroom. Every child has gifts and together they can help each other and the class as a whole in rich and wonderful ways. Also, celebrate the diverse heritage of class family traditions and ethnicity that will help children appreciate on a local level some of the vast differences in the worldwide church. When possible, bring in guests who can show other ways of worship, praying, singing, and musical expression, including those from other countries.

Drawing it all together

We have only touched the surface. We could go on to look at many other theological foundations for educational ministry in the church, but those described here should illustrate how profoundly theology lies at the heart of Christian education with children.

Here we have explored just a few of the possible theological bases for teaching and learning, including the work of Christ in justification, baptism, ministry in Two Kingdoms, the Word, and the church. In your own congregational setting, sit down with the Christian education committee and reflect seriously on your faith. You could start with the suggestions in this chapter or with any of the traditional theological themes, such as the Trinity, God as Creator, humanity and sin, the person and work of Christ, the Holy Spirit, the church, ministry, the sacraments, and the Last Things (what we call *eschatology*). A case for educational ministry can be made on the basis of many great themes of the faith. The important thing is to have such a basis, to think through why your congregation should be involved in teaching and learning with children, and the implications of your theological basis for content and method in teaching.

Such a theological foundation deserves to be shared with your whole congregation so that they understand why your congregation is passionate about the educational task, and so they can participate or at least pray for the congregation's educational ministry with children.

Of course, a good theological basis for educational ministry with children will be an excellent theological basis for educational ministry with youth and adults as well. The entire educational program of the church must be thoroughly grounded in the gospel and should clearly be a whole. When adults and youth learn on a regular basis, then there is little reason for children to suppose that they should "graduate" from learning when they complete sixth grade, or when they complete the catechetical process.

When the theological basis is clear, there should never be an argument that pits one age level over against another, and rejects children's learning in favor of older age levels. All age levels are equally important in the learning enterprise, and the church does well when it calls all of its baptized members to serious learning at every stage in their lives.

FOR REFLECTION AND DISCUSSION

• What theological basis lies at the heart of the Christian education ministry in your congregation? How might you express that basis to the new-member class? How might you explain to a child why your congregation wants children to learn and why teachers want to teach in this congregation?

• How do your educational practices reflect your theological basis? Would the linkage be obvious to an outsider? To long-time members?

Notes

1. Robert Kolb and Timothy J. Wengert, eds., *The Book of Concord* (Minneapolis: Fortress, 2000), p. 348.

2. Charles P. Arand, *That I May Be His Own: An Overview of Luther's Catechisms* (St. Louis: Concordia Academic Press, 2000), p. 95.

3. Ibid., p. 92-93.

4. *Book of Concord*, p. 383.

5. Arand, *That I May Be His Own*, p. 93.

6. Cf. Norma Cook Everist, *The Church as Learning Community* (Nashville: Abingdon, 2002).

7. *Book of Concord*, pp. 38-39.

8. See Paul Tillich, *Systematic Theology*, vol. 2 (Chicago: University of Chicago, 1957), p. 178; and "You are Accepted," Tillich, *The Shaking of the Foundations* (New York: Charles Scribner's Sons, 1948).

9. For example, Rudolph Bultmann, *Theology of the New Testament*, trans. Kendrick Grobel (London: SCM Press, 1952), vol. 1:302.

10. Martin Stallman, "Contemporary Interpretation of the Gospels as a Challenge to Preaching and Religious Education," in Charles W. Kegley, ed., *The Theology of Rudolph Bultmann* (London: SCM Press, 1966), pp. 251-252.

11. Paul Tillich, *Theology of Culture* (New York: Oxford, 1964), chapters 11 and 15.

12. Timothy J. Wengert, "Forming the Faith Today through Luther's Catechisms," *Lutheran Quarterly*, xi:4 (1997), pp. 382-383.

13. Arand, *That I May Be His Own*, p. 132. For a much more detailed and technical examination of Paul's and Luther's understanding of law and gospel, see Wolfhart Pannenberg, *Systematic Theology*, vol. 3, trans. Geoffrey W. Bromiley (Grand Rapids: Eerdmans, 1993), pp. 58-96.

14. As Paul Tillich also reminds us, in a secondary way the sources of theology include church history and the history of religion and culture. *Systematic Theology*, vol. 1 (Chicago: University of Chicago, 1951), pp. 34-40.

15. A good description of children's development of thinking is provided in David Elkind, *A Sympathetic Understanding of the Child: Birth through Sixteen*, 3rd ed. (Boston: Allyn and Bacon, 1994), chapters 2, 7, and 10; and in Anita E. Woolfolk, *Educational Psychology*, 8th ed. (Boston: Allyn and Bacon, 2001).

16. See Woolfolk, *Educational Psychology*, 7th ed. (Boston: Allyn and Bacon, 1998), pp. 29-39.

17. Points on teaching theological concepts to children are also developed in Margaret A. Krych, *Teaching about Lutheranism* (Minneapolis: Augsburg Fortress, 1993), sections in the chapters "With Young Children" and "With Elementary Grades."

18. For a fuller account of children's experiences of alienation and estrangement, see Krych, *Teaching the Gospel Today: A Guide for Education in the Congregation* (Minneapolis: Augsburg, 1987), pp. 56-61.

19. This is an attempt to deal on a child's level with the five areas in which Tillich expounds questions and answers throughout his *Systematic Theology*—that is, he correlates the ambiguities of reason with revelation; human finitude with God the Ground of Being; estrangement and sin with the New Being in Jesus as the Christ; the ambiguities of life with the Presence of the Spirit; and the ambiguities of history with the kingdom of God.

20. Tillich would call this "participation" in the world of children, which he says is necessary in any communication of the gospel. See *Theology of Culture*, pp. 205-206.

21. Paul Tillich, "Creative Love in Education," *World Christian Education* 18:3 (3rd quarter, 1963), p. 70.

22. Tillich, *Systematic Theology*, vol. 3, p. 212.

23. The Augsburg Confession rightly puts ministry (Article V) immediately following justification (Article IV).

24. Holy Baptism, *Lutheran Book of Worship* (Minneapolis: Augsburg, 1978), p. 121. Italics in original.

25. Krych, *Teaching about Lutheranism*, p. 34.

26. *Luther's Works*, vol. 45, pp. 339-378.

27. *Luther's Works*, vol. 46, pp. 207-258.

28. Ibid., p. 220ff.

29. "To the Councilmen of All Cities in Germany that They Establish and Maintain Christian Schools," *Luther's Works*, vol. 45, pp. 359-366.

30. Ibid., pp. 369, 376.

31. *Luther's Works*, vol. 40, pp. 269-320.

32. Article VII, Augsburg Confession, *Book of Concord*, p. 42.

33. Explanation of the Creed in the Small Catechism, *Book of Concord*, p. 356.

34. David Elkind, *Sympathetic Understanding*, 152-154. For the original research on children's concepts of religious affiliation, see Elkind, *The Child's Reality* (Hillsdale, N.J.: Lawrence Erlbaum, 1978), chapter 1.

CHAPTER 2

The Child Grew: Understanding Children's Development

Diane J. Hymans

THREE-AND-A-HALF-YEAR-OLD Beth wandered into a chapel on the campus of a theological school with her visiting parents. After carefully examining the room, she asked her mother, "Is this a church?"

"It's like a church," her mother replied.

Beth wandered down the center aisle, deep in thought, and then announced, "Let's play church! I'll be the minister and you be the people." The adults who were with her took their seats and waited to see what would happen next.

Beth moved up behind the pulpit. She could not see over it, so she peeked around it to speak. "First, I'll read the Bible," she stated with confidence. These were her words: "Dear God, we love you a lot, but we don't know very much about you."[1]

I n our relationship with God, there is a sense in which all of us—children, youth, adults—stand with young Beth as she prays those words. God is so much more than any of us can grasp. No matter how old we are, we continue to struggle to make sense of our faith, and to understand fully the breadth and depth of God's love for us and what that means for the living of our lives. In spite of this, each of us, no matter what our age, is able to come into God's presence with confidence because of baptism. It is important to keep this truth in front of us as we think about the growth and development of children, especially in relation to faith. Before God, the faith of a child and the faith of an adult stand on equal terms. God chose us all through our baptisms because of God's grace, not because of the size or maturity of our faith. Faith is not an achievement. It is a gift.

Yet we know that children are different from adolescents and adults. They see the world differently and make sense out of things in ways unique to their own abilities and experience. The apostle Paul recognized this when he stated in 1 Corinthians 13:11, "When I was a child, I spoke like a child, I thought like a child, I reasoned like a child." All of us begin life as infants who grow and change in remarkable and dynamic ways throughout our lives. We change physically as our bodies move through childhood, on to adolescence and adulthood, finally reaching old age. Our mental abilities adapt over time, allowing us to absorb and understand more complex concepts and ideas as we grow older. Those physical and mental changes affect the way we respond emotionally to the joys and sorrows life presents to us along the way.

This chapter will explore the psychological and intellectual development of children from birth to the beginning of adolescence. We will examine the question of how those dynamics relate to the growth of children in their life of faith. It is important to stop at this point to think about how we are using the word *faith* here. This word carries a multitude of meanings for most of us. We often use it interchangeably with *belief*. Although there are beliefs that shape and give meaning to our faith, faith itself is more than the sum of what we believe. Sara Little says, "Faith *is* a trust, loyalty, confidence, but it is more than a 'feeling.' It is a trust qualified by the One who is trusted. It is, in fact, a gift from that One who reveals himself."[2] For those us who hold to the Christian faith, the One in whom we place our trust is the God who has been revealed to us in Jesus Christ and is known to us through the work of the Holy Spirit. Faith is recognizing our need for this God, receiving the love that has been freely given to us, and responding to that love by seeking to live a new kind of life—a life of faith.

As we think about the growth of children, we recognize that our faith is tangled up in our development as human beings. To be sure, faith is something more than these human processes and is never determined by them. Faith is not a product of human development. But as we grow, we know intuitively that something in us changes and has an impact on our faith. So when we talk about the development of the child, what we mean to say is that the child changes as she grows—and something about her faith changes as well. One way to make sense of all of this is to frame the matter in terms of the way we hold our faith and how the processes of human development affect that dynamic. As we grow and change physically, cognitively, and emotionally, we understand faith differently, we experience it differently, we live it differently—that is to say, we *hold* it differently.

So the question before us is, how do children change intellectually and emotionally as they grow, and what do those changes mean for their growth in faith, and for educational ministry with children? To help us find the answer, we will consider the ideas of some of the major developmental theorists, along with others who provide insight into children and their development. Religious educator John Westerhoff has suggested that as we progress through the life span, our faith can be characterized as having four distinct styles that he has identified as experienced faith, affiliative faith, searching faith, and owned faith.[3] Although Westerhoff talks in terms of styles of faith, we will borrow his categories to provide a context to help us consider how the dynamics of children's growth and development affect how they hold their faith at various ages. While we will briefly mention the latter two, it is John Westerhoff's first two styles that are of interest to us as they represent the years of childhood that are the concern of this book.

Getting started

Before we explore John Westerhoff's styles of faith and some of the patterns of development that shape a child's growth, it will be helpful to have a brief introduction to the theories of two of the major thinkers in child development—Erik Erikson and Jean Piaget. These individuals may well have articulated two of the most important theories of human development in the 20th century, both of which have become foundational to all that have come after them. We will refer to the specifics of their ideas throughout the rest of the chapter, but at this point we will simply consider the basic structures of their theories.

We begin with Erik Erikson. A German-born Dane whose life spanned most of the 20th century, Erikson (1902-1994) was interested in the changing dynamics of the emotional lives of individuals. His theory finds its roots in the psychoanalytic tradition and focuses on the relationship between our psychological lives and the social and cultural environments where we live. According to Erikson, each of us passes through a series of eight stages that emerge naturally during our lives. Each stage presents a unique "crisis," to use Erikson's own term, which must be satisfactorily resolved for the individual to continue to grow into a psychologically healthy person. These psychological crises, which could also be called challenges or even opportunities, are a result of the interaction between the forces of biological growth and the social context that shapes the life of the developing person. Erikson describes the crises that constitute each of his stages in terms of opposing tensions. The eight stages appear below:

1. Trust vs. mistrust   0-1 year
2. Autonomy vs. shame and doubt   2-3 years
3. Initiative vs. guilt   4-5 years
4. Industry vs. inferiority   6-12 years
5. Identity vs. role confusion   Adolescence
6. Intimacy vs. isolation   Young adulthood
7. Generativity vs. stagnation   Middle adulthood
8. Integrity vs. despair   Old age

The way an individual resolves the tensions present at one stage influences the way that he or she responds to the challenges presented by all of the following stages. In spite of this, there is hope inherent in Erikson's theory, because it is possible to revisit the tensions operating in any of the early stages later in life to work through them. The question that interested Erikson was: How does the interaction between our biological growth and the people and groups who make up our social world affect the way we grow into emotionally healthy people who are able to withstand the storms and vicissitudes of life? Although Erikson proposed that we progress through eight stages from birth to death, it is the first four that are of interest to us. They are the stages that span the years from birth to the beginning of adolescence.[4]

Jean Piaget (1896-1980), a Swiss scientist whose life span roughly parallels Erikson's, focused his attention on the intellectual growth of children. Although Piaget's theory does not provide the complete picture, his ideas are foundational to any discussion of children's development. As a result of his work, we have come to understand that children's thinking is qualitatively different than that of older youth and adults. It is not just that children know less than adults do. Piaget helped us realize that they make sense of the world in a manner unique to their age and experience. We cannot change children's thinking by simply giving them more information. We have to let the developmental processes work. As they grow, their thinking will become more complex and their reasoning more flexible. Piaget developed his theory though careful observation of children and through open-ended interviews with them. His own children served as three of his primary subjects.

Like Erikson, Piaget proposed that children pass through an invariant series of stages. In each stage, a child's thinking takes on a different quality that represents a more comprehensive way of understanding the world. Piaget identified four stages of development: *sensorimotor intelligence, preoperational thought, concrete operations,* and *formal operations.* Although Piaget was not especially interested in the ages associated with a particular stage, his first three stages correspond roughly to the periods of infancy, the preschool years, and the elementary years, with the final stage emerging in adolescence. Even though the sequence of stages remains the same for all children, each child moves through them at her or his own rate.

One of the important elements of Piaget's theory is that children's thinking grows as a result of their active engagement with their world. Children constantly act upon their environment in an effort to understand it. Through this active exploration and manipulation, children construct cognitive structures that give form to their thinking. Piaget borrowed the language of biological adaptation to describe this process. As children encounter many objects or experiences in their environment, they simply fit them into the cognitive structures that already exist for them, that is, they assimilate them into their current patterns of thought. For example, very young children who know what a dog is will simply fit new dogs they encounter into the concept of dog that they already possess. But when they encounter a new kind of four-legged, furry creature that doesn't fit this concept of dog—one that goes "meow," for instance—they must make an accommodation to their existing mental structures to account for it. Through this ongoing process of assimilation and accommodation, children adapt to and come to understand more and more about the world around them. Piaget's theory is sometimes called a constructive-developmental approach because it describes the process of development as one in which the individual interacts with the world to construct meaning. This is what children do. As they grow, they are actively engaged in a process of attempting to make sense of the world, to interpret what it means, and they do so in a way appropriate to their age and level of development.[5]

With this brief background on the theories of Erikson and Piaget in mind, we begin our exploration of children's development with a look at John Westerhoff's experienced style of faith that extends from infancy to the beginning of the elementary school years.

Experienced faith

The beginnings of faith, according to Westerhoff, are rooted in our experiences of the world around us. Through his active exploration of the world, through his responses to the adults around him, and through the emotions that accompany them both, a child begins to form the foundation from which he will gradually begin to make sense of his faith experience. "A person first learns Christ not as a theological affirmation but as an affective experience."[6] Westerhoff reminds us that at this stage of life especially, the actions and emotions that accompany the words we use with a child may be more important in shaping his faith than the words themselves. Words and experience are connected. A child who hears the word *love* spoken when he is being abused will grow up with a distorted understanding of the meaning of that word. That misunderstanding will have a powerful impact on the child's life and relationships with others. Experienced faith grows out of our interactions with other people of faith and the larger faith community during the first years of our lives. According to Westerhoff, the question we need to ask as we interact with young children is, "What does it mean to be Christian with this child?" [7]

Infancy

A baby enters the world as a totally dependent creature. At birth, she is able to do nothing for herself and must rely on the care of the adults around her to provide for all of her most basic needs. The roots of faith are found here. In the first years of life, as individuals are learning how language works and how to control the motions of their bodies, whatever it is that faith means for an infant is based on experience

We have suggested that one way to describe faith is to think of it as a profound attitude of trust in God and God's promises to humankind. To say we have faith in God is to trust that God will do what God has promised. Erikson's first stage focuses on the alternative attitudes of *trust versus mistrust*. This stage constitutes the first year of life during which the child's dependency on others to meet her basic needs is total. The social realm where the child's emotional responses are being formed is made up of those who are responsible to provide that basic care—usually her parents, and most likely her mother. When the child comes to realize that her caregiver can be depended upon to come when she cries, to feed her when she is hungry, to change her when she is wet, and to comfort her when she is afraid or hurt, she is likely to develop the sense that in general people are worthy of her trust. Although there are cultural variations in the way that parents respond to the needs of a child, what is important is that, whatever form the response takes, it is consistent and ongoing.[8] When this is true, a baby is able to develop this basic sense of trust in herself, in other people, and in the world in general—essential elements in growing into a dependable person who is able to relate to others in healthy ways. A sense of trust that the world is a good place to be includes a sense of trust in one's self, in one's ability to handle the circumstances of life and to make a difference.[9]

The opposite of a sense of trust, as Erikson suggests, is a mistrustful attitude toward the world and other people. Erikson believed that all infants need to have some sense of both trust and mistrust to survive. Not everyone is worthy of our trust, and children need to be able to discern when mistrust is an appropriate reaction. Erikson's concern is the need for a healthy balance between the two polarities. In general, trust should outweigh mistrust, but all of us need a little of both.[10] This need for balance is true for all of Erikson's eight stages.

Unfortunately, too many infants do not experience the loving and dependable care of a parent or other caregiver to provide them with what they need to thrive. These children grow up with an imbalance of mistrust and the consequences are profound for children and for society. Infants need particular kinds of emotional support that include attention, warmth and touch, interest in what they are doing, and empathy. When these basic emotional needs are not met, a child is not able to sense the world as trustworthy, and the possibility of healthy future development—emotional, social, intellectual, and spiritual—is compromised.[11]

As we have said, the presence of an adult who pays attention to a child and responds appropriately to her needs in a consistent and loving manner provides the basis for the child's sense of trust. The result of this healthy attention is the infant's attachment to the caring adult. Attachment is that strong bond that develops between a baby and the significant adults in her life that provides her with a sense of security and comfort.[12] Attention, attachment, and trust are all related to a child's need for adults who show interest in her actions and behaviors. Infants need someone who responds to the sounds that they make by talking back, for that is where the roots of spoken language are found. They need caring people who will react to their facial expressions and their physical actions—who smile back when they smile, make silly faces at them, and tickle their feet as they wave them in the air. The warmth and touch that are embodied in these kinds of responses nurture the child's future ability to express compassion and sensitivity to others.[13]

Children who lack strong attachments to caring adults may fail to develop the capacity for empathy, the ability to put themselves in the place of another and to understand what others are feeling. The consequences for both the child and for the larger society may be severe, even violent.[14] What is more, the failure to develop trust and to attach strongly to a caring adult has implications for the child's life of faith. A child who has not learned to trust other people may find it difficult to trust God and God's care for her. The lack of empathy will limit the child's ability to love others as Jesus has loved us. The child's ability to trust and respond to those who have primary responsibility for her care is foundational for her future development and critical in the way she holds her faith. Basic trust makes it possible for the child to have hope.

One way we can tell that an infant is developing a healthy sense of trust is her willingness to let her mother out of her sight without becoming overly upset. The child is able to do this when she knows that her mother can be depended upon eventually to return.[15] This development is related to the child's growing intellectual abilities. To understand more about what this means, we turn to what Piaget has to say about infants.

The beginnings of intellectual development occur during the first 18 months of life in what Piaget called the *sensorimotor* stage. During this period, the infant comes to know the world around her through her senses and through physical actions. At this stage, we can appropriately say that a child's actions are her thoughts. At first these actions are no more than random reflexes. For example, as she waves her hands in the air, the child may happen to hit a mobile that hangs over her crib, which startles her and draws her interest. If this occurs a number of times, the child may begin to hit the mobile intentionally to see what happens. She has begun to construct a mental image based on motor activities of what her hand does when it come into contact with a movable object.[16] During the period of *sensorimotor* intelligence, the child gradually builds a system of mental structures related to space, time, and cause-and-effect relationships as a result of her growing ability to coordinate her physical movements and her perceptions.

According to Piaget, one of the most important mental structures that the child constructs during her first year of life is that of object permanence, or the realization that something exists even when she cannot see it.[17] In the first months of life, when an object disappears from view, an infant will not look for it. She seems to assume that it no longer exists and as a consequence shows no further interest in the object. Over the course of the first year of life, the infant will learn to look for an object, even when it has been deliberately hidden from her view. She has come to realize that the object has its own existence apart from her experiences of it.

Although we adults can no longer remember this phase of our lives, this is a monumental achievement for the child, for she has begun to construct a world filled with many separate objects of which she is only one. At birth and during the first months of life, the child experiences the world around her as simply an extension of herself. Over time, there is a gradual shift in her sense of herself and of the world, until a world outside of her experience comes into being. At that point, the child is able to construct a sense of *me* and *not me*, and the seeds of a personal identity are planted. The child can now begin to relate in intentional ways to people and things in the larger world, beginning with members of her family.[18] One of the most important external objects of which the child becomes aware is her mother, or her other primary caregiver if there is one. Only when she knows that her mother is someone separate from her, can the child begin to trust. This discovery that her mother is something other than herself is also the beginning of separation anxiety. When an infant discover that her mother exists somewhere else when she is not present with her, the infant often cries to try to bring her back. Through experience, a child learns that when the people she cares about go away, they do return.[19]

What does this mean for educational ministry in the church? Much of our contact with infants in the congregation will come through our interactions with their parents. At this point in the child's life, that is where the focus of much of our attention should lie. Churches can provide opportunities for parents to learn about child development and to strengthen their parenting skills. For some congregations, this ministry to parents may extend beyond their own members. There is a need for quality, affordable childcare for infants and toddlers in many communities. Many churches have stepped into the void to offer this important service to parents. This is ministry to children by means of nurturing their families.

When congregations do provide direct care for infants, whether in a Sunday morning nursery, or through weekday childcare programs, it is absolutely essential that they be staffed with adults who will offer loving, consistent care. In Sunday morning nursery settings, it is a gift to children and their parents to have the same caregiver present every week. When babies can depend on the same person to care for them at church each time they are there, it helps to reduce their separation anxiety and supports their growing sense of trust in the world. Caregivers can help parents by assuring them that the crying that accompanies separation anxiety is a normal reaction, and that in time it will pass.

Toddlerhood

Between the ages of 18 months and 3 years, the child makes significant leaps mentally and physically that set the stage for Erikson's second stage, *autonomy vs. shame and doubt*. First of all, because he has acquired an understanding of object permanence, the child sees himself as a separate being in a world populated by other people and objects with which he can interact. Second, he has gained a great deal of control over his physical movements.

He can use his hands to feed himself. He can stand on his own two feet, and use those feet to begin to explore the world on his own. As he is toilet trained, the child gains control over the muscles related to these bodily functions as well. Finally, he has begun to acquire language skills—another monumental achievement. The use of language requires that he understand how symbols work. He must comprehend that one thing can stand for another for that is how words function. They represent something else and make it possible to talk and think about something even though it is not present.

All of these achievements are the basis for the child's increasing sense of his own autonomy and the desire to exercise his will in exerting it. As any parent knows, some of the first words a child enjoys using are *me, mine,* and an emphatic *No!* [20] "I do it myself" is a regular refrain during this period, along with behaviors and words that say in effect, "You can't make me do it." It is the task of parents, who provide the primary social context for the child during this stage, to make room for the child to exercise his new found autonomy in appropriate ways.

A 2-year-old does not have the wisdom and experience to regulate himself completely. He needs to learn the limits that society has set on certain forms of behavior. The challenge for parents is to figure out how to provide those limits. This is a delicate balancing act. Parents who are too controlling may resort to excessive shaming to get their child to respond. But shaming has consequences. Erikson understands shame to be a sense of self-consciousness, of being exposed and looked at by others. It includes a desire to disappear so that others cannot see us. Too much shame can lead to a sense of inner rage and a desire to defy those who are shaming us. Shame's partner, doubt, reveals itself as a wish for excessive self-control. As in the first stage, there is a need for balance here. It is not healthy for a child to be utterly shameless. We all need to understand which forms of behavior are appropriate, and which are not, as we move into larger social contexts. As Erikson states, "This stage . . . becomes decisive for the ratio of love and hate, cooperation and willfulness, freedom of self-expression and its suppression. From a sense of self-control without loss of self-esteem comes a lasting sense of good will and pride." [21]

This can be a time a great emotional turbulence for toddlers and their parents as the child strives to hold onto his new-found self-control. Yet he does so with mixed emotions, still wanting to maintain the intimacy he so enjoyed with his primary caregiver during the first year of life. The child's emotions during this stage range from great joy in his ability to explore the brand new world that is suddenly available to him, to anger—even rage—when his will is thwarted, to anxiety that he will lose that closeness to his caregiver. A new relationship between the child and his parents is being forged. One moment they are good parents who love and care for him, and the next they are bad parents who make him go to bed when he doesn't want to, or who won't let him have all the cookies he wants. One writer has suggested that the child has a great need for constancy during this period when the good parent and the bad parent are embodied in the same person. Constancy is another necessary ingredient for living the life of faith.[22] Trust again plays a role. Toddlers who have developed a sense of trust as a result of the dependable care of a parent can move out into the world in confidence that the world will hold them just as that parent did. The constancy provided by parents who are experienced as both good and bad, who are present even when the world does not respond the way the child had hoped it would, makes it possible for the child to pick himself up and keep on going even in the tough times. As toddlers come to terms with these contradictory feelings about their parents, they are able to develop realistic expectations about others, and about God who does not always seem to do what we want God to do for us.[23]

Intellectually, the child is moving out of Piaget's *sensorimotor* stage and into the *preoperational* stage. If the primary intellectual achievement of infancy is the conquest of the object in relation to the self, the primary achievement of the years of early childhood is the conquest of the symbol. We will explore this more in depth in the next section on preschoolers. For now we can say that one of the signs of the child's developing mind is his growing ability to reason things out internally rather than being totally dependent on physical activity. The baby's "body mind" has become a "thinking mind."[24]

As we consider educational ministry with children during this stage, we must again think about ways to support and include parents. The church can help parents understand the importance of balancing their need to hold on to the child and his need to exert his autonomy. Children who are struggling with their own conflicting desires to hold on and to let go need appropriate limits to keep them safe, and to help them learn to manage their own behavior. Parents and teachers who work with children in the church need to understand what behaviors are developmentally appropriate so that they will not shame children unnecessarily. We can help parents think about where to set boundaries and what kinds of choices to give children to allow them to experience the independence they need and want. Young children can exercise choice in their classrooms at church when the space is arranged with low shelves and tables so that toddlers can help themselves to the materials they want to use during periods of free play. Our time spent with these children should always include periods when they can exercise their autonomy by choosing which activity they would like to do from a range of acceptable options.[25] At the same time, we must take care not to offer false choices to young children. It is not appropriate to ask a child, "Would you like to take your medicine?" They do not have a choice in this matter and to give them one may lead to frustration. On the other hand, we can ask a child, "Would you like to take your medicine now or after we read a story?" This is an option we are able provide and to do so allows them an appropriate sense of control.

Preschool years

By age 3, the child has grown in amazing ways. Because she has gained enormous control over her muscles, she can now do things like throw a ball and draw simple pictures. She walks and runs with confidence. Having acquired a much larger vocabulary, she is able to talk in complete sentences, even if they are not always grammatically correct. Socially, she is able to carry on a conversation with the people in her world of experience. She has some distance to go in all of these areas, but adults who interact with children need to appreciate how far she has come. She has attained proficiency with a great many skills and has learned a staggering amount of knowledge about the world. The preschool child is moving into an exciting stage of wonder and discovery. As she now engages the world with boundless energy and enthusiasm, this child can be a great joy to be around.

For Erikson, preschoolers are moving out of the stage of *autonomy versus shame and doubt* and into the stage of *initiative versus guilt*. While 3-year-olds are living on the border between the two stages, by age 4, children have fully arrived in the third stage in Erikson's theory. The task for children in this stage is to develop a sense of purpose. With all of the knowledge and skills that they are acquiring, these children are ready to conquer the world. Erikson states that "according to the wisdom of the ground plan the child is at no time more ready to learn quickly and avidly, to become bigger in the sense of sharing obligation and performance than during this period of his development."[26] At this stage, children have left behind many of the battles of will that are typical of the previous stage, and can now act less out of a need to establish their own control over things and more to get things done.[27]

The challenge for adults who work with children during this time in their lives is to give them room to act on their own so that they can acquire a sense of their own competence. They need to be offered experiences and resources appropriate to their level of ability so that they can act on their own initiative wherever appropriate. They will make mistakes, and these must be handled gently to help children learn from them and not to feel guilty about them. The danger at this stage is that we will expect more of children than they are capable of because preschool children often seem to know more than they actually do. They can say more than they know, so it is easy to assume that they can do more than they actually can. Their language may exceed their abilities. There are a number of possible consequences here. To please the adults who matter to them, children sometimes try to live up to adult expectations even when they are unrealistic. When they cannot, they may begin to see themselves as incompetent. If they do somehow succeed against the odds, they may develop an unrealistic picture of what they ought to be able to do. Because they cannot succeed every time, the result may be an unnecessary sense of guilt and inadequacy.[28] Guilt may also result when the child senses that her energy and natural curiosity are becoming overly intrusive. A healthy resolution of this stage occurs when the child has achieved an appropriate sense of self-control; when she can impose her own limits on her behavior. A child who has achieved a balance between initiative and guilt has learned when it is socially acceptable to move exuberantly into the world to achieve the plans she has in mind, and when she needs to curb her enthusiasm to accommodate the needs and expectations of others.

The preschool child is in the throes of *preoperational thought*, the second of Piaget's stages, which begins during the second year of life and extends roughly to ages 6 or 7. The thinking of a child in this stage is no longer shaped by motor activities. Because she has figured out how symbols work, the child can now carry mental pictures and ideas in her head. Her thinking is now symbolic rather than based on her physical actions. One of the things that adults notice about the thinking of preschool children is that it is highly imaginative.

Preschool children think intuitively. They observe the world around them, drawing their own conclusions about what they see. Those conclusions are based on their own points of view, not what they are told by others. Piaget identified this tendency of young children to see everything from their own perspective as *egocentrism*.[29] Intuitive, egocentric thinking often has a magical quality about it. It is not unusual for a young child to think of non-living objects as alive. For example, very young children may believe that the moon has a life of its own, and that that life has a purpose that is to light up the night so that the child can see where she is going even though it is dark. Preschoolers often believe that the wind or their own shadows are alive because they move. For young children, these entities that we know to be inanimate have a kind of consciousness that leads to what the child believes to be purposeful behavior.[30] God also takes on a magical quality for the young child. For many of them, God is a magician in the sky who makes all things happen. While this is not an adequate concept of God for youth or adults, we should not worry when young children see God in this way. It is a natural outcome of where they are in the developmental process. Their encounters with the community of faith and conversations with pastors, teachers, and parents as they grow will help them come to a larger understanding of who God is and how God acts in the world.

A child may also believe that her own thoughts and wishes have magical powers. If a child wishes for something that actually comes to be, she is likely to assume that it happened because she wished for it. This can cause a child emotional problems when what happens is something disturbing. A young child, in a fit of jealousy, may wish that her new baby brother would disappear. If that terrible thing did occur, if the brother were to die, the child may believe that her wish caused it to happen. Parents may not realize that a child is trying to deal with the guilt that comes from this kind of intuitive reasoning. A child may try to undo what she believes her wish has caused by promising to be good forever, or giving up some prized possession as an act of contrition.[31]

These examples of the thinking of preschoolers represent *transductive reasoning*. Transductive reasoning moves from one concrete example to another, usually focusing on only one aspect of each, and drawing conclusions based on intuition. The example of magical thinking in the previous paragraph represents this type of reasoning. For a child, if two events happen in succession, the first one caused the second. Although adults know this is not always a rational conclusion, it is a natural outcome of the kind of thinking of which young children are capable. It is difficult to avoid our tendency to want to explain to young children that they are wrong and why that is so, but a preschool child simply cannot understand our logical explanations. What we can and must do is to reassure children who fear that they have caused something terrible to happen. When someone dies, it is important to let the child know that that happened because of an accident, or because the person became ill and the doctors were not able to fix them, not because the child wished it. Even though the child may not completely understand our reasoning, it is the emotional content of the warmth and care that accompanies our words that will matter most.

The reality of transductive reasoning helps us understand why the conversations we have with young children so often feel disconnected to adults. To illustrate, a teacher who has just told the story of Jesus feeding the 5,000 people to her preschool class, may want to engage them in some discussion about the story. If he were to ask them what they liked about the story, it would not be unusual to get comments similar to the following:

Child 1: We had fish sticks for lunch.

Child 2: My grandpa took me fishing once.

Child 3: I went in a boat and I was scared.

Teacher: *(To Child 2)* You went fishing with your grandpa?

Child 2: My grandpa tells funny stories.

From the teacher's point of view, it's difficult to follow the logic of this conversation, much less uncover much meaning related to the story he has just told. But the children here are not trying to connect to each other's stories or to the story of Jesus feeding the crowd. For them, a single element in the story or in another child's comment triggers their thinking about something from their own experience and that is what they want to talk about. This is how transductive logic functions. It is a way of thinking that focuses on one element in a situation as seen from the point of view of a particular child.

Most Sunday school teachers would hope to draw the children's attention to something deeper in this wonderful story, certainly something related to what Jesus was doing and what that might mean for our lives. But the teacher would be attempting to have a conversation appropriate to his level of intellectual development, not the child's—a relatively hopeless task. The child has found something in the story of Jesus that, in her own system of logic, is connected to something in her experience. That is all she is capable of at this point in her life, and perhaps for now at least, that is enough. If a child has found something in the story of Jesus that has something to do with her concrete experience, that story has meaning for her. As the child's intellectual capacities expand with age, there will be other opportunities to explore the story at deeper levels.

This does not mean that children are not capable of thinking about God and Jesus and what they mean for our lives. But just as children's thinking at this age is tied to their concrete experiences in the world, so too is their theology. We do not often think of children as possessing a theology, but they surely do. The word *theology* simply means the study of God, and children who live in families and faith communities where they hear people around them talking about God will certainly include God in their thinking. They will do so, however, using the intellectual abilities available to them.

Four-year-old Alex ran up to me as I sat in his Sunday school classroom one morning. "Do you know that God is inside us?" he asked.

"Yes," I replied, "we often say that God is inside us."

"Where do you think God is in there?" Alex asked.

"Where do you think God is?" I responded.

"In my stomach!" he announced with great relish, then bounded off to resume playing.

Alex is working at his level of intellectual development and drawing on his experience to understand a fairly abstract idea about God, that is God's presence with us in a personal way. He is engaging in what religious educator John Hull calls *concrete theology*. Many teachers assume that because children think in concrete terms that they cannot understand abstract ideas. Children are concrete thinkers because their thinking is confined to objects, people, and situations with which they have had direct experience. Hull differentiates between abstract thinking, of which we are usually not capable until we reach adolescence, and thinking about abstract concepts. Abstract thinking is being able to think about ideas in our heads. Although young children cannot do that, they do have to make sense of abstract concepts all the time. They simply do so in concrete terms.[32] *Big* and *little*, for example, are abstract ideas. We cannot point to *big* anywhere, but we can point to an object that is big and compare it to one that is little. Children come to understand *big* and *little*—and any other abstract concept—by using concrete objects from their environment.

That is what Alex is doing. For him, God can be understood only in concrete terms, so God has to be located somewhere. If God is inside of us, as he has probably been told, then God must be in a particular place. Alex has decided that his stomach is the most likely location. His parents may have told him that when he eats his food, it goes into his stomach. Alex has connected that knowledge with what he has been told about God and made a logical connection.

Stories provide a wonderful context for helping young children deal with the ideas and concepts of the Christian tradition. One educational theorist has suggested that children come to comprehend many abstract concepts that they could not explain otherwise within the context of a story.[33] Stories have the capacity to carry children beyond their world of concrete experience. Fairy tales, for example, are full of kings and queens, fairy godmothers, talking animals, and other creatures that children do not encounter in their daily lives. Although most children have virtually no direct experience with the strange and wonderful world of fairy tales, they have no difficulty understanding them because the story itself provides a structure that allows them to know where it is going and how it works. The same may be said of stories in the Bible, which are also set in a world where children have no experience.

One dimension of the structure of a story holds special interest for us here. Many of the best stories, those that hold children's attention, are built around a conflict between opposites, such as good and evil, fear and security, love and hate, and so on. When we think of some of the familiar children's stories, such as *Cinderella* and *The Three Pigs*, we often find these dynamics operating in them. These opposites get to the heart of human experience and emotion, and are, in fact, very large and abstract concepts. Although young children would not be able to articulate what any of these concepts means, it is clear that they understand what they are about when they are part of the underlying structure of a story. It is striking how the binary opposites mentioned above, along with many others, are part of the language of our faith.

The Christian tradition is blessed with a wealth of wonderful stories in the Bible that have been used for thousands of years to help us know who

God is and what God has done for us. Just as children are able to move into the strange world of fairy tales, they are able to move into the world of the Bible, which is also strange to a child, because they are familiar with the structure of a story. Many of the stories of the Bible include the dynamic tensions represented by these polar opposites. These stories can help children get inside many of the abstract concepts and ideas that are related to our faith and find meaning there, meaning that they would not be able to comprehend were we to try to explain it to them. We need to share our stories with young children as a pathway into the language faith.

Just as stories have an important role in the lives of young children and contribute to their development, the pretend play of young children also helps them understand the world. In pretend play, children engage the world around them as a way to comprehend it and to appropriate the meanings that they discover for themselves. This is not something of which children are conscious. For the child, genuine play serves no purpose outside of itself. It is simply fun.

Pretending begins with the ordinary world and transforms what is found there into a new reality where the child determines what things mean. She makes the rules and can change them at will. Play provides a context in which the child can fully exercise her initiative. Play also has a significant role in helping children become integrated into the patterns of belief and behavior of particular cultures. As children work out an understanding of their world in their play, they become part of that world. In a sense, play provides children an opportunity to practice the roles and behaviors of their culture.

Pretend play is sometimes called *symbolic play* because of the way children use objects, actions, words, and roles to represent something else found in their real or imagined world of experience. There are two levels to children's pretend play.

The first is the "as if" dimension. A child acts "as if" she were a mommy or a queen or one of Jesus' disciples. A block is used "as if" it were a telephone or a gun or a communion chalice. While playing, a child's imagination runs free, and anything is possible. Here, children simulate their everyday reality. Early forms of this type of play emerge when children in their early 2s imitate the behavior of Mommy and Daddy. Just watch a 2-year-old pretending to talk on a telephone and you will recognize "as if" play.

In the second dimension, the "what if" level, anything is possible. Here, children do not simply represent the real world, they begin to play with it to see what might happen. Some developmental theorists suggest that for young children, play is the context in which they try out new ideas. Older youth and adults are able to try out new ways of thinking about things in their conversations with others. Children do not always have the words to say all that they know, so play becomes a kind of language for them through which they can begin to make their own meanings out of their experience in the world. One theorist has said, "Children do not just say it otherwise, they play it otherwise."[34]

This has significance for faith communities. Because pretend play has a significant role in the growth of the child, we need to make room for it in our educational ministry with young children. Classrooms must provide space and materials with which children can play. The "as if" play of children helps them practice the patterns of language and behavior of the faith community—to learn them well. Here, children receive what the church has to pass on to them. But in their "what if" play, children have the freedom to look at the world from a different angle, to try things out in the safety of the play context. In so doing, they may discover new levels of meaning in the Christian tradition—meanings that are appropriate for them at their level of development. Those meanings will be their own, not ours.

An example might help here. Suppose a group of young children have been participating in the worship of their congregation when one Sunday they observe the baptism of a baby. What if the next time they are in the church school classroom, they find basins of water and baby dolls available to them to use however they want. Not all of them will choose to reenact a baptism, but some may. If they do, on the first level they will reinforce for themselves what they observed in the worship service—the "as if" dimension of play. Now suppose some of them go a bit further. Children who are part of a congregation where the pastor dips his hand or a shell into the water during baptism and pours it on the baby's head may try immersion instead. That is not to say that they will understand that this is what they are doing, but play gives them room to try other ways of doing things before they have the language to accompany them. Pretend play provides a framework of experience into which the child can insert later more direct experiences and later conversations with teachers and parents who can help them develop alternative understandings.

Piaget reminds us that children are meaning-makers, but the meanings that they construct from their world of experience and within the life of faith are their own. We can teach preschool children to say things about God or about Jesus that are important for them to know. For example, children can learn to say, "God is a spirit," but we cannot predict the way that a young child understands what that phrase means. Because children have no direct experience with "spirits," they may decide that God is a ghost, like Casper.[35] Children will willingly learn to say what they know we want them to say, but they will make sense out of these things only as they are able because of where they are developmentally. Because their logic is transductive, their feelings about God may change instantaneously. One moment God is nice. Then, after hearing the story of Noah's ark, when all the animals and people die, the child may declare, "God is mean. I don't like God." [36] Although we long to explain to young children why this is not so, our logic will make little sense to them. Their ability to understanding these complexities has yet to develop.

That does not mean that we should stop telling them about God, sharing all of the stories of God, and loving them as God loves them. If children form many of their concepts about the world through their experiences and the language adults use that accompany them, we want to be sure that their experience of God through us confirms that what we know to be true. But there is more to be said about this matter. Piaget seemed to regard children as solitary learners who came to understand the world primarily through their personal experience. However, we are discovering that learning is a much more complex activity. Russian psychologist Lev Vygotsky, among others, has reminded us of the significance of cultural factors in all of human development. Vygotsky was a contemporary of Piaget's, but because he worked in what was once the Soviet Union, his ideas have not been available to us until recent years. One of his convictions is that the social world where children live plays an important role in their cognitive development. Their world, and the way they understand it, is influenced in many ways by the values and beliefs of their families and their communities. Their learning occurs through interactions with the people who inhabit these worlds. Where we once thought that the best way to help children learn was to teach to their level of development, Vygotsky's work with children revealed that with the assistance of others, such as parents, teachers, and even other children, a child can develop skills and concepts that are beyond her level of development. Vygotsky introduced an idea he called the *zone of proximal development*, by which he meant the space between the actual developmental level of a child, in which she can solve problems independently, and the potential level of development where a child can solve problems with the assistance of an adult. According to Vygotsky:

> The zone of proximal development defines those functions that have not yet matured but are in the process of maturation, functions that will mature tomorrow but are currently in an embryonic state. These functions could be termed the "buds" or "flowers" of development rather than the "fruits" of development. [37]

Learning happens beyond a child's level of development, but with the assistance of others in her world. This assistance has been called *scaffolding* by some. Scaffolding is not so much simplifying a task or concept so the child can understand it, as it is providing a structure by breaking down a task, or asking questions to guide a child's thinking so that she can solve a problem on her own.[38] This is the kind of teaching, for example, that occurs whenever a parent helps a child find something she has lost. The parent may ask a child where she last saw the object. If the child replies, "I can't remember," the parent may continue with additional questions—"Did you have it in your room? Is it in the car?"—until the child recalls where the item might be. The parent is teaching the child a mental structure to help her think about a situation and solve a problem. The child is not passive in this process. Her mind is actively engaged in making sense of the situation, just as Piaget described children's thinking. For Vygotsky, however, development occurs through the reciprocal interaction of the child with her social context.[39]

Vygotsky has helped us to see that children learn not just by doing, which we concluded from Piaget's discoveries, but also by talking with adults and with one another. The simple act of conversation offers a rich context where teaching and learning can occur.[40] Our conversations with children about God and about who God calls us to be in the world can help stretch their understandings beyond where they are developmentally and reach toward the next stage of growth. That stage is where we will move to now.

Affiliative faith

Between the ages of 6 and 11, the style of faith held by children begins to take on a different quality. John Westerhoff suggests that they don't leave behind completely the faith that characterized the years of early childhood, but there are new dimensions to the way that they hold their faith that result from their social, emotional, and intellectual growth. Westerhoff calls the faith of the elementary school years *affiliative faith* because its primary context is the faith community. Affiliative faith is about becoming part of that community, about the child being accepted by others who are its members, and feeling that he can make a contribution to the group to which he now knows that he belongs.[41]

Jason was a third-grader whose family belonged to a downtown congregation. On Mondays, this congregation served lunch to people who lived on the streets of the southern city where the church was located. When school was not in session, Jason's father, who regularly volunteered to assist with the lunch, would often bring him along to help. Jason's father was also an usher during Sunday morning worship. Now this was a congregation whose beginnings dated back to before the Civil War. Its style of worship was formal, and ushering was serious business. Children were not usually allowed to share that responsibility, but when Jason's father was assigned ushering duty, Jason stood alongside him to help. Jason, rather than his father, was the one who carefully passed the offering plates to the people sitting in the pews and who carried the offering forward when the time came to do so during the service. Jason's father was doing what congregations ought to be doing for all of their children. He was helping him find a place where he could contribute in a meaningful way to the life and mission of that church. It was clear that Jason's father had prepared him for how he was to carry out these responsibilities. Jason knew what he was supposed to do, and he did it well. This is what affiliative faith looks like in action.

In addition to learning what it means to belong to a community of faith, this is the time when children begin to dig into the story that gives that community its identity. For the church, that story in found in the Bible. Even though we surely tell stories from the Bible to younger children, for them it is the lived and experienced faith that is most formative. For elementary-aged children, the stories of the faith community begin to give a more comprehensive form and shape to their faith. We will explore this in more depth later in this section. This shift in the style of faith that is characteristic of children ages 6 to 11 comes as a result of developmental changes that reshape the way that they experience and make sense of the world. It is to those changes that we now turn.

Elementary-age children

These are busy, active years for the child. His world is expanding at a rapid rate. The family is no longer the primary social context in his life. He is now a part of a host of other organizations—school, first of all, but also peer-related groups such as sports teams, music groups, scouting, and groups at church. Erikson identifies this as the stage of *industry versus inferiority*. During this period of life, the child's primary task is to acquire the basic skills and knowledge necessary to function in society. As Erikson put it:

> One might say that personality at the first stage crystallizes around the conviction "I am what I am given," and that of the second, 'I am what I will." The third can be characterized by "I am what I can imagine I will be." We must now approach the fourth: "I am what I learn." The child now wants to be shown how to get busy with something and how to be busy with others. [42]

This is the stage when children receive some form of systematic instruction so that they may become contributing members of society. In our culture, the place where all this happens and where the child spends a significant portion of his time is the school. Developmental theorist Robert Kegan says that for children in our culture, there is more to be learned at school than the content of the formal lessons taught there. A child is also learning about going to school, which means he must figure out how to live with rules to which he must conform and roles that he is expected to play. The egocentric behavior of the preschool child is not tolerated in the elementary school. [43]

This period is one of accomplishment and, we hope, recognition for work well done. It is a time of productivity—of industry—for the child, and we see him busy with many kinds of tasks. Where the preschool child's play is free flowing and imaginative, the play of the elementary child is more rule-governed and structured. This child is learning how to follow the rules and how to function cooperatively through his membership on sports teams and other groups. Traditionally, this is the stage in life when the child is involved in making and doing activities—building things, craft activities, cooking, and so on—that are possible because he now has good control of both his large and small muscles. This has changed somewhat in recent years as computer games, television, and organized group activities, such as team sports, now absorb more of children's time. In many ways, these are the activities of adulthood rather than childhood. Although some worry that childhood itself is fading because of the proliferation of these new kinds of activities, children at this age become part of a peer culture consisting of rituals, games, and understandings passed on through an informal oral tradition. Jokes, riddles, songs, chants, and playground games all belong to the culture of childhood of which every child is now a part, and help him learn about the role he is to play in this new world. [44]

The activities of this period in the child's life contribute to helping the child learn about himself and what he is capable of doing. Is he a good student? An athlete? A musician? The responses of others to what he does provide information that helps the child discover these things about himself. [45] When the reactions that the child receives are not positive, he may develop a sense of inferiority. There are many possible reasons for this. Difficulties at this stage may be related to unresolved problems at an earlier stage. For example, a child who developed a greater sense of doubt than autonomy during that period in his life may feel unsure of himself as he attempts new tasks. [46] Adults may expect more of children than that of which they are capable, putting pressure on children to perform. When they cannot meet our expectations, they may see themselves as failures. Children who are members of minority groups may have experiences in school or elsewhere from which they wrongly conclude that their racial or ethnic background means that they are not capable of doing all that they desire. Schools and teachers have an important role to play in helping *all* children become strong, healthy, competent individuals who can contribute to society. Churches can do a great deal to help children discover that God has gifted all people with abilities they can use in service to the world.

Children at this age have a strong desire to play a significant role in the communities to which they belong, which is one of the characteristics of the affiliative style of faith. Congregations can support children in the elementary years by finding appropriate and meaningful ways for them to contribute to the life of the faith community, just as Jason's father did for him. While we must be careful not to impose unrealistic expectations on them, children are often capable of far more responsibility than we are willing to give. As many congregations already know, they can sing in choirs, serve as greeters and ushers, and help in a variety of mission projects. Because children at this age love ritual, it is appropriate to ask a child to assist with the leadership of the worship service. But when we do, we must work with them to make sure they are adequately prepared. Like adults, children do not want to be embarrassed. For children who are wrestling with feelings of inferiority, this is especially important. They want to help, but they also want to do well so that they will be perceived by others as being competent and successful. For example, when we prepare children for their first experience of communion, we adults are most concerned that they understand the meaning of what they will be doing. The children are more concerned with what they will be expected to do when the elements are shared with them. As we help them explore meanings, we must not forget the latter.

This child who is working hard to become a productive member of his world is also undergoing a qualitative shift in the way he thinks about that world. In Piaget's theory, beginning around age 7 the child enters the stage of *concrete operations* in which he begins to master the elementary patterns and structures of logical thinking. In this stage, the mental activities of a child remain concrete because they are still tied to the real world where he lives. But he is now able to engage in mental operations related to that world. An operation is a mental action that can be reversed. As Piaget studied them, operations have to do with the child's ability to deal with such matters as space, time, quantity, and the classification of objects.

Piaget's famous conservation experiments provide us with a picture of what he meant by reversing an operation. There are several versions of this experiment. In one, a child must judge whether two mounds of clay that appear to be the same size continue to contain the same amount of clay when one is rolled into a sausage or flattened into a pancake. In the latter case, a preschooler is likely to say that the pancake is larger. Because he draws conclusions intuitively based on perception and because he tends to focus on only one facet of a situation at a time, the fact that the pancake now covers more area may cause him to judge it to be larger. A child who has reached the stage of *concrete operations* will usually be able to determine that the amount of clay has remained the same. He can reverse his mental operation to conclude that if you reformed the clay into its original ball, it would be the same as it was at the beginning. Nothing has been added or subtracted. This is what Piaget meant by reversibility—the ability to reverse a thought process in one's mind. [47]

Conservation and reversibility are two primary characteristics of concrete-operational thinking. Classification is another. Classification has to do with groupings and relationships. A 5-year-old may know that his class at school is made up of 15 children, including six boys and nine girls. If you ask him whether there are more boys or more girls in the class, he will easily reply, "More girls." But if you ask him whether there are more girls or more children in the class, he will likely be puzzled and still reply, "There are more girls than boys." He does not have a grasp of the concept of class in which the larger class of children subsumes both the class of boys and the class of girls. In a similar manner, if a preschool child is asked whether he has a brother, he might answer, "Yes, his name is Andrew." But if he is asked whether his brother has a brother, he will answer, "No." Fitting the concept of brother into a larger pattern of brother relationships is beyond his cognitive abilities. By age 7, this idea poses no problem for a child.[48]

What all of this means is that the concrete-operational child is no longer bound by his perceptions. Even though he is still very much tied to the real world, he is now able to take into account multiple factors of a situation at once and perform logical operations related to them in his head. He cannot yet think abstractly as we described it earlier, but his thinking about the world is becoming more logical and organized. We need to remember that Piaget argued that this change in the way a child thinks has to do with more than the fact that his knowledge of the world is expanding. That is happening. But for the child, it is not just a matter of carrying more information in his head. Around age 7, he begins to process knowledge differently than he did as a preschooler. There is a qualitative shift in the way that he thinks.

A child in this stage of cognitive development is very interested in figuring out how the world works. His newfound mental abilities may lead him to question many of the ideas he has carried from preschool years. "Is it real?" is a common question that is applied to everything from the tooth fairy to Santa, and perhaps to God as well. This child is a gatherer of facts and information. If we tell him the story of Jesus feeding 5,000 people and ask him what he finds interesting in that story, he may want to know how Jesus did it. How did he manage to feed that many people with five loaves of bread and two fish? The concrete realities of the story are likely to grab his attention, and he may begin to work out the math involved.

Because of this focus on the concrete, the elementary-age child is in many ways a biblical literalist. In the case of Bible stories, the question "Is it real?" may shift to become "Is it true?" For many of us, answering his question about the truth of a Bible story is a complicated task. We may choose to let the facts speak for themselves and let the child draw his own conclusions. Or we may use the question as an opportunity to work within this child's zone of proximal development and push him to think further about his question. As we enter into conversation with the child about this matter, we may invite him to consider the story in ways that move beyond *true* and *untrue*. For example, by the middle elementary years, we can begin to introduce children to the concept of literary forms in the Bible and how they might distinguish between those forms. They can be helped to understand that we do not read the book of Psalms the same way we read an epistle, and that we ask different questions of one of the stories of Jesus miracles than we do of one of his parables. Opening up the notion of literary forms for children is one way that we may help to stretch them developmentally. [49]

Piaget assumed that his understanding of a child's intellectual development provided a comprehensive view of children's intelligence. As the examples above illustrate, Piaget focused his attention on how children make sense of things such as numbers and quantity. He was a scientist primarily interested in a child's scientific thinking. [50] While Piaget's research was foundational for what we understand about children's cognitive development, a number of theorists are expanding on the groundwork that he has laid. One of those is Howard Gardner who has proposed that all human beings really possess eight different kinds of intelligence. Gardner believes that Piaget's theory accounts for just two—linguistic and logical-mathematical intelligence.

For Gardner, an intelligence is "*a biopsychological potential to process information that can be activated in a cultural setting to solve problems or create products that are of value in a culture.*" [51] Through work with people with brain injuries, with gifted children, and through the study of psychology, neurology, biology, sociology, anthropology, and the arts, Gardner identified a number of criteria that he used to determine whether a particular human capacity counts as an intelligence according to this definition. There is not space here to explore the criteria Gardner selected. [52] What we do need to note is that he is very deliberate in using the word *intelligence* to describe the capacities he discovered using these criteria. According to Gardner, they are not skills or gifts or talents. They are mental tools we use to come to understand something about the world.

The eight intelligences that Gardner has identified

- **Linguistic intelligence:** The ability to use written and spoken language. Writers, public speakers, and lawyers excel in this form of intelligence.

- **Logical-mathematical intelligence:** The ability to analyze problems, do mathematical operations, and engage in scientific investigations.

Gardner believes that these first two intelligences are the most valued in schools, and that children with high intelligence in these areas usually do well academically.

- **Musical intelligence:** The ability to perform, appreciate, and compose works of music.

- **Bodily-kinesthetic intelligence:** The ability to use one's body, or parts of the body, to solve problems or create products. Athletes and dancers rely greatly on this intelligence, as do craftspeople and surgeons.

- **Spatial intelligence:** The ability to recognize and manipulate spatial areas, both large and confined. People with high spatial intelligence include pilots, navigators, chess players, visual artists, and architects.

- **Interpersonal intelligence:** The ability to understand the intentions and motivations of other people and to work well with others. Teachers, salespeople, ministers, and counselors need a high level of this intelligence.

- **Intrapersonal intelligence:** The ability to understand oneself and to use that knowledge effectively in living one's life.[53]

- **Naturalist intelligence:** The ability to recognize and classify the various species—both flora and fauna—in one's environment.[54]

Gardner originally proposed the first seven categories of intelligence. Then, using the criteria he has specified, he later concluded that the naturalist intelligence also qualified. In addition, he has explored the possibility of the existence of two more intelligences—a spiritual intelligence and an existential intelligence—but he is not yet ready to add them to the list.[55] Gardner contends that all of us possess the potential for all eight intelligences, but that we do not develop them all. The particular combination of intelligences we each possess depends on which ones are valued by our culture, our personal environment, and the opportunities we are given to develop particular intelligences, such as music; plus our own inclinations. Each of the children with whom we are engaged in educational ministry brings to the faith community his own blend of intelligences. Each engages the world through his distinctive framework for understanding it, which means that the way that a child engages and holds faith is also shaped by the unique combination of intelligences that he possesses. In our planning for educational ministry, the multiple intelligences with which God has gifted children—and all of us—open up a variety of possibilities for engaging them in teaching/learning experiences.

Although elementary children are inclined to focus on concrete realities and are most interested in facts, they haven't entirely lost the ability to engage in the more imaginative thinking that we see in preschoolers. In fact, imagination can play an important role in their learning. Kieran Egan defines imagination as "the capacity to think of things as possibly being so." [56] It is the ability to envision alternative ways to look at the world, not unlike the "what if" aspect of the play of the preschool child. The imaginations of children of this age, says Egan, are especially captivated by the extremes and limits of human experience—the most terrible and the most wonderful, the cruelest and the most courageous.[57] They are drawn to heroes and heroines whose stories allow them to imagine all that they might be. The stories of the Bible provide an arena in which their imaginations can be engaged. These stories are filled with acts of love and hatred, of courage and cowardice, and of sacrifice and generosity, all of which help to reveal the nature of authentic discipleship. For children to discover this, we will need to stop treating the stories as lessons in how we are to behave. Children need encouragement to engage the stories on their own terms to discover what meanings they can find there.

We can invite them to imagine themselves in the stories: What if you were Abraham or Sarah, and God told you to leave your home and move to a new land that you had never seen? Imagine what that was like. What if you had been one of the disciples standing below the cross on what we now call Good Friday? Imagine what you would have felt.

We worry that because the world of the Bible is so far removed from our own, children will not be able to understand its stories. But children's fascination with strange and distant worlds might mean just the opposite. The "strangeness" of the Bible could be a vehicle for engaging their imaginations and drawing them into its world and its message—if we allow this to happen. While this is an appropriate stage in their development to encourage our children to learn the practices and stories—the facts, if you will—that constitute the content of our faith, it is also an ideal time to help them capture the wonder and mystery of God.

Growing in faith

We began this chapter by affirming that faith is a gift from God to which we respond in trust and gratitude. Children come to God on their own terms and the way they express their trust and gratitude is shaped by where they are in their own development. Robert Kegan suggests that a person is more an activity than a thing—to be human is to be in motion.[58] He does not mean by this that to be human is to be busy *doing* things, but that human *being* itself is activity. We are constantly about the business of making meaning out of the things that happen to us, out of the experiences of our lives.[59] If this is true, it is surely true of faith as well. All of us throughout our lives are engaged in the activity of making sense of the experiences of our faith, sometimes successfully and sometime not so successfully, and we do so in ways appropriate to our level of development. Children do not make sense of their faith like adults do. They do so in ways appropriate to where they are emotionally and cognitively. What they discover may not seem adequate from an adult point of view, but may be just fine from a child's perspective. We need to trust that as they grow in the ways that God intends, the way they hold their faith will expand to meet them.

The styles of faith that Westerhoff describes give us a framework for understanding all of this. Experienced and affiliative faith, which we examined in this chapter, lay the groundwork for the next two styles. The faith of the adolescent is a searching faith. From Erikson's perspective, this is a time of exploration and experimentation during which youth search for an identity that will connect who they were as children with who they will be as adults. Because they can now think abstractly—Piaget's stage of *formal operations*—they may begin to ask questions that test the faith of their childhood to see if it is strong enough to carry them into adulthood.[60] They are reaching for an owned faith—the faith of the adult. This is a faith that is claimed and lived. It is not a resting place, but a continuation of a journey that began in infancy.[61] As we travel that journey, we do not leave behind the styles of faith that characterized our childhood and adolescence, but incorporate them into the faith that we now claim as our own.

For those of us in ministry with children in the church, it is a privilege and a joy to walk with them as they grow in faith. Along the way, we do well to remember that God's Spirit travels with us and works both in the lives of the children and in our own. The writer to the Ephesians has articulated where it is that we are heading, which is to the place where all of us come "to the unity of the faith and of the knowledge of the Son of God, to maturity, to the measure of the full stature of Christ" (Ephesians 4:13). May God be with you on your way.

FOR REFLECTION AND DISCUSSION

1. Why should the church pay attention to the processes of human development? What do these things have to do with growing in faith?

2. Think about children you know who are at various stages in the developmental process. What have you read here that helps you understand something about their behavior or the conversations that you have had with them?

3. Based on what you have read in this chapter, are there things that you would change in your congregation related to how you go about your ministry with children? What are they?

Notes

1. This illustration is taken from Diane J. Hymans, *The Role of Play in a Cultural-Linguistic Approach to Religion: Theoretical Implications for Education in the Faith Community* (Ed.D. dissertation, Presbyterian School of Christian Education, 1993.), p. 1.

2. Sara Little, *To Set One's Heart: Belief and Teaching in the Church* (Atlanta: John Knox, 1983), p. 17. Italics in original.

3. John H. Westerhoff, *Will Our Children Have Faith?* (New York: Seabury, 1976), pp. 89-99.

4. A complete discussion of Erikson's theory appears in Erik Erikson, *Childhood and Society* (New York: W. W. Norton, 1950, 1963).

5. A useful overview of Piaget's theory appears in Jean Piaget and Barbel Inhelder, *The Psychology of the Child* (New York: Basic Books, 1969).

6. Westerhoff., p. 92.

7. Ibid., p. 93.

8. Erikson, p. 247.

9. Carol Garhard Mooney, *Theories of Childhood: An Introduction to Dewey, Montessori, Erikson, Piaget, and Vygotsky* (St. Paul: Redleaf, 2000), p. 40.

10. William C. Crain, *Theories of Development: Concepts and Applications*, 2nd ed. (Englewood Cliffs, N.J.: Prentice-Hall, 1985), p. 163.

11. Stanley N. Graven, "Things That Matter in the Lives of Children," in *Exploring Children's Spiritual Formation: Foundational Issues*, Shirley K. Margenthaler, ed. (River Forest, Ill.: Pillars, 1999), pp. 50-52.

12. Mooney, p. 40.

13. Graven, pp. 50-51.

14. Mooney, p. 41.

15. Erikson, p. 247.

16. Mooney, p. 64.

17. Jean Piaget and Barbel Inhelder, *The Psychology of the Child* (New York: Basic Books, 1969), pp. 14-15.

18. Robert Kegan, *The Evolving Self: Problem and Process in Human Development* (Cambridge: Harvard University, 1982), pp. 30-31.

19. Mooney, pp. 65, 67.

20. Crain, pp. 164-165.

21. Erikson, p. 254.

22. Alice S. Honig, "The Roots of Faith: The Crucial Role of Infant/Toddler Caregivers" in *Faith Development in Early Childhood*, Doris A. Blazer, ed. (Kansas City, Mo.: Sheed and Ward, 1989), p. 41.

23. Ibid., pp. 40-41.

24. Ibid., p. 41.

25. Mooney, pp. 48-49.

26. Erikson, p. 258.

27. Mooney, p. 51.

28. Ibid., p. 53.

29. Jean Piaget, *Six Psychological Studies* (New York: Vintage Books, 1967), p. 29.

30. Ibid., p. 26.

31. David Elkind, *A Sympathetic Understanding of the Child: Birth to Sixteen*, 3rd ed. (Boston: Allyn and Bacon, 1994), p. 59.

32. John Hull, *God-talk with Young Children* (Philadelphia: Trinity Press International, 1991), pp. 8-9.

33. See Kieran Egan, *Teaching as Storytelling* (Chicago: University of Chicago, 1986), pp. 13-15.

34. Quoted in "Let's Play: The Contribution of the Pretend Play of Children to Education in a Pluralistic Context," by Diane J. Hymans, *Religious Education Journal*, vol. 91, no. 3 (Summer 1996), p. 374. This article provides a more complete discussion of the ideas discussed here.

35. A. Roger Gobbel and Gertrude G. Gobbel, *The Bible: A Child's Playground* (Philadelphia: Fortress, 1986), p. 104.

36. Ibid., p. 106.

37. L. S. Vygotsky, *Mind in Society: The Development of Higher Psychological Processes*, ed. Michael Cole, et al (Cambridge: Harvard University, 1978), p. 86.

38. Roland G. Tharp and Ronald Gallimore, *Rousing Minds to Life: Teaching, Learning, and Schooling in Social Context* (Cambridge: Cambridge University, 1988), pp. 33-34.

39. Ibid., pp. 29-30.

40. Mooney, p. 91.

41. Westerhoff, p. 94.

42. Erikson, *Identity and the Life Cycle* (New York: International Universities, 1959), p. 82.

43. Kegan, p. 163.

44. Elkind, pp. 96-97.

45. Ibid., p. 102.

46. Crain, p. 167.

47. Ibid., pp. 99-101.

48. Elkind, pp. 135-136.

49. For a more complete discussion of this issue, see Gobbel and Gobbel, pp. 119-122.

50. Howard Gardner, *The Unschooled Mind: How Children Think and How Schools Should Teach* (New York: Basic Books, 1991), p. 29.

51. Gardner, *Intelligence Reframed: Multiple Intelligences for the 21st Century* (New York: Basic Books, 1999), pp. 33-34. Italics in original.

52. Ibid., pp. 35-41, for a complete discussion of the eight criteria.

53. Ibid., pp. 41-43.

54. Ibid., pp. 48.

55. Ibid., p. 64.

56. Kieran Egan, *Imagination in Teaching and Learning* (Chicago: University of Chicago, 1992), p. 43.

57. Ibid., p. 72.

58. Kegan, p. 8.

59. Ibid., p. 11.

60. Westerhoff, p. 96.

61. Ibid., p. 98.

CHAPTER 3

Who Is the Child?
Whose Is the Child?
A Theology of Children

Norma Cook Everist

EMMA SHOWED ME THE FLOWERS, the prettiest ones, especially a large pink peony bush way to the back of Concordia Cemetery. As we walked hand-in-hand, we passed a new grave and this just-turned-seven child noted how easy it is to plant flowers in freshly turned earth. Since the time she was 2, Emma has lived in the parsonage between the church and the cemetery with her father and mother (who is pastor of this rural congregation), and her older sister and brother. Emma knows about death as a part of life. She knows about Jesus who loves the little children buried in this graveyard. She knows about the Creator God of the frozen northern plains and of late spring peonies. Surely the Holy Spirit has created a deep, solid faith in Emma who calmly and confidently trusts in and witnesses to the God of abundant, steadfast love.

W ho is the child? Whose is the child?[1] We find the answers by watching Emma. We discover a theology of children by focusing those questions in a number of directions. In this chapter we shall first ask those questions of the society in which we live. Then we shall look at the three articles of our Christian creeds, followed by a brief look at the Bible. Next we look at two of the writings of Martin Luther. Finally we observe six children, ranging in age from infancy to age 12. At each stage we invite the reader also to reflect on the two questions, culminating in a call to see the ministering child.

Answers in the news

The world responds to the questions "Who is the child?" and "Whose is the child?" in multifaceted ways. I have been fascinated with these questions and the gradually changing answers for more than a quarter century. To note the range of responses, I watched for explicit—but more often implicit—answers in three weeks of local, regional, and national news media.[2] I did not do statistical analysis (which would have been invalid research). My goal was for us all to see how society views children today, through hard news, features, sports,[3] as well as in photographs, ads, and even in an advice column.[4]

Whose is the child?

Problem or promise?

Is a child "naturally" good (innocent) or bad (evil)? Who determines that judgment? A 7-year-old boy was found kept in a closet in filth. He was unfed, weighing 36 pounds, being punished for "being bad." The parents were not contrite but tried to justify their actions, holding, as many parents throughout history have done, that children not only have problems, or are sometimes problematic to parents, but are themselves a "problem" (bad and need to be reared using punishing correctives).

On the other hand, when people hold a working theology that children are "innocent," incapable of the wrongdoing that characterizes adults, their response to reporters' questions when boys took bombs to school was,

"They didn't look like they could do that." When teenage girls hazed and injured other girls (society holds a working theology that girls in general are more "innocent" than boys), adults told reporters, "Not our children" and "We have a good school." Such common comments imply that children of other parents, perhaps less economically advantaged or of other races or religions, or living in urban not rural areas might be "bad." The potential in children for hurting others, even killing, is present in every child, intensified greatly in a culture that promotes and glamorizes violence.

Who is responsible when children cause problems? "Child driving car; dad held responsible." "Teenagers at high schools where condoms available are not more likely to have sex than other teens." "Juvenile detention centers not meant to serve as mental hospitals." What does this society believe about psychiatrically ill children and youth? About sex? About breaking the law?

News stories clearly showed that those children society deems more "problematic" by race (higher arrest rates), or economic class (sent to a detention center rather than a mental health facility) "fall through cracks." "Teaching boys manhood isn't measured in sexual conquests" was a story that showed a group of men not abdicating responsibility ("boys will be boys") but addressing sexuality in communal accountability.

Protégé or pride?

We may associate stage mothers and proud fathers grooming their sons to take over the family business with scenes from the past,[5] when children had less choice of their own vocations. But today we find new forms of children as extensions of parental dreams.[6] Because my search was done at the beginning of summer, I found numerous stories on children's summer activities, including camps for drama, science, and even hair-styling. It is gratifying to see children today encouraged to explore their interests and gifts, but when the child is merely an extension of parent's dreams and the main source of adult pride, children and their accomplishments can become idols. The busyness of children may be extensions of adults' activity-obsessed culture. Children's lives are measured in lists of activities.[7]

On the other hand, I saw children's accomplishments, not just in sports, but in education, a source of pride not only for their family but for the whole community. (For example: "Area youth advances to spelling bee finals."[8]) Pictures of high school graduates from area schools were displayed daily through the season in local newspapers. Scholastic achievement was recognized on local television. (One grocery store took out a full page add picturing, individually, all their graduating student employees.)

Possession

Child custody battles fill the news, often pictured by a child being ripped from the arms of one parent or another. News reports often follow a romantic search for a grown child's "real" parents. At times foster parents are demonized, adoptive parents ignored. "Whose is the child?" insinuates, "To whom does this child belong?" Does giving birth to children make them the possession of parents? When does the state have the right to sever ties? How does a state carry out its communal responsibility toward children? If children are not possessions like property, do we find stories of people appropriately, courageously caring about the well-being of children? Two news organizations carried the story of African-American families that a century ago moved north for opportunity, now moving back South with and for their children. "Tragedy Turns Dad into a Father"[9] featured a moving account of the physician father, after the space shuttle death of the child's mother, changing his overly busy life: "When you're a dad you're always on call." In the same issue was a story of unmarried men learning how to be fathers.

In need of protection

From what and from whom do children need protection? In "Doors Galore in Cuba City School," regional news of a Wisconsin town noted that 13 doors might be good for fire escapes but not for security. In another state, "Police may be pulled from high school. This popular program is in jeopardy."[10] People are savvy to the danger of strangers, but sometimes children need protection from their own caregivers. Stories abound of overzealous parents at little league games. Parental abuse at home is so common that it often no longer makes the news. "Parents uncork teen alcohol debate," headlined a story asking, "Is supervised drinking by youth at home a safety issue or flouting the law?" In whose protection are children?

A number of morning national TV shows featured segments on child safety. "Children should be in child booster seats much longer than parents expect." Resources were provided on topics such as "Keeping baby safe:

a guide to childhood injuries." A story on "Trend in flextime" providing a greater variety of benefits, showed that what began as part of the women's movement, now helps men and women care and provide for their children. There is still a call for protection for all children in the area of health care. Neither a working theology of "We can protect our children completely" nor of "It's not our responsibility to protect other people's children, only our own" suffices. Still we ask, "What do I do when I cannot protect a child from all danger and disease?" The question "Whose is the child?" has no easy answers.

Who is the child?

Voiceless

Many illegal immigrant children are imprisoned in the United States each year. Their stories rarely make the news. Without vote, 12 million children were quietly excluded from a tax credit bill. News carried stories of the work of Marian Wright Edelman of the Children's Defense Fund, and of babies in strollers, children and adults protesting on Capitol Hill to move legislators to reconsider.

The old adage "Children should be seen and not heard" is rarely enforced today. Yet children, particularly those born into poverty, are voiceless, and their plight not heard except for the advocacy of others. "Sick and without insurance" headlined a story of children of immigrant families, but it was not on the front page. "Build a better system" called for improvement in a state's child welfare system that is being stripped of services in economically strapped times.

A banner headline, "School Closings Likely," appeared in a local paper. Similar articles abound, such as "Milwaukee schools may seek waiver," reporting freezing of funds for mandated school improvements, an ironic response to the "No child left behind act." Who speaks for the children? And on whose behalf and for whose benefit?

Meanwhile children's faces are seen in the news. See the section later in this chapter on "the child as symbol and sign." A local newspaper add for Mercy Hospital shows pictures and lists names of all babies born each month. How might we listen to the needs of the child?

Victim

Children are victims of child abuse, child abduction, natural disasters, disease, war, and much more. In my piles of newspapers, I seldom found children victims of natural disasters ("Fire kills Muscatine boy"). In the days of Martin Luther, one-quarter of all children died before age 5, while today we almost take for granted that most U.S. children will live to adulthood.

Television gave seasonal coverage to children drowning, often accompanied by tips on how to prevent such tragedies. Lacking in U.S. news are global stories of the hundreds of thousands of children who die from disease and malnutrition. While we feed our fear on continuous coverage of one U.S. child who is missing, only a few inside page paragraphs report on thousands of children killed and maimed in wars around the world.

The victimization of children in this society comes in other forms. Headlines scream: "Child's murder shocks Texas border town." "Father kills 3 kids and hangs himself." "Mother acquitted in killing newborn." "Two-car crash kills woman and child." and, the front-page article: "Bishops Work to Regain Trust." (These articles focused on the bishops, not on the children who were sexually abused.)

This society has been aware of lead poisoning for decades. Unwilling as a society to make a commitment to mandatory inspections, children become the first line of detection. Only when they show signs of delayed development are landlords notified that they must do something. By then children have permanent brain damage. Children are victims of a disease for which at this time there is no cure, but which is totally preventable.

Hero

Children are not simply victims. A news account of an 8-year-old girl who was abducted reported that she had the presence of mind and creativity to tell her abductor that she was asthmatic and that if she didn't get her medicine she would die. She also took note of the house number where she was confined and the cell phone number that her abductor used to order pizza. All that information was used to arrest the man. Yes, vulnerable, yes, object of abuse, but children are also brave and bright and capable.

A 7-year-old pulled his 19-month-old sister out of a wading baby pool. He was deemed a "hero" for his life-saving efforts. The story aired in part to inform the public that a child can drown even in three inches of water. Life is precious; life is fragile. Children are strong; children are precious.[11]

There was a newspaper picture of a child athlete in a wheelchair and the story of a youth group's mission project to spend time at an animal rescue league. (Church periodicals often carry articles about youth serving.) People need to hear not just of dramatic survival but also of children who daily are capable of genuine service. Also in the news were pictures of boy soldiers, of a girl suicide bomber, seen as heroes because the adults in their world have not yet been able to establish and maintain peace. At what price are such heroics?

Immature people

For centuries, children were portrayed as immature people. Artwork did not show correct proportions. They were "incomplete" and therefore lacked adult privileges.[12] Today we understand child development. Yet, ironically, in a society where childhood is portrayed as a time of innocence, today the word *adult* privileges one not only to vote, but to be killed in war, to drink, to gamble, and to purchase pornography.

This society is criticized for extending childhood and also for shortening childhood. News and feature stories about children in transition to adulthood capture conflicting attitudes. "R-rated hit-movies draw teens but not I.D. checks." A business section front-page article: "Entrepreneurship inspires teens at Lutheran High School" is particularly noteworthy because of providing business skills to minority youth. "College students find paid internships scarce." "Student loans consolidated both an advantage and disadvantage." TV and news magazine features offer new rules for parent-child relationships when graduates move home after college or divorce. How do we determine who is a child? By age? By economics? By independence?

The child as symbol and sign

Sign of an affluent society: consumer

Today one enters a secondary school and sees halls lined with soda machines and junk food dispensers. Aware of nutritional information and with the rising rate of childhood obesity, why provide children such blatant opportunity to spend their money and consume what adults know is not good for them? (Approximately 13 million children in the United States are at risk for hunger,[14] and millions more suffer health risks because they are overweight.) An early-morning news report showed results of tests that if children are exposed to the option of purchasing milk, it will increase the amount of milk they drink that day, not only from machines at school but also at home.[15] Children's buying power now must contribute to funding public schools that face severe budget cutbacks. Some school administrators, securing large contracts from soft-drink companies, are expected to place soft drink machines at every strategic corner so that children will have to pass them often, particularly on the way to the cafeteria.

Easily noticed, but rarely opposed is the phenomenon of marketing to children on Saturday-morning television and through movie character products. In a consumer-oriented society, the child becomes a symbol of conspicuous consumption. We have exported consumerism as a symbol of worth to the world. (The news story of an emerging middle class in China is told through a picture of children eating pizza.)

Symbol of success and celebration

The term *trophy wife* is not very common today, but today we have *trophy children* instead. On an afternoon talk show,[16] a mother is stressed out because she could not send her preschool children out the door unless perfectly groomed (with ironed clothes, including jeans). A newspaper advertisement promoted, "The quiet of St. Bens neighborhood. The quality of Bell school. The opportunity you've been waiting for." The pictures of happy families with children promised an "extraordinarily private city enclave with homes from $859,000."[17]

An intriguing paragraph in a story of Queen Elizabeth of Great Britain's 50th anniversary of coronation, told of 500 children invited to the castle grounds for a party. A good gesture for "poor, orphaned, and disabled children," but a gesture nonetheless.

More troubling, because the Queen's party was *for* the children, is "Parents spare no expense for kids' birthdays." "Kids birthday parties now are a full-blown industry fueled by increasing amounts of disposable income." Some cost $1,000 or more and "prove" a family's ability to provide entertainment for their children. Giving to one's children to help them be happy is a genuine desire for parents everywhere, but it crosses over to trophy children, or even child-worship when a parent says, "I wouldn't give her the moon, but I will do what I can within reason!"[18] Are we justified by our trophies? How do we celebrate childhood and children?

Sign of the holy and symbol of terror

Is the child a holy symbol? Two newspapers carried the story of a town keeping the memory of a "mystery baby" alive.[19] Abandoned at birth and forever anonymous, the community sensed this child was more than throwaway waste. Life is holy.

Children are frequently spotlighted in pictorial coverage of war: a child holding a picture of the missing Thailand leader; children peering from a balcony over soldiers in their street; a baby in the arms of a mother greeting a U.S. soldier back from war. Are these children being used as heart-tugging symbols? What do we do to change a world that still glamorizes adult-spawned wars? Children are also symbols of the open future. Children symbolize promise. Among the many seasonal stories of children graduating, from kindergarten through college, a front-page story of high school graduates had this third-page continuation subtitle: "Journey to the Unknown."[20]

A symbol security

What is more calming at the end of a stressful day than to see children's faces on the front page of the newspaper? Pictures abound of children with animals, kids selling lemonade, children riding a carousel in a park, a man and his granddaughter attending Greek Fest together, a 13-year-old in a beautiful front page picture in scenic Eagle Point Park.

Even if the children are named, they are placed there not for singular notoriety but to assure a society that things are secure. Pictures feature parents and children running together and cycling together. This is an active society, and people are bonding.

This is "good news" in a world that is titillated by bad news ("If it bleeds it leads" is a newspaper editor's mantra.) But still one wonders: In a society in which children are still victimized and voiceless, and in a world where millions of children die of preventable disease and are homeless because of war, why do we use children to symbolize what we seem unable to attain?

Sign of unsolved issues in society

Where in this list would one place the issue of abortion? An unborn child in need of protection? (A fetus on a billboard.) A possession? A symbol of what the family should be? I place it here as a sign because often the child is a pawn in hands of those who want to judge and to control women's bodies. It is also a symbol of the challenge to have women and men fully take responsibility for their own relationships and for bringing into the world children they are willing and able to care for.

How will we as adults deal with issues that face not only children but the entire society? Unsolved issues are often played out in the school yards of America. A generation ago, battles over integration and bussing were played out at the school door. Today the issues of evolution and creationism determine school board elections in some areas. The growing disparity between the wealthy and the poor show up in school budget debates and school voucher decisions. "New Schools for Pine Ridge" signals that the presence of children in a Native American reservation are symbols of the health—even the continuing identity—of a community. School bombings and security checks for weapons signal our inability to turn from our addiction to violence.

The images and impressions from the media that answer our questions, "Who is the child?" and "Whose is the child" continue to change. They give us much to ponder.

For Reflection and Discussion

1. Listen, watch, read the news. What do you find? What other word categories would you use?

2. If you were preparing the news, what would you report?

Grounding in the creeds

What do our creeds say in response? Christian churches throughout the centuries and around the globe share a common confession of faith in the words of the Apostles' Creed:

The First Article

I believe in God the Father almighty, Creator of heaven and earth.

The Second Article

I believe in Jesus Christ, God's only son, our Lord, who was conceived by the Holy Spirit, born of the Virgin Mary, suffered under Pontius Pilate, was crucified, died, and was buried; he descended to the dead. On the third day he rose again; he ascended into heaven; he is seated at the right hand of the Father, and he will come to judge the living and the dead.

The Third Article

I believe in the Holy Spirit, the holy catholic church, the communion of saints, the forgiveness of sins the resurrection of the body, and the life everlasting. Amen.

The creating God

It sounds so simple! Of course we believe that this little baby born to or adopted by a family was created by God. Who of us could have crafted those tiny fingernails? Who else but God could have shaped those small limbs that stretch and wiggle and will grow to carry this child out to discover the world? Of course we believe in the almighty Creator of heaven and earth.

But do we believe that?

The creating God

Luther's explanation to the First Article in the Small Catechism says:

I believe that God has created me together with all that exists. God has given me and still preserves my body and soul: eyes, ears, and all limbs and senses; reason and all mental faculties. In addition, God daily and abundantly provides shoes and clothing, food and drink, house and farm, spouse and children, fields, livestock and all property—along with all the necessities and nourishment for this body and life. God protects me against all danger and shields and preserves me from all evil. [21]

This God who has created the children for whom I am parent, for whom I am teacher or pastor, has also created all the other children in the world. This has consequences. This God who created my child who needs food and shoes and books, created the environment. To believe in the Creator God is to believe that children are created to grow and designed to develop.

The providing God

Luther's Large Catechism says:

What kind of person is God? What does [God] do? How can we praise or portray or describe [God] in such a way so we may know [God]? . . . Aside from this one alone I regard nothing as God, for there is no one else who could create heaven and earth.[22]

Thus, we learn that none of us has life by ourselves. None of us can create, live, nor perfectly provide for our children. "None of us has life by ourselves" could also be interpreted to mean that if we seek to provide only for our own children, or as children, want things provided only for ourselves, we will not truly have life. God provides life not just for one person or one family, or one church. God is the provider of all, and God uses us to participate in God's providing for the needs of the young.

The preserving and protecting God

"God protects me against all danger and shields and preserves me from all evil." [23] This is more difficult to believe. After the natural disaster of a tornado, a newscaster asks, "How do you think you and your child survived when your house was blown away around you?" "God protected us," the survivor responds. This is a moment to confess belief in a loving God. But what about the child down the street that did not survive the tornado? And what about the millions of children killed, maimed and displaced by wars, disasters that are caused by human beings?

To say we believe in God the Creator is to commit to caring for, protecting, and being an advocate for children throughout the world. The first realm of creation includes all human institutions (family, church, governments).[24] In order to protect us, God has provided God's righteous law to restrain harm and ensure just well-being of all people, which certainly must include children everywhere. We are dependent upon God who calls us to use appropriately our parental, pastoral and teaching authority to care for children so that they will develop and grow. Children are not our possessions. All children are God's children.

The liberating God

We believe the living God works among us in a second way (the second realm of God: Law and Gospel). God liberates humankind from bondage to sin and death not with missiles or might, but by coming to live among us as a child. We believe that Jesus was conceived in a woman's womb, born homeless, that no children, even the homeless ones, no matter how poor, might be left outside the arms of God. Luther wrote:

> Behold Christ lying in the lap of his young mother. . . . Look at the Child, knowing nothing. Yet all that is belongs to him, that your conscience should not fear but take comfort in him. Doubt nothing. Watch him springing in the lap of the maiden. Laugh with him. Look upon this Lord of Peace and your spirit will be at peace. See how God invites you in many ways. God places before you a Babe with whom you may take refuge. You cannot fear him. . . . Trust him! Trust him! Here is the Child in whom is salvation. . . . Now is overcome the power of sin, death, hell, conscience, and guilt, if you come to this gurgling Babe and believe that he is come, not to judge you, but to save.[25]

God in Christ was vulnerable, but not victim because of that vulnerability. Jesus was whisked away to Egypt as an infant because King Herod felt threatened enough by the potential power of this little child to slaughter all of the children in and around Bethlehem who were 2 years old or younger (Matthew 2:16). Unnamed and even unnumbered, these children—"collateral damage"—are remembered liturgically each December 28. Jesus the child, was carried, presented in the temple (Luke 2:22-39). He grew, listened, and discerned his own calling when he was just 12 years old (Luke 2:41-52).

Who is the child? Sinful and redeemed. Lost and now found. We need no longer punish children for sins through military might. We dare not be willing to sacrifice thousands of children of people whom we call our enemies. The enemy is no longer an enemy. We need to be careful that we do not see Christ's atonement only as appeasement of an angry Father God. Too often this has resulted in the mistaken view that fathers are God, kings of the castle, masters of their domain. Too often this gives parents excuse for their own anger and abuse.

The Large Catechism

Here we get to know the second person of the Godhead, and we see . . . how he has given himself completely to us, withholding nothing. [In his usual colorful language, Luther continued:] Those tyrants and jailers [disobedience, sin, death and all evil] have now been routed, and their place has been taken by Jesus Christ, the Lord of life, righteousness, and every good blessing.[26]

The Small Catechism

[Jesus] has redeemed me, a lost and condemned human being. . . . He has purchased and freed me from all sins, from death, and from the power of the devil, not with gold or silver but with his holy, precious blood and with his innocent suffering and death.[27]

We hear parents say how much they have sacrificed for their children. Jesus alone is the sacrificial lamb. We cannot justify our idolatry of children or our abuse of children. A child cannot serve as the scapegoat of a family. Nor are parents to sacrifice themselves. Jesus' atonement for reconciliation of relationships is complete. Christ has created a new community where no one need be sacrificed.

FOR REFLECTION AND DISCUSSION

1. Who is Jesus for you? Throughout the life cycle we may think of Jesus differently. Tell each other. Is Jesus your brother? Your Savior? Your friend?

2. No matter what your age, 7 or 77, talk about your relationship with Christ the Savior in your education class, in a small group, or at home. Now think of at least one time this next week when you can naturally share Jesus with someone at work or at school. If they seem lost, show them Jesus, who looks for and finds the lost. If they seem sad, show them Christ, who loves them. If it seems their lives are torn apart, tell them of Christ, who makes them whole.

The empowering God

We confess we believe in the forgiveness of sins and the communion of saints. In Christ we are sanctified, made holy. We are saint and sinner. The child is neither "innocent" nor "evil." Children and adults alike are in need of God's work of redemption and sanctification. Sometimes we hear children referred to as "God's holy angels," or hear a grieving parent say, "God wanted another angel in heaven." God does call all children to God's self, but children are not automatically little cherubs. At each stage of the life cycle God is making each of us holy, freed from bondage to sin for service in the world and for life together with God forever.

The Small Catechism

I believe that by my own understanding or strength I cannot believe in Jesus Christ my LORD or come to him, but instead the Holy Spirit has called me through the gospel, enlightened me with his gifts, and made me holy and kept me in the true faith. [28]

The Holy Spirit calls, gathers, enlightens, and makes holy the whole Christian church on earth and keeps it with Jesus Christ in the one common, true faith. [29] It is the Spirit who calls our children, gathers them, teaches enlightens—them and makes them holy. We, members of Christ's body, are called to participate in God's calling, enlightening, sanctifying mission action.

The Large Catechism

[The Holy Spirit] first leads us into his holy community, placing us in the church's lap, where he preaches to us and brings us to Christ. [30]

[The Holy Spirit] reveals and proclaims [the Word of God], through which he illuminates and inflames hearts so that they grasp and accept it, cling to it, and persevere in it. . . . For where Christ is not preached, there is no Holy Spirit to create, call and gather the Christian church, apart from which no one can come to the Lord Christ. [31]

In this multicultural world of many religions (very different from the Germany that Luther knew), we do have a mission to respect, listen to, and learn from people of many faith traditions. We teach clearly the gospel of Jesus Christ. Such instruction of God's unconditional love equips children to share their faith in words and actions and to live together in God's interdependent world as peace-makers and workers for justice. [32]

We do not educate our children in the faith to keep them safely tucked inside the home or the church building. The empowering work of the Spirit sends children out to share God's love and to be Christ's arms and legs and voice in God's work of healing the world.

The Large Catechism

Neither you nor I could ever know anything about Christ, or believe in him and receive him as Lord, unless these were offered to us and bestowed on our hearts through the preaching of the gospel by the Holy Spirit. The work is finished and completed; Christ has acquired and won the treasure for us by his sufferings, death, and resurrection, etc. But if the work remained hidden so that no one knew of it, it would have been all in vain, all lost. In order that this treasure might not remain buried but put to use and enjoyed, God has caused the Word to be published and proclaimed. [33]

Teach the Word, publish resources, proclaim. We are to teach the child. "It takes a village to raise a child," as the African proverb states. In the Apostles' Creed we say to each other: "I believe in the communion of saints." God is creating villages for us to raise each other's children. The United States, with its heavy emphases on the civil religion doctrine of freedom of the individual and rights of private family, has much to learn from cultures and churches around the world that practice communal care for each other. We sometimes worry about with whom our children might associate. We are called to care for the children next door, across town, and around the world. God in Christ has not only associated with us, but binds us all to one another for mission and ministry and reconciliation among all peoples. We need not fear when we confess we believe in the living God.

FOR REFLECTION AND DISCUSSION

1. How does thinking about the creating, liberating, and empowering actions of God help you answer the questions "Who is the child?" and "Whose is the child?"

2. Look at children in your community and around the world. To what mission and ministry is God calling you?

Seeking the Scriptures

Other authors in this book will have referred to Scripture in a number of ways. Here I shall look briefly at only a few portions of the Bible, asking the specific question, "How does Scripture answer our questions: 'Who is the child?' and 'Whose is the child?'"

In those societies thousands of years ago, where women and children and slaves were of much less significance than adult males, one might expect that *child* and *children* would be rarely mentioned in the Bible. But not so! These words are used hundreds of times. Rarely are children spoken of negatively. The word *childish* appears only once in Scripture (1 Corinthians 13:11), and then not disparagingly. Paul simply says that when he grew up and became an adult he "put an end to childish ways." In its own way, this is a positive acknowledgement of the unique nature of childhood: "When I was a child, I spoke like a child, I thought like a child, I reasoned like a child."

The child as measure of women's and men's worth

Our question "Whose is the child?" is answered in some ways that should trouble us today. A woman who did not have children was categorized negatively: "childless," "barren." From Sarai in Genesis 11 to Rachel in Genesis 29 to Hannah in 1 Samuel 1 to Elizabeth in Luke 1 women are scorned and pitied because they had not become someone's mother. A woman who had no children was considered less than a woman, of less value by men, by other women, and even, it was thought, by God. Her childless state was attributed to God, for God "closed her womb" (1 Samuel 1:5). Women were divided from one another by whether or not they had children. (n.b. Hannah and Peninnah in 1 Samuel 1: "Her rival used to provoke her severely, to irritate her, because the Lord had closed her womb.") Elkanah, the husband, did not understand and even furthered the division (verses 3-8). The structure of the biblical passage itself is formed around the presence and absence of children: "There was a certain man (Elkanah). . . . He had two wives: the name of the one was Hannah and the name of the other Peninnah. Peninnah had children, but Hannah had no children" (verses 1-2).[34]

A man who had no children was bereft of property. The wealth, and the blessing of God, was measured for a man in children, lands, and herds. For example, in Genesis 45:10, Joseph sent these words to his father, Jacob: "You shall settle in the land of Goshen, . . . you and your children and your children's children, as well as your flocks, your herds, and all that you have." A man with no children was less than successful. For example: "Record this man as childless, a man who shall not succeed in his days" (Jeremiah 22:30).

From sign to the significant One

In Matthew 18:1-14, Jesus seems to "use" a child to answer a question meant to force him to rank people's worth. The disciples ask, "Who is the greatest in the kingdom of heaven?" (verse 1). Jesus calls a child, "whom he put among them," as an object lesson of sorts: "Truly I tell you, unless you change and become like children, you will never enter the kingdom of heaven" (verse 3). Lest we see this response to their inappropriate question as merely an objectifying answer, note that Jesus goes on: "Whoever becomes humble like this child is the greatest in the kingdom of heaven. Whoever welcomes one such child in my name welcomes me" (verses 4-5). Jesus carefully moves from perfunctory question and disarming reply, to a call for repentance ("change," verse 3) and ministry to children.

Jesus not only uses the child as sign of what the reign of God will be like, but he clearly states children's significance in that reign of God. Amazingly, he likens himself to a child. When someone receives children, welcomes them, ministers to them, that person is ministering to Christ himself ("welcomes me," verse 5). The God who put on flesh (John 1), the Savior who came as a child (Matthew 1-2 and Luke 1-2) also as an adult identifies with the children. Who is the child? Jesus the Christ.

To make certain there is no doubt that Jesus is merely using the child as a symbol, he goes on to warn against the disciples' misusing children, or putting a "stumbling block before" them. Jesus acknowledges, almost takes for granted, that children can believe in him, do believe in him ("one of these little ones who believe in me" Matthew 18:6).

We might ask ourselves what stumbling blocks we might have today? What do we do that hinders their belief? That does not take seriously their faith development? Do we disregard or dismiss them? For those who put such "stumbling blocks" before children, Jesus warns, it would be better if they had a real stone fastened around their necks and they be drowned in the depth of the sea (Matthew 18:6-7).

Jesus continues at length about our stumbling blocks, and God's unfailing search for us (verses 7-13). "If a shepherd has a hundred sheep, and one of them has gone astray" (verse 12). Often these verses about God's search and God's joy at finding the one who was lost (verse 13) have been used in sermons and lessons about people in general. Indeed, they are inclusive. But note that Jesus never leaves the subject of children: "Take care that you do not despise one of these little ones" (verse 10), and it is not the will of God "that one of these little ones should be lost" (verse 14). The message is clear: We are not to disregard nor despise children, nor hinder their growth in belief, for they *do* believe and minister,[35] and are the heart of the reign of God. They and Christ are one.

The child as the people of God

Who are children? Scripture turns our question around to have "children" as the answer. In *Jeopardy!* game fashion, the response "What are children?" could be given for "chosen ones" and "people of God" in the category of "God and God's people." Who are God's people likened to? Children!

In the Old Testament, God's chosen ones are sometimes spoken collectively as "a child." For example: "When Israel was a child, I loved him, and out of Egypt I called my son" (Hosea 11:1). In the New Testament, those who believe in Jesus are called, "children of God." There are many such references, including Mark 10:24; John 13:33; Galatians 5:1; and 1 John 2-5. John's Gospel states, "But to all who received him [Jesus], who believed in his name, he gave power to become children of God" (John 1:12). At the end of John's Gospel, Jesus asks the disciples, "Children, you have no fish, have you?" (John 21:5). Then, after their nets were full, they recognized the Christ who would commission them to feed his people.

Likewise, those who have been commissioned to be leaders of God's people address the Christians as children, not because leaders are to take the role of parent, or of God, but because we all have become children of God together in baptism. In the book of Galatians, Paul uses not only the image of children but of childbirth (a man using such an image would have been almost unheard of in the Roman world) to show his urgency and even anguish for these new Christians to grow in faith. "My little children, for whom I am again in the pain of childbirth until Christ is formed in you, I wish I were present with you now" (Galatians 4:19-20).

The child develops. The child is healed. The child eats.

Who is the child? Without mistakenly laying modern child-development theories over scriptures written thousands of years ago, we do see that biblical writers believed that children grow. For example, the boy Samuel "continued to grow both in statue and in favor with the LORD and with the people" (1 Samuel 2:26). Similar words are used concerning Jesus, who "increased in wisdom and in years, and in divine and human favor" (Luke 2:52).

The Bible includes some remarkable stories of children being healed. The child, created by God, becomes sick, then is touched by God's healing hand through God's people. In 2 Kings 4, we see a lengthy account of the child of the Shunammite woman. Even though the child is unnamed—children in the Bible rarely are—the story is one of pain, a touch, and a sneeze. Although the child's father dismisses the mother's persistence, she rushes for help. "Urge the animal on; do not hold back for me unless I tell you" (verse 24). She insists Elisha aid the child who has been pronounced dead: "As the LORD lives, and as you yourself live, I will not leave without you" (verse 30) Elisha does come and through his touch, God revives the child. The child sneezes seven times and opens his eyes (verse 35).

We see another remarkable story of healing a child in the Gospels (Mark 5:21-43). Intertwined with the story of the woman who has been bleeding for 12 years—who dares to reach out to Jesus for a healing touch—is the story of the 12-year-old girl. Both are "daughters" in need, and neither are named. But whereas the woman is commended for her faith, "Daughter, your faith had made you well; go in peace, and be healed of your disease" (verse 34), those around Jairus's house thought Jesus could do nothing for the child and laughed at him (verse 40).

So Jesus kept them outside and "went in where the child was. He took her by the hand and said to her, "Talitha cum," which means, "Little girl, get up." The girl immediately got up and began to walk. The bystanders were overcome with amazement. Therefore, Jesus could not use their witness to his healing of the child. "He strictly ordered them that no one should know this" (verse 43). Then Jesus added an important word, in concern for the child, not just the healing of the child. He told them "to give her something to eat." Being able to eat is a sign of wellness, then, and when our children are ill today.

The child as sign, the significance of children, Jesus' identification with, calling and healing children, our being called children of God: all of these ideas and more intrigue us. "Who is the child?" and "Whose is the child?" raise even many more questions for us in Scripture.

For Reflection and Discussion

1. Tell some stories from the Bible to one another. Which ones about the nature of children come to mind? Look them up. What new insights about how the Bible views children can you find?

2. What does it mean for you that you are a child of God? What does it mean t hat Christ says he is the Child?

Martin Luther on children and education

Martin Luther was a man of the Middle Ages, and his view of children was profound for its day. Some scholars have said that Luther brought about as important a reformation in education as in religion.[36]

Three main sources give us a glimpse of Luther the reformer of education. The first two are primary sources written by Luther. The first, "Letter to the Mayors and Aldermen of All the Cities of Germany in Behalf of Christian Schools,"[37] was written in 1524. The second, "Sermon on the Duty of Sending Children to School," was addressed to preachers in 1530. The third source is a work written in the United States in 1889, entitled *Luther on Education,* by F. V. N. Painter, including his translation into English of the above works by Luther.

It is true that during the century before the Reformation, schools probably were as numerous as during the century following. However, for the greater part of the Middle Ages there were three well-marked social classes: clergy, nobility, and peasants. Painter says that no general effort was made to provide the common child with education.[38] Knowledge was held in and dispensed from repositories, often monasteries. Through careful dispensation, the clergy retained power over both peasants and nobility, because they kept salvation and knowledge in their hands. Luther would say that all people, including children, have the right to education.[39]

Luther's emphasis on the priesthood of all believers creates a connection between religion and daily life. The freedom Christian people experience thrusts them forth into the world in their vocation. Yet how can people fulfill those vocations without education? No one can be left in ignorance, no matter what her or his class. Education becomes the interest of the state no less than that of the church. Its aim should be to fit the young for useful living in every relation. In his address to mayors and aldermen Luther wrote:

> Now if (as we have assumed) there were no souls, and there were no need at all of schools and languages for the sake of the Scriptures and of God, this one consideration alone would be sufficient to justify the establishment everywhere of the very best schools for both boys and girls, namely, that in order to maintain its temporal estate outwardly the world must have good and capable men and women. . . . Now such men must come from our boys, and such women from our girls.[40]

> If the government can compel such of its subjects as are fit for military service to carry pike and musket, man the ramparts, and do other kinds of work in time of war, how much more can it and should it compel its subjects to keep their children in school.[41]

Luther went on to make a more personal appeal to those charged with governing the people:

> There must be civil government. For us, then, to permit ignoramuses and blockheads to rule when we can prevent it, is irrational and barbarous. Let us rather make rulers out of swine and wolves, and set them over people who are indifferent to the manner in which they are governed. It is barbarous for men to think thus: "We will now rule; and what does it concern us how those fare who shall come after us?"[42]

This is an issue for our day, too, when many people, indeed many Christians, believe warfare to be inevitable to hasten the end of the world. Can you imagine Luther's words to those who say, "We will now rule; what does it matter what comes after us? Who cares if we educate our children?"

Education for boys and girls

For Luther, a schoolmaster was as important to a city as a pastor. He could do without mayors, princes, and noblemen, but not without schools for children. Luther was familiar not only with the importance of education, but also with its difficulties. He said:

An industrious, pious school-master or teacher, who faithfully trains and educates boys, can never be sufficiently recompensed, and no money will pay him, as even the heathen Aristotle says. Yet the calling is shamefully despised among us, as if it were nothing, and at the same time we pretend to be Christians! If I had to give up preaching and my other duties, there is no office I would rather have than that of school-teacher. [43]

Although Luther mentions only boys here, he repeatedly urged the establishment of schools for girls, which besides religious instruction were to include reading and writing. He says, "And would to God each town had also a girls' school, where girls might be taught the gospel for an hour daily, either in German or Latin." Luther declared that the maintenance of civil order and the proper regulation of the household require "the establishment of the best schools everywhere, both for boys and girls." [44] Although he often spoke only of sons, this inclusive position of Luther on the education of daughters is remarkable for his time.

Luther believed all children were called by God to be believe in Christ and to be educated to prepare them for service to their neighbor. No longer was education merely for boys who might enter the priesthood. No longer was education merely for nobility. Luther went beyond mere pity for the poor. He assumes they can learn! He cared about the rich, the poor, men, women, boys, and girls from all stations of life. He honored them by his care.

Theology of children

Luther's care about education for children was not an incidental interest. It was directly related to his theology. "Just as certainly as the call to God's kingdom seeks to lift us infinitely above everything that our everyday duties by themselves could give us, just that certainly the call does not take us away from these duties but more deeply into them." [45] This call is the forgiveness of sins. Life organized around the forgiveness of sins encompasses Luther's idea of call. It is primarily gift, and only secondarily duty. From such a call, from such forgiveness, the Christian is able to move forth into vocation. [46] Education for vocation is education for life and throughout life.

The ongoing care for and education of children in the home, city, and province was a consistent concern for Luther. In this he might be compared to Horace Bushnell who, in the mid-19th century, challenged Jonathan Edwards in New England. Edwards's prevalent writings emphasized the total depravity of humanity.[47] In light of his view of humankind and his understanding of God's sovereignty, Edwards believed nothing could be done for children but to hope and pray that they might experience conversion during seasons of revival. Otherwise they would be lost. Bushnell increasingly trusted the influences of family life and a Christian home without giving up his belief that human nature was corrupted by sin. He came to believe and state as his philosophy of Christian education: "that the child is to grow up a Christian and never know himself as being otherwise."[48]

Luther believed the child was sinful, but he also was committed to the nurturing of the baptized child. He also realized the difficulties of the task:

> In my judgment there is no other outward offense that in the sight of God so heavily burdens the world, and deserves such heavy chastisement, as the neglect to educate children. . . . Parents neglect this duty from various causes. In the first place, there are some who are so lacking in piety and uprightness that they would not do it if they could, but like the ostrich, harden themselves against their own offspring, and do nothing for them. Nevertheless these children must live among us and with us.[49]

On another occasion, Luther remarked:

> Such great works can your [children] do . . . if you send [them] to school . . . [think of your child as] a cornerstone and foundation of temporal peace on earth . . . it is a shameful contempt of God that you do not bring up your children to such an excellent and divinely appointed calling, and that you strengthen them only in the service of appetite and avarice, teaching them nothing but to provide for the stomach, like a hog with its nose always in filth, and do not bring them up to this worthy station and office. You must either be insensible creatures, or else you do not love your children.[50]

Luther had more to say about parents and children:

> Parents are not free to do with children as they please. . . .This is a sad evil, that all live on as though God gave us children for our pleasure or amusement, and servants that we should employ them like a cow or ass, only for work, or as though all we had to do with our subjects were only to gratify our wantonness.[51]

Whose is the child?

Whose is the child? The child is God's and not ours: not our possession, product, problem, or protégé. Luther said that our children are not so entirely our own that we can withhold them from God; they are more God's than ours. Through education our children enter into the world's work in risky, bold ways, but always held carefully in the hand of their Creator and Redeeming God. Luther believed that "God is a wonderful Lord. God's business is to take beggars and make them into lords, even as God makes all things out of nothing, and no one can disrupt God in this work." [52]

Luther said the child is someone with whom we "play and prattle." The great learned Doctor took time to observe children. Luther called for us to love our children, to care for them, to educate them in a risky world. We are to help them learn from the world so that they can take their place in it, living out their vocations.

Almost 500 years ago, Luther wrote to councilmen in all the cities of Germany to establish and maintain schools for children. Today we are called on as citizens to discern our calling to provide education for all children, not just our own. We must see who we are as a pluralistic people. We are a people of many faiths who need to come together in a public world. We cannot simply say the child belongs to the parents, nor seek privatized or corporately run for-profit education which in a competitive world elevates our own children (our trophies) above others, for then we would fall back into the classism against which Luther wrote. We must discover how to live together safely as people of different faiths in God's public world. Only then will we be able to answer in an inclusive way the question: Whose is the child?

For Reflection and Discussion

1. Gather some members of your education team, staff, or council, and compose a letter to the mayor or newspaper in your area. What would you say about your concern for all the children in your community in regard to education?

2. Draft a letter for your congregational newsletter, or to post on your Web site, about education for children in your parish ("parish" meaning not just children of members, but all children living in the neighborhood). What would you say?

Seeing the children

We need to look around and see the children in our midst. What follows are simple observations. Children are created to grow and designed to develop. Created by God, they are liberated to learn and to serve in the church.

Jody, age 14 months

It is 9:25 A.M. and the church is filling. A couple sits together with Jody on their collective laps. The child has the undivided attention of both parents and most of the surrounding adults. She is the center of things and likes it that way. Suddenly the activity level subsides; the service is about to begin. Also suddenly, Jody is placed on one lap and told to be quiet. She squirms a little and puts forth a small whine. Another squirm gets her to the floor and a chance to explore. After just a few steps, hands reach out to limit her range. The child is returned to the lap of her mother who places Jody's head on her shoulder and rocks her quietly from side to side. The child accepts this for a short period of time. Then the cries become louder and more frequent. Finally, her father takes the child and they leave the sanctuary for a short period of time. Eventually, the father and child return to worship.

The child is not really so ill-mannered. Actually, manners are a foreign concept at this stage in her life. Right now, according to Jean Piaget's work in the field of cognitive development. See the chapter "The Child Grew: Understanding Children's Development." Jody's world is a collection of objects, people, and actions. Everything is present time with the child at the center. At this learning stage, the child is just beginning to learn to separate herself from other objects and people. She compares all things to herself and thereby continues to learn and expand her experience.

After worship is over, Jody is with her parents and the rest of the community during fellowship hour. She is once again on the floor, exploring. The child moves from her parent's table but only to the limit that she can still see them and return quickly if she feels uncomfortable. Erik Erikson calls this stage *trust versus mistrust*. The child moves out from her safety net to explore and to expand her experience, but mistrust keeps her close to her primary caregivers. The distance between caregivers and the world beyond grows with experience and age.

What can we do with children of this age and development in educational ministry? Is baby-sitting the only option? Infants and young children belong in the worshiping community. They can be quietly busy with objects on the pew where they can enjoy them while standing on the floor. Can we offer an explorative type of worship experience for those children capable of moving on their own? Can we provide biblically based picture books and toys for them to see and handle? Can we surround them with a caring community where they feel safe and trust the love of God?

Todd, age 2
(as told by Beth, a young adult)

We danced. First, there was one. Then there were two. Then a third quietly came up and joined. And a fourth! Before I knew it, I was dancing in a circle with five children. Five beautiful, unique, and amazing children made the brave decision to come out and join the dance. I was astonished, not so much that they came to dance, but that I was included in it. When the music played and the first girl asked me to dance, I accepted, and I felt comfortable. Being comfortable, I think, is what made all the difference for them and for me. So, we danced.

Todd caught my attention. He was no older than 2, and he really wanted to dance. I was impressed with this very brave action: a very big step for this young child. Independence is an important part of the second year of a child's life. Children at this age are stepping out to explore the world on their own. Todd came over to us completely on his own, without any help from anyone. He knew what he wanted to do. Todd was very confident in holding our hands, jumping and turning with us. The best thing for Todd was that his parents let him go. They didn't try to stop him from dancing with trusted people whom they and he knew.

Todd has been learning how his body works, and is beginning to see how he is a part of the larger world. He is able to associate events with words or symbols. During our dancing I tried to physically get down to Todd's eye level. He was so much smaller than the rest of the children, so I went down to my knees. Well, Todd must have thought this was a new way to dance because he went down to his knees as well. It took me by surprise. It was a special moment.

According to Erikson, this is a stage of *autonomy versus shame and doubt*. Children developing autonomy learn that they can do things by themselves, a great discovery, and so want to do things their way. Hence, they discover the power of the word *no*. When the dance was over and Todd's parents wanted to go home, Todd made it clear that he did not want to go. Todd didn't use the word *no*, but he proceeded to lie down on the floor. A parent must have patience, patience, patience.

Children at Todd's age are really fun to teach. They need a lot of hands-on, experiential learning: objects to play with and things to do. They need to explore on their own at their own pace. This allows a child to develop his or her individual autonomy in a safe and structured place. It is a time when we can work on their language skills by beginning to help them associate words with events. Creating a safe environment at home and at church is important when teaching this age, or any age. The goal should be for an environment where one can learn to be who he or she is and do what he or she wants, but also has a healthy balance of boundaries to work within.

Sam, age 3

The children were running through the backyards. Most of them were second- to sixth-graders. Sam is not quite 3 ¹/₂. The other children ran with a strategy—someone was "it." There was a place they were running from and a place they were running to. They traveled in groups, sometimes whispering and sometimes shouting rules to their game. But this little boy just ran. Sam's purpose was to run and to be a part of what the "big kids" were doing. He was always last but, he ran close enough to the speed of the group so that he remained a part of it. Sam was encouraged by a few of the other children. One older boy talked to Sam; he addressed Sam with a tone of voice that was different than was used among the older children—higher in pitch, with a kind, gentle tone. No one was impatient with Sam. He didn't whine or cry. He didn't shout out orders or plead for the other kids to slow down.

Dressed in his loose-fitting t-shirt and soft, knit shorts, white socks and tennis shoes, Sam's run was different from the older children. He didn't have well-defined muscles like the older boys. His solid little frame had the coordinated movement typical of a child who is 3 to 4 years old. He ran at one speed—on. He didn't dart in and out. There were no quick changes of direction or speed. He was operating in his own little world both physically and socially.

Sam seems to be attaining autonomy rather than shame and doubt and is moving into the stage of *initiative versus guilt* (described by Erik Erikson). He can freely develop within safe boundaries with other children. He still lacks the social understanding of the total picture of what he is doing, however. Those understandings will come with his school-age years. He is gradually learning about the world that extends beyond his family and home. He is also in the early stages of using his imagination in play. He will learn by doing, by play, and by imitation.

During this stage, as his imagination grows, so will his early understandings of God grow. As be begins to talk about God and Bible stories, he will use his imagination to fill in storylines where there are gaps in knowledge. During infancy, he would have viewed himself as a part of his mother or father. Now is aware of himself as a separate person.

The majority of Sam's faith formation takes place in the family. This does not mean that children of this age cannot learn in the church environment. Images and ideas that are used in Sunday school curriculum resources are simple: "God loves me." "God made the trees." Bible stories are repeated: told by teachers; sung in songs; drawn on pieces of paper. In all of that repetition, children hear the words of Christ. They also experience Christ— in the love of a parent, the smile of their teacher, and the consistency of other children being there with them week after week.

Sam is experiencing the growing importance of participation. What does it mean to be of service to others? Even a child as young as Sam can begin to experience what service is like. He enjoys being a part of something bigger. Young children love helping. Some could help at church in a role that is outside the classroom: walk to Sunday school classrooms with a teacher or a "big kid" to pick up offerings or deliver notes. He might enjoy helping to put up children's artwork on the wall in an entryway or bulletin board in the church. "Helping" could carry over from home to church and back. Sam's learning need never end.

Rebekah, age 5

Rebekah is the youngest of three children in her family. She is 5-years-old. She wants to go to school like her older brother and sister, so she loves the classroom setting of Sunday school. She always sits in the same seat, works diligently whenever given a task, and desperately wants her chance to read the lesson, even though she cannot yet read.

Rebekah exhibits many of the aspects of Erik Erikson's psycho-social stage three: *initiative versus guilt*. Rebekah definitely takes on new challenges and feels much satisfaction in learning new skills and taking on responsibilities as she is able. She loves to imagine, and play make-believe. Rebekah uses symbols to represent other objects. She is able to look at one thing and give it the characteristics of something else. She is able to draw those connections. Taping three used food containers together, Rebekah proudly declares, "Here! I made a cat for you!" Because she sees things primarily from her own point of view, she automatically assumes that adults will make the same conclusion she does and see a "cat."

Rebekah knows that when she hits her brother or yells at her sister that consequences occur, and she is careful not to be in that situation. She knows the guilt of not doing what her mommy says and tries to act in ways so as to not have to experience that guilt and possible punishment.

In this stage Rebekah can use words and mental pictures to think, but she is unconcerned about logic. However, she is able to remember and make connections between two situations. One Sunday in church while listening to the reading of the Gospel, Rebekah leaned over and whispered, "This is what we learned about in Sunday school today." Rebekah is showing some aspects of organizing facts, which is characteristic of Piaget's *concrete operational* thought period.

When teaching Rebekah in a Christian educational setting, it would be wise to make use of her imagination and love of play. It would be helpful for her to act out some Bible stories or use concrete objects as symbols of some of the abstracts of the Christian faith. Since Rebekah loves learning new things, she could be introduced to a broader range of Bible stories and visit places in the church that she isn't aware of such as the sacristy. Rebekah is growing to be an active member of the body of Christ.

Jens, age 8

Jens is an active child who enjoys many types of physical and mental activities. He plays organized soccer and also loves gymnastics. He can hardly keep himself from doing some of his gymnastics wherever and whenever he can, including his living room. He loves to show people in public what he can do.

Although Jens is very bright and an excellent student in school, he would tell you his favorite part of school is recess. Jens can be fairly loud, which sometimes causes him trouble. He can get wound up at school and in Sunday school, especially if there are not clear guidelines. When something holds his attention, he can be a very polite, involved participant.

This child is in the *concrete operational* stage of cognitive reasoning. Jens is capable of patterned acts of transformation, can make generalizations from specifics, understands reversibility and is capable of coordinating things into overall systems. He is in Erikson's stage of *industry versus inferiority*. Jens has learned how to use physical and intellectual abilities in potentially productive work. He has learned how to contribute as a part of cooperative groups in school, in children's choir, and on sports teams. Jens is sorting out the real from the make-believe. This may be why he does not want to read Bible stories on his own. He wants and needs the guidance of an adult to discuss his questions. With his new capabilities of reversible thought, taking other perspectives, and understanding cause and effect, he is ripe to hear stories and appropriate them.

Jens could benefit from a Christian education setting where there are "stations" all geared toward the hearing and understanding of a particular story or theme. Dramatization, in a small group, would give Jens and his classmates a chance to hear and discuss in their own words the different perspectives that are so important to faith development. For Jens, who prides himself on knowing hundreds of cartoon and computer game characters, memorization of Bible verses and whole stories would not be a problem and would actually be a source of pride.

Music and crafts, connected to the lesson, help Jens discover what the story he heard that day meant. Jens needs the opportunity to move around and be a bit loud (he likes to sing out) without getting into trouble! Jens and his friends could benefit from taking home one question each week to ask a parent, preferably as soon as possible after class. At home, Jens should continue doing Bible stories and devotions with his parents.

Christopher, age 12

Christopher is sweet, outgoing, and curious. He constantly asks questions and makes observations about the world around him. His stepfather is the church choir director, and his mother directs some other congregation musical groups, so he attends choir practice with them. Christopher sits patiently in one of the upper rows of the choir loft, slightly slouched in his chair, and plays a video game that has the volume turned down. Once in a while, Christopher will look up and watch the people singing. He feels that he isn't old enough to participate in what is going on around him. Therefore, he stays quiet in his seat and tries to focus on his game.

Christopher has grown in many ways. When Christopher was 6 he was very industrious. He was a very confident child who wasn't afraid to try new and different things. Now that Christopher has become older, he is still very eager, but he has become more introspective. More often than not, Christopher will now sit back and watch what is going on around him, rather than engaging in the situation. He is more contemplative and doesn't seem to feel as confident as he used to. According to Erikson, he is moving from the stage of *industry versus inferiority* to the stage of *identity versus role confusion*. If someone were to invite him to participate, he would probably be more than happy to try.

When Christopher was 6, he wasn't afraid to approach anyone. He was very open and thought that his ideas were great and trusted everyone to accept what he imagined to be true. Now Christopher's faith is more literal. He no longer feels that he can address his needs to just anyone; it might be possible that his ideas could be shot down. He is starting to see things more for what they are, instead of what he perceives them to be. His faith in God, and life in general, have taken on a different meaning. He is starting to explore these meanings.

Christopher is starting to think about new stages of his identity. This 12-year-old child can understand the dynamics of his environment and knows something of where he stands. His church has a youth group of children ranging in age from 6 to 13. It is challenging to find activities that would engage and challenge this age range. But Christopher is able to teach the 6-year-olds and is self-differentiated enough to be open to receiving the ideas of the younger children. The most important thing is that each child be heard. A 6-year-old's feelings are just as valid as a 12-year-old's, and vice versa. A 12-year-old needs just as much attention as a flamboyant 6-year-old. Faith needs to grow at every age.

Ministering children

A book from the mid-19th century, *Ministering Children*, tells the stories of "Ruth and Patience," "The Little Comforter," and "Little Rose":

> Difficulty being sometimes felt in training children to the exercise of those kindly feelings which have the Poor for their object, it was thought that an illustrative tale might prove a help toward this important end. . . . Let the truth be borne in mind, that the influence of the giver far exceeds that of the gift . . . let children be trained, and taught and led aright—and they will not be slow to learn that they possess a personal influence everywhere.

> The youngest child of God who is able to understand anything, can learn to be a ministering child!" [53]

Children today are more than problem or protégé. Both sinner and saint, created, redeemed and empowered by a loving God, they are welcomed into the body of Christ to minister in the community of faith and in the world:

- Andrea's art adorns her downtown congregation's worship bulletin cover.

- Thomas came with his new foster parents to church for the first time and joined them in ushering. In his ministry, week after week, of handing out bulletins, lighting the candles, and carrying the offering plate and food pantry basket to the altar, he heard the gospel, asked questions, and learned about the life of faith and service.

- Jennifer, a neighborhood child, heard about the church's food pantry and thought about hungry people. She asked her parents not to give her Christmas or birthday presents, but money instead. With it she bought food, put it in her red wagon and knocked on the door of the parsonage saying, "Here is food for the poor."

- After our noon walk through the cemetery, Emma wanted to ride with me to the final afternoon of vacation Bible school. She showed me the way down the gravel road. More than 50 children gathered in this rural church, using their money to buy chickens and sheep for children's families around the world. [54] Emma made sure I had a song sheet (she knew the words), as all boarded a bus to go into town to sing at the nursing home.

Who is the child? Whose is the child? God's child. Where are the children? Ministering in Christ's image in God's world.

Notes

1. While "Whose is the child?" is not the grammatical form one would use in ordinary conversation, it is used here, obviously, to complement its companion question, "Who is the Child?" It also is used to purposely avoid "Whose child is this?" or "To whom does this child belong?" which tend to objectify the child as someone's possession.

2. Issues of the following were used, primarily during the time frame of May 25, 2003-June 15, 2003: *Telegraph Herald*, Dubuque, IO 52004-0688, published daily by Woodward Communications; Des Moines Register, 715 Locust St., Des Moines, IO 50309; *Chicago Tribune*, 435 N. Michigan Ave., Chicago, IL 60611, Tribune Publishing; *Newsweek*, Box 2120, Radio City Station, New York, NY 10101; television news, primarily ABC. Also consulted: *Christian Science Monitor*, Box 98, Boston, MA 02117; *International Jerusalem Post*, 401 North Wabash Ave., Ste. 732, Chicago, IL 60611; *National Geographic*, National Geographic Society, Box 98199, Washington, DC 20090; and *Time*, Time and Life Bldg., Rockefeller Center, New York, NY 10020.

3. The more local the newspaper, the more children and youth sports activities were reported. Noteworthy is the fact that for more than 25 years the *Telegraph Herald* in Dubuque has reported girls' sports on an equal basis with boys' sports. The proportion of coverage of men's and women's sports in national media is quite different.

4. "Children's Tussle Results in Family Feud," *Telegraph Herald*, June 3, 2002, p. 8A.

5. "Town Enjoys Annual Festival as Farm Faces Uncertain Future" *Des Moines Register*, June 15, 2003, p. 2B. This article recounts the sad fact that in Brooklyn, Iowa, (population 1,367) and many rural areas, farm economies are making it impossible for children to own their land and farm. "The end of family farms is a tragedy to the community." The negative side of globalization touches rural children here and around the world.

6. Although there are still some remnants of the concept of children carrying on work of their parents: "Firemen Spawn Little Firefighters," *Des Moines Register*, June 13, 2003, p. 1A. The headline was more suggestive of dreams for their children than the article. Interestingly, however, the feature used much more suggestively open language than a generation ago, the lead being, "They never had that little vasectomy party at the Pleasant Hill firehouse after all." It went on, however, with candid and poignant accounts of women suffering through miscarriages and the resulting joy of bearing children together.

7. *Telegraph Herald*, June 11, 2003, p. 1A. This front-page story featured parental support for their daughter graduating a year early to pursue a dance career. Her accomplishments listed included ballet practices and performances, choir, band, math club, French club, cheerleading, varsity dance team, Christian leadership class, teaching at a local academy of ballet, and working part time. This is not to say that children's activities are not noteworthy, but it is questionable to quantify them as marks of parental success.

8. *Des Moines Register*, May 29, 2003, Metro section. A full-column, front-page story in this regional newspaper: "Madrid student missed only 1/2 day of school." His mother debated the half-day missed in kindergarten. He had a "perfect" 4.0 grade average. When asked if he intends to continue that attendance record in college, the youth replied, "I don't know if my parents would be pushing me as much."

9. *Chicago Tribune*, June 15, 2003, pp. 1, 19.

10. *Telegraph Herald*, June 14, 2003, p. 3A; and *Des Moines Register*, June 3, 2002, p. B1.

11. *Good Morning America*, June 11, 2003.

12. For a thorough review of how children were viewed by theologians and the church through Christian history, see Marcia J. Bunge, ed., *The Child in Christian Thought* (Grand Rapids: Eerdmans, 2001).

13. "Job dearth deprives kids of more than money," *Christian Science Monitor*, May 21, 2003, p. 1. This article explores the importance of youth developing pride in work skills. Almost a century after child-labor laws were enacted to protect children from danger and provide time for schooling, important again is the question of the place of work in children's lives.

14. *Chicago Tribune*, June 8, 2003, *Parade* section, p. 7.

15. KCRG-TV, Cedar Rapids, Iowa, "U.S. Farm Report" 5:15 a.m., June 28, 2003.

16. *Oprah Winfrey Show*, June 23, 2003.

17. *Chicago Tribune*, June 15, 2003, section 16, p. 5R.

18. *Chicago Tribune*, June 17, 2003, section 2, p. 2.

19. *Des Moines Register*, May 31, 2003, p. 1A ; *Telegraph Herald*, June 1, 2003, p. 5A.

20. *Telegraph Herald*, June 2, 2003, p. 3A.

21. Robert Kolb and Timothy J. Wengert, eds., *The Book of Concord* (Minneapolis: Fortress, 2000), p. 354. Hereafter references are from the Large Catechism and Small Catechism, *The Book of Concord*, pp. 345-480.

22. *Book of Concord*, p. 432.

23. *Book of Concord*, p. 354.

24. Martin Luther's "Two Kingdoms" theory, often referred to today as the "Two Realms of God." In the First Realm, God uses the First Use of the Law to restrain wickedness and assure order, justice, and peace. In the Second Realm, God uses the Second Use of the Law to show people their sin and drive them to Christ so that people might truly hear the Gospel, God's saving work in Jesus Christ (Law and Gospel).

25. Roland H. Bainton, trans. and arr., *The Martin Luther Christmas Book* (Philadelphia: Fortress, 1948), p. 40.

26. *Book of Concord*, p. 434.

27. Ibid., p. 355.

28. Ibid., p. 355.

29. Ibid., p. 355.

30. Ibid., pp. 435-436.

31. Ibid., p. 436.

32. *Newsweek*, December 15, 1997, cover and pp. 49-56. "Whose faith for the kids?" describes how religion plays a bigger role in the home today than expected.

33. *Book of Concord*, p. 436.

34. This division of women if remarkably overturned in Luke's Gospel when the annunciation to Mary is marked by it being in the sixth month of Elizabeth's pregnancy. Rather than being divided, Mary, carrying Jesus Christ, goes to serve Elizabeth during her own pregnancy (Luke 1-2).

35. John's account of the feeding of the multitude includes the boy with five barley loaves and two fish. Jesus used the resources and ministry of the child to feed the hungry (John 6:9-14).

36. Portions of this essay first appeared in Norma Cook Everist, "Luther on Education: Implications for Today," *Currents in Theology and Mission* 12 (1985), pp. 76-89.

37. Luther, "Letter to the Mayors and Aldermen of All the Cities of Germany in Behalf of Christian Schools" (1524), in F. V. N. Painter, *Luther on Education* (Philadelphia: Lutheran Publication Society, 1889), pp. 169-209.

38. Gustaf Marius Bruce, *Luther As an Educator* (Minneapolis: Augsburg, 1928), p. 24.

39. See also Jane E. Strohl, "The Child in Luther's Theology: For What Purpose Do We Older Folks Exist, Other Than to Care for . . . the Young," in Bunge, *The Child in Christian Thought*, pp. 134-159.

40. Luther, "To The Councilmen of All Cities in Germany that They Establish and Maintain Christian Schools" (1524), in *Luther's Works*, Walther I. Brandt, ed., vol. 45., *The Christian in Society II* (Philadelphia: Muhlenberg), p. 368.

41. Luther, "A Sermon on Keeping Children in School," 1530, in *Luther's Works*, vol. 46; *The Christian in Society III* (Philadelphia: Muhlenberg), pp. 256-257.

42. Luther, "Letter," in Painter, *Luther on Education*, pp. 178-179.

43. Painter, pp. 142-143.

44. Ibid., pp. 138-139.

45. Einar Billing, *Our Calling*, trans. Conrad Bergendoff (Rock Island: Augustana, 1958), p. 6.

46. Ibid., pp. 8, 11.

47. For a brief overview of Edwards and Bushnell, see "Catherine A. Brekus, "Children of Wrath, Children of Grace: Jonathan Edwards and the Puritan Culture of Child Rearing," and Margaret Bendroth, "Horace Bushnell's Christian Nurture," in Bunge, *The Child in Christian Thought*, pp. 247-299, 350-364.

48. Horace Bushnell, *Christian Nurture* (1888; New Haven: Yale University, 1967), p. 4.

49. Luther, "Letter," in Painter, *Luther on Education*, pp. 178-179.

50. Luther, "Sermon," in Painter, pp. 247-248.

51. Ibid., p. 116.

52. Luther, "Sermon" in *Luther's Works*, vol. 46, p. 250.

53. Marie Louis Charlesworth, *Ministering Children: A Tale* (New York: American Tract Society, ca. 1850s), pp. vii-viii, 279.

54. Through Heifer International, 1015 Louisiana St., Little Rock, AR 72202 (www.heifer.org/kids).

PART II

Contexts

CHAPTER 4

Family Ministry

Mary E. Hughes

LISTEN, PLEASE. I GO TO CHURCH. I take my family . . . that's me and my 9-year-old daughter and my 6-year-old son. Their father lives only a few blocks away since our divorce last year, but I'm the primary parent. Of course, they spend a lot of time with him and at his apartment. He and I try to do what is best for our children, so we try to communicate and be friendly, even if we are divorced. And even if he is dating another woman now. It's hard to stay connected, but we have to because of the children.

I think we're all a little embarrassed about our family situation. Sure, there are lots of divorces, but still the kids feel awkward about dad not living at home. It's like they have to explain it all the time. It's like everything is set up for moms and dads and perfect children. Well, Dad's not home, I work full time, and I feel guilty because I'm tired and grumpy with the children.

The children are wonderful, most of the time, but Sarah wants to play every sport that comes along (that takes time, money, and energy) and Danny has ADHD (that takes energy and patience). I just don't have enough time, money, energy, or patience for life these days. I don't know what I'm doing, but I'm doing the best I can do.

Church is especially hard. The kids enjoy Sunday school and vacation Bible school, and they don't complain very much about going. I sing in the choir. But the whole church thing doesn't seem to have much to do with my *real* life.

I don't know how to help us be a Christian family, if there is such a thing. Am I supposed to be doing devotions with the kids? And the church wants my time, money, and energy, too. They even asked me to teach Sunday school!

I have an idea: How about if the church looks at my life and me a little differently. How about if the church helps me be a better parent, helps me raise a Christian family, helps me learn how to have devotions with my kids, helps me know how to prioritize the time-money-energy demands in my life. How about if the church remembers that I am a mature, single parent? How about if the church recognizes that I feel like a failure in my marriage and I always doubt my parenting?

Doesn't the church get it . . . that I'm scared to death about holding life together day-to-day, but, in spite of it all, I'm doing a pretty good job? All that doesn't even begin to touch on my aging mother, my stressful/satisfying job, and my newfound interest in leading Sara's scout troop.

It seems like the church usually wants more of me. How about if the church becomes more of a team player with me, a partner in life . . . in *real* life. Do you think the church is interested in that?

> *Amy, age 29*
> *Anywhere, U.S.A.*

The ABC's of family ministry

Why is there a chapter called "Family Ministry" in a book on children's education?

Children come in all kinds of families. Whatever happens to a child, happens to the whole family. Whatever happens to the family, happens also to the child. There is much to know about children themselves and the church's ministry with children, but ministry with children must happen within the context of their families. Within their families and their homes, children have most of their physical and emotional needs met, spend a majority of their time (especially in early childhood), and catch the values and priorities of their parents or caregivers. When thinking about ministry with children, it is important to consider a larger ministry . . . ministry with the entire family.

What is a family?

The term *family* refers to whatever family configurations are being lived— singles with the people who surround and support them, sometimes including children; couples with and without children living at home; small groups of households who choose to share life closely; adults and children; adults and older adults—you get the picture. *Family* refers to all those intentional ways people choose to live their lives together most intimately.

Not everyone agrees with this description of family and will modify their understanding of family ministry accordingly. Unfortunately, the greatest debate about family comes when someone tries to identify the "correct" family and uses family ministry as a way to support only the families that fit that description. However, families yesterday and today come in great variety and naming one family pattern to be best tempts us to miss our opportunity and responsibility to help all families live as faithful families.

Who is your family? Family is identified in two ways: (1) those related to one another because of birth, adoption, marriage or other legal bond, and (2) those with whom we have formed connections of caring, commitment, and support. When we speak of family ministry, we take into account the reality of both families formed by choice and families formed by kinship.

Throughout much of the 20th century, the same people were part of both "related family" and "chosen family" in middle-class, Euro-American households. In other times and cultures families have included people with no legal or birth connection, and bonds of care and support were formed within those larger households.

A few questions can help clarify the "related" and "chosen" family theme. If you become ill, who can you count on to take care of you? When you have the joy of good news, who do you tell? Since my "related family" lives hundreds of miles away, special friends and neighbors help in times of need and celebration. They are my family, too, just as much as my brother, sister, and other relatives.

Why should the church be doing family ministry?

If faith should be nurtured within caring relationships through which God is constantly being revealed, if our most powerful relationships happen with the family, and if families (especially parents and adult caregivers) feel inadequate and alone in their faith-nurturing responsibilities, then it is the church's delight and obligation to help build up families to be effective "faithful families" that are both growing in faith and living out their faith.

How can a congregation organize for family ministry?

There's no one, right way to organize for implementing family ministry. In fact, many congregations are already engaged in family ministry because their congregational life takes into account the challenges and resources of families in that church. However, without a more intentional system of organizing family ministry, such efforts will be effective in some areas with some families, less effective in other areas, and may totally ignore some families and some areas of concern. The following organizational possibilities might be useful:

1. An individual volunteer or staff person might take the responsibility to oversee family ministry, helping all church committees and leaders see their potential and responsibilities.

2. An existing committee may assume the responsibility for oversight.

3. A special group might be gathered to reflect on current family ministries with the intention of making suggestions for the future. This might be a one-time gathering or a longer-term process.

4. A special group might be gathered from neighboring churches, either within or beyond one's denomination, to study the topic of family ministry and to help the churches find their way into the endeavor.

5. Within several of these suggestions, a competent resource person might be invited to give guidance as the study of family ministry begins.

What resources can help us get started in family ministry?

Some of the best resources are right in your congregation and community. These are people with special interest and expertise in family life. Make a list of family counselors, parent educators, family physicians, attorneys specializing in family law, child and family service specialists, college professors specializing in family life, pastors, schoolteachers, and principals. Some of those people are members of your church and others are members of neighboring churches. Regardless of their religious affiliations, most are eager to help strengthen family life and can be a helpful resource to you.

1. Other congregations and synagogues may already have an intentional family ministry, or they may have an interest in developing one. Combining ideas and efforts can be an energizing for everyone.

2. Other resources are programmatic: parenting education programs, books and media, workshops. The professionals you have already identified probably will be aware of many of these programmatic resources in your community.

3. Every denomination has resources in the form of curriculum, ministry guides, and personnel to offer assistance in areas of family ministry. Visit your local bookstores and church resource centers to find assistance. Visit your denomination's Web site or call your church's headquarters to learn of the resources available.

Living together as family members

Family ministry includes helping families live together faithfully in their daily relationships: parents with children, adults with one another, children with one another. These relationships are intense and powerful because they are constant and long lasting.

How can we be more effective in our parenting?

Parenting is a complex adventure. Our parenting will be more effective when we practice the following 10 suggestions:

1. Work at understanding our own parents and how we were parented.

2. Reflect on the values and beliefs we wish to instill in our children, and consider how those values and beliefs can be shared. This is especially important for the Christian parent.

3. Seek the knowledge and resources to ensure the good physical health and safety of our children.

4. Understand our child's development. That is, what can be expected at this age and what's driving her or his behavior.

5. Develop and use our best communications skills for listening, having open conversations, and solving problems.

6. Develop a considered and consistent strategy for discipline, especially an approach to daily behavior that is age appropriate.

7. Have put into place an overall legal and financial plan that fits our goals and yet is flexible enough for life today . . . a plan that provides for the legal and financial well being of our children in times of crisis.

8. Develop a network of professional and personal support that we turn to for friendship, feedback, advice, and perspective, especially in emergencies.

9. Regularly give our children focused time.

10. Take the time to ensure our own physical, emotional, and relational stability.

That's an overwhelming list, of course. However, every parent is already at work on every statement. A church can use the above suggestions in two ways:

1. Invite parents to consider how they are doing on each endeavor and to identify if some need more attention. Help parents, then find ways to go about addressing the concerns identified.

2. As a planning committee, consider the resources available within the church and community for addressing each of the 10 concerns. Some of them may be addressed through traditional parenting classes. Some require other community resources. Family ministry leaders can help ensure that parents accomplish every one of these areas.

How do we help parents to parent faithfully?

Does parenting education belong in the church? If we want to help families live together faithfully, then helping parents can be a centerpiece in family ministry. Adults wishing to adopt a child spend hours answering questions about discipline methods, childcare logistics, support networks, financial obligations, family history and stability, and education plans. Otherwise, children usually arrive with a minimum of required preparation by parents. No instruction manual comes with children . . . although every parent has occasionally yearned for one. Yet every parent wants to be a good parent. We seek advice from friends and family. Books, magazines, workshops, and TV specials abound on the topic of raising children. We rejoice when parent-child relationships are good, and we despair when they are bad. What can a church do?

A family ministry program can ask the following questions and be guided by the answers:

- Are opportunities for good parenting education available to everyone? Do cost, schedule, childcare arrangements, or location prevent participation? Can family ministry ensure that everyone has access to good parent education?

- Does our community have adequate and accessible resources for parents and families in crisis? Can the staff of our church guide people to needed resources?

- Do families in special circumstances have places of support and resource?

• What are the strengths of this congregation on which we can build good parental education and support?

What does good parent education look like?

Dozens of parent education programs exist, such as Positive Parenting (from the University of Minnesota Extension Service), Parenting with Love and Logic (developed by Jim Fay), STEP: Systematic Training for Effective Parenting (from the American Guidance Service). These types of programs offer organized multiple-session workshops, sometimes with videos or trained leaders, to train and encourage parents. Additional programs address parents with special parenting concerns, such as divorcing parents, stepfamilies, adoptive families, chronic or terminal illnesses.[1] Some of the elements most current parenting education programs have in common are:

1. Understanding the normal development and characteristics of children at different ages.

2. Reflecting on your own parenting style.

3. Learning skills of good communication and appropriate approaches to discipline.

4. Creating family relationships of respect, cooperation, and acceptance of responsibility.

Focused attention often is given to replacing punishment with the "natural or logical consequences" that result from a child's choices or behaviors.[2] A critical component of these parent education programs is the sharing and mutual support experienced among the parent participants. It appears that the group experience is often as beneficial as the program content. Parenting couples that participate together benefit further from the content and their shared dialogue during the days surrounding the program.

Within your church and community, you will find educators, social workers, and therapists who work with children and families that are knowledgeable about such parenting programs. They can help select and implement parent education that is most valuable in your community. Sometimes a church takes the lead in such endeavors; sometimes a church cooperates with or complements them.

What's Christian about Christian parenting?

Watch two families in a restaurant or in a store and guess which one is Christian. Except in extreme situations, it is probably impossible to tell. Many parents interact with their children in loving ways that reflect the values as honesty, generosity, and respect. Such parenting is not limited to Christians.

A Christian parent's faith, however, shapes all of parenting. A Christian parent understands parenting to be a vocation, not simply a challenging or desirable task. In addition, children are not seen as possessions to enjoy, but as gifts given by God, created in love, and shared with us to nurture, love, and care for. With the relationships of family, faith is nurtured and expressed, and Christ is revealed. While those principles may not be spoken aloud by parents, they are theological underpinning of Christian parenting.

Children are especially vulnerable to exploitation, neglect, abuse, misunderstanding, and violence. Jesus not only showed great compassion, even preference, for children and other vulnerable people, Jesus insists we do the same. In the Bible we find guidance about parenting, including the example of Jesus' interaction with children.

The long-term, intimate relationships within families provide rich opportunity to grow in faith. In its study *Effective Christian Education: A Summary Report* (1990), Search Institute examined the impact of various factors on the faith maturity of youth. The study concluded:

> . . . factors with the two most powerful connections to faith maturity for youth are family religiousness and lifetime exposure to formal Christian education. . . . Of the two strongest connections to faith maturity, family religiousness is slightly more important than lifetime exposure to Christian education. The particular family experiences most tied to greater faith maturity are the frequency with which an adolescent talked with mother and father about faith, the frequency of family devotions, and the frequency with which parents and children together were involved in efforts, formal or informal, to help other people. [3]

There is no doubt that the faith of children is strongly tied to the experiences within the home and family. The topics of conversations about faith, devotions, and actions to help others are addressed later this chapter in the section "Creating homes that are sacred spaces."

Finally, Christian parents know they are not alone in parenting. Not only is Christ present in family relationships, but the whole Christian community of the church is committed to helping be the family of God surrounding children. While nuclear families are central, no family is adequate for raising children . . . it takes the whole community of faith.

FOR REFLECTION AND DISCUSSION

- What's different about Christian parenting? What's different is the parents' whole perspective on parenting . . . grounded in Christ? For more information on this concept, see the chapter "Who Is the Child? Whose Is the Child? A Theology of Children."

- How can parents be reminded and encouraged in their distinctive Christian vocation of parenting? Consider the church library, newsletters, special events, classes, and parent conversations.

What else beyond parenting education?

While family ministry focuses on parenting education and support as central to living together as family members, family ministry must recognize also the essential need to support marriages and the dynamics of adults in their own intimate relationships. In fact, strengthening the primary relationships between adults may have long-lasting positive effects for both adults and entire families.

Enriching adult relationships

This is about marriage enrichment . . . and lots more. While two-parent families are common, they can no longer be assumed. Think about all the families you know. The adults in those families bear many descriptions: parent and stepparent, single parent, grandparents, parents plus grandparent, unmarried parents, same-gender parents, parent plus another adult relative or non-relative, foster parents. Many of us know a surprising number of parental relationships in the families around us.

In addition, the adults in families without children at home also carry many descriptions: adults married to each other in first marriages, those in second or third marriages for one or both adults, single adults, empty-nesters, double-incomes-without children, unmarried partners, same-gender relationships, widows and widowers, adults living in assisted living or various residential communities.

All these adults live in complex relationships with other adults. Family ministry has the opportunity to help adults enrich those relationships. Topics such as effective communication and resolving differences are common components of programs to enrich adult relationships. The church has the opportunity to center relationships within the Christian faith, where people are valued as God's creation, given gifts for sharing, and called into the body of Christ. They are our brothers and sisters in faith, people in mission in God's name.

FOR REFLECTION AND DISCUSSION

- In your community or neighborhood, where can adults participate in events designed to strengthen marriages and other adult relationships?

- Which adults are targeted in those events, and who is left out?

- Are adults encouraged to examine their relationships in light of their faith?

- What is the work of family ministry in this area of enriching adult relationships?

Special challenges for families

Violence

"She's not coming with us to the movies. Her dad's upset about something and she's afraid to ask him. So she's just gonna stay in her room and watch TV." My 8-year-old daughter was disappointed . . . and sad, too. Her friend Bee, also 8, gauged life by the moods of her father, usually fun and upbeat, but sometimes angry and violent. Asking to go to a movie when he's upset might trigger a slap or profane outburst. "He'd hit her, you know," my daughter continued. "He hits her mom when he gets like that."

It was similar to other conversations my daughter and I had had about her friend Bee, but this time she added, "It's not right. Can't somebody do something? Can't we do something?" What do I tell my 8-year-old who is learning much too young about violence that can happen right in your own home?

FOR REFLECTION AND DISCUSSION

- What options do I have to do something about Bee's situation? How would I go about those options? What would be the consequences of my actions?

- In what ways are children in your church touched by violence?

- You can assume that in every classroom, every retreat, every children's choir practice, every children's sermon, one or more children are touched by violence. What does your church do to protect children from violence?

- I've never tried to do anything about a situation like this. In what way can your church help me know what to do about Bee, and how to do it?

Disabilities

Kathie had been the organist at Peace Lutheran Church for several years when her third child was born. She was a beautiful baby girl, with Down's syndrome. Because of Kathie's public leadership role, her daughter was well-known, and Katie's special concerns and challenges were "out there in plain view of everybody, it seems."

It didn't take long before members of the congregation began to talk with Kathie about their own experiences with special needs, disabling or limiting conditions . . . and talk about how the church was more a part of the problem than part of a solution. Some families had quietly become inactive, seldom at worship, never participating in other congregational activities. Not only had the church neglected to help them bring faith together with daily life, the church had appeared impatient and unwelcoming.

Because of her staff position, Kathie had more members of the congregation talking about her daughter and other children in the church and surrounding community. A parents' support group emerged. Leaders planned to help make worship and congregational events more available to every member and every family. Hard questions about life were talked about more openly, and members of the congregation began to interact with others of all levels of ability. Some people made public the limitations they had once kept secret, now receiving support and nurture, not ridicule and ostracism.

FOR REFLECTION AND DISCUSSION

- Why did it take the birth of Kathie's daughter to begin changes in this congregation?

- How could the church building and ministry be more accessible to people with physical disabilities?

- What attitudes and logistics keep people from feeling welcome in your church?

- In your community, who takes seriously the needs of families with special needs such as limiting physical conditions? Who takes seriously the faith lives of these same families?

- What steps can your church take to include families with special needs in your family ministry?

Death

Gramma lives 400 miles away from Maya, a full day's drive. Yet the relationship between this 5-year-old and her 85-year-old grandmother has been close. At Christmas, Maya and her mom spent three wonderful days visiting Gramma at her retirement apartment. Two weeks later Gramma suffered a stroke from which she never regained consciousness. Maya's mom was at Gramma's side when she died two days later.

Adult friends will bring Maya to be with her mom for the funeral and a few days afterward. Through telephone calls and conversations with her adult friends, Maya has been told that Gramma died. Death is not a totally new concept to Maya. Her dog died two years ago. A friend's dog died last year. And an adult neighbor died within the last month. There has been conversation about all these deaths.

Now Maya's mom faces a decision. Gramma's casket will be closed at the funeral, as it was at the visitation the night before. Should she allow, encourage, discourage, or prevent Maya's seeing Gramma's body? Maya will arrive late tonight, after the visitation. Tomorrow afternoon is the funeral.

There's time to go to the funeral home and open the casket, but is this a good idea? And if Maya will see Gramma's body, how can her mom help make it a good experience . . . if that is possible?

FOR REFLECTION AND DISCUSSION

- What advice do you have for Maya's mom? Why do you offer that partic-ular advice?

- More than we may think, children are surrounded by images and experi-ences of death. In what ways are children helped to grapple with their questions, misconceptions, and fears of death?

- In what ways can family ministry help parents find age-appropriate ways for children to explore the concept of death?

Sexual abuse

Research suggests that 1 in 4 girls and 1 in 6 boys will be sexually abused before the age of 16. It may be the most publicized, least talked about subject today: the sexual abuse of our children. We prefer to talk around the topic, discuss problems revealed in some distant state, lament over the scandal surrounding a well-known public figure. Unfortunately, we spend less time considering the vulnerability and safety of our own children. Additionally, 75% to 95% of these victims know their abusers.[4] There is no more imme-diate crisis in family ministry than the physical and emotional safety of our children within their own homes.

FOR REFLECTION AND DISCUSSION

- Who in your community is already at work to prevent the sexual abuse of children, and what are they doing?

- Has your church found its voice in protecting children from abuse?

- How can family ministry help families face the issues surrounding sexual abuse—protecting children, confronting offenders, supporting those in crisis?

- How can family ministry help ensure the safety of children throughout this community?

Creating homes that are sacred spaces

How can a home be a sacred space?

Spiritual life is not reserved for church. We are spiritual beings all the time, not just on Sundays. We spend more time, have our most long-lasting and intimate relationships, and are shaped and nurtured most in our homes and families. The home is a center of faith in many traditions. Therefore, the home can be recognized as a sacred space. Jewish families share Friday evening meal (Shabbot) together, and blessings accompany the lighting of candles, pouring of wine, and sharing of bread. Hindu families have home altars for worship. Muslim families have a place facing Mecca to pray five times a day.

The Bible often refers to the natural and vital place of the home in one's faith. For example, Deuteronomy 6:4 states, "Hear, O Israel: The LORD is our God, the LORD alone" begins a statement of faith to be shared with "your children and talk about them when you are at home and when you are away, when you lie down and when you rise." We can help make this sacred space called home even more effective as a place for faith nurture and expression.

How can my home be a sacred space?

There are at least six ways that our homes can be shaped as sacred spaces—spaces where faith is shared, nurtured, enriched, and expressed through the following:

- Conversation and storytelling
- Rituals and celebrations
- Prayer
- Books, art, and other media
- Patterns of daily living
- Relationship with a larger faith community

For resources in each of these areas, contact your denominational publishing house or church headquarters (visit their Web sites), or visit your local religious bookstores.

How do conversation and storytelling contribute to the sacredness of home?

What stories do you tell in your family? When do you talk together? Where do you have conversations? Who does the most talking? Who is the best listener? Would it be okay for others to overhear your conversations?

Good communication is necessary for families to live together well. Communication in the form of stories and conversation is ideal for sharing and enriching faith. We love to hear and tell stories about the things we cherish. Stories about special events, special people, emergencies, happy days, the house where we used to live, how it was when a grandparent was growing up, how I spent last summer, a favorite pet's new trick, getting ready for a big family trip bring families closer together. Talking about those things comes naturally to us.

There are stories to tell in our faith lives as well. Stories of kindness and hospitality, stories of faithful people we know and remember, stories from and about the Bible, stories about God and how we have experienced God in our lives, comments about a recent worship service or church event, ideas about an up-coming work project or mission trip help nurture faith in families.

When I was a child, my family talked while sitting on the front porch of our old farmhouse on hot summer evenings. I heard and overheard the adults talking about farm crops and weather and daily activities. I also heard them talk about launching satellites and people into space, about the assassinations of national leaders, about neighbors fighting in a war somewhere far away. They spoke of their own childhoods and early adult lives. Through those stories, I learned what my parents valued, the principles they lived by, how they made sense of a world that sometimes confused and frightened me. Our conversations with and around our children about the tough topics in life are critical for helping share our values, our principles, and our faith.

For Reflection and Discussion

• Most homes don't have big front porches waiting for conversations. Conversations just don't happen when and where they once did. So when and where do you talk? In the car? On long walks? After school or work? On vacation? While shopping together?

- Do you sometimes talk about the most important things in life: what you cherish, what you believe, what you fear, who you are as a child of God?

- What can you do to help your conversations include your life of faith?

How do rituals and celebrations contribute to the sacredness of home?

We love traditions . . . fixing pancakes on Saturday mornings, hosting the annual Halloween party, picking strawberries at the farm each summer, visiting Aunt Imma on Thanksgiving. We create rituals and symbolic actions to express what we cherish. If we are sports enthusiasts, we prepare for the big games, planning to attend the event or watch on television. Those preparations often become repeated rituals themselves, and our children learn how important these events are to our family.

When our faith is important, we create rituals and celebrations surrounding our spiritual lives. Some of these rituals may happen daily, such as table grace and evening prayers. Some may happen with special events in life: the ways we observe or celebrate confirmations, baptisms, birthdays, weddings, tragic events, and deaths. What rituals exist in your home? Which ones involve your life of faith? Which ones could be modified to reflect your spirituality?

Decorating the Christmas tree is an annual event for some families. Why not include reading of an appropriate Bible passage and discussing the celebration of Christmas this year in your family? Perhaps celebrating baptismal anniversaries could become special for you. One woman looks forward to listening to Handel's *Messiah* throughout the Saturday before Easter and on Christmas Eve day, and she arranges her schedule to make this happen.

One important feature of these kinds of ritual celebrations is physical symbols and actions. Rituals are not just talk; they include symbolic activity. Just think of birthdays—lighting the candles on the cake, blowing out the candles, singing "Happy Birthday," opening presents, receiving cards, wearing something festive. Birthdays lose some of their special qualities when we neglect the symbolic activities.

For Reflection and Discussion

- What occasions are we going to make special? How will we prepare for those occasions?

- What will we do as a symbolic activity? What part of the story will we reenact or retell? How will we involve any children present?

How can prayer contribute to making home a sacred space?

Most Christians agree that prayer is a centerpiece of a life of faith. Our invitation to "pray without ceasing" gives us encouragement and challenge to live a life filled with prayer, including prayer in our homes.

Perhaps you can think bigger and more creatively about praying together than you now do at home. Here are a few ideas.

- Find and organize prayers you love and want to remember and perhaps memorize. Keep these prayers where you can find and use them. Collect them into a folder or booklet or post them on a bulletin board. Look together for books of prayers at the library or bookstore, or find some on the Internet.

- Pray for your children. Pray for your siblings. Pray for your spouse.

- Let your family hear you pray,

- Keep a family prayer list. Each day or week, put on the list the names or situations for which the family is asked to pray—individually and together. If you keep those lists you may reread them later to remember God's faithfulness.

- Keep your family prayer list in a spot no one will miss—on a card in the center of the kitchen table, taped to the bathroom mirror, on the refrigerator door.

- Practice spontaneous prayer. Although we might be intimidated by the thought of praying aloud without something written to read, people of every age can become more comfortable with spontaneous prayer and public praying. It just takes a little practice. It helps if children hear and observe adults praying. An adult may ask everyone to name something to include in prayer, then pray aloud including those things.

How can books, art, and other media contribute to making home a sacred space?

Our homes reveal much about us. What does your home reveal about your faith life? We surround ourselves with physical symbols of what we cherish. Let's walk through the home of Judy and Frank, and their son Jonah. On their front porch is a small sign that reads, "Peace to all who enter here." Artwork on their walls gives the visitor a clue about the family's activities. Ask about the wall hanging from Peru and they will tell you about their church's mission trip to build a children's center there. Soon you are looking at pictures from that trip in the scrapbook they created.

Because it is Christmas, a nativity set is placed near the tree, with sheep, goats, and other nativity pieces collected from all over the world by friends who travel and remember their love of various Christmas traditions. The Christmas tree would not win a decorator's award. It is cluttered with every imaginable expression of the coming of the Christ child—children's simple artwork, sophisticated Christmas decorations from many countries, nationalities, and ethnic groups. With every decoration there is a story of a person, place, or tradition. A young adult friend who has found art to be a therapeutic response to his battle with a chronic disease made the angel at the top.

Judy and Frank's framed marriage certificate hangs in their room. In Jonah's room, his framed baptismal certificate hangs above his bed. On the end table in the family room is a book of devotions. Near the breakfast table is a bulletin board with the words "We thank you, God, for . . ." followed by photographs and words of special significance in their lives that week.

Why is it important to have these symbols of our faith around us? First, they remind us continually of our faith, strengthening us and giving us joy. Second, they make an unspoken witness of our faith to others who see them, a witness we often find hard to make publicly. Third, when people ask about them, they give us opportunity to tell the stories behind them, stories of faith and faithful people.

- Look around your home. Will a visitor have a clue about your values? About your faith?

- What symbols of your faith can be placed in more visible places for others to see? For further discussion about the role of media in the family's life of faith, see the chapter "Growing Faithful Children in Media Cultures."

How does my pattern of daily living contribute to making my home a sacred place?

"Now, Jeremy, because you are a member of this family, you will behave in the following ways . . . and you will speak in the following ways." We seldom use the classroom lecture to teach our children what it means to be a member of our family. In fact, those kinds of lectures often remain unheard, even when the child's head is shaking up and down in response. More frequently, our children catch our values simply by watching and being part of the everyday life of the family. Truly, faithfulness is more caught than taught.

FOR REFLECTION AND DISCUSSION

- What images of God do children have through living with you? For instance, what do you say to God when you are happy? What names and titles do you use for God? How do you relate to God in a crisis?

- What acts of service and kindness do children see you perform? What service activities do you perform together? What attitude accompanies such service? For instance, when you visit an aging relative, is that visit anticipated with pleasure, resentment, thankfulness, ridicule, graciousness, or anger? The attitudes that surround our words and actions teach more than the actions themselves.

Giving ourselves in acts of compassion, kindness, and service to others has a remarkable effect upon ourselves and others who share those activities, particularly our children. That positive effect is increased when I think and talk about what I am doing and why. Action based in God's love, action centered in being Christ-like, action motivated by love for others, that kind of action strengthens the faith of all involved. Do you know a better way to share your faith with your children than by living it out every day?

How does my relationship with a faith community contribute to making home a sacred space?

Families of faith are strengthened when they are connected strongly with a larger faith community . . . a congregation. Just as we surround ourselves with traditions, actions, and physical symbols of our faith, so we also become part of a larger community that shares our values and faith. No, this is not meant to isolate us from others unlike ourselves in faith. Instead, sharing community enriches us, encourages us, and joins us in faithful family living.

FOR REFLECTION AND DISCUSSION

- What role does your church play in your life? That is, what habits and traditions include your church? Is "going to church" a habit or a weekly decision?

- Is participating in congregational life built into weekly life? What part of your schedule includes church-related activities? Does this level of participation in your faith community adequately enrich and strengthen your family's life of faith?

- Do your children know why you participate in church and why you want them to participate?

We often assume that our family and friends know why we make the choices we make. Don't make that assumption; tell them. It may not be easy to put into words, but telling others why you choose to go to church, why you teach Sunday school, why you visit people who are sick, or why you contribute money clarifies your own values and gives you opportunity to invite others to join you. If you find it important to do something, you naturally want others to find similar value by doing it also.

How can you prepare your children for what is going on in church today? Preparation pays off. Even if it is a trip to a friend's house, we prepare our children with reminders, such as "Be home by three o'clock" or "Joe's been sick, so don't play outside" or "Remember to say 'thank you' for dinner."

Preparation for church participation also pays off. Is there a special guest? Is it a special festival day? Will there be a baptism? Where will the work project be held? What is the purpose of this family night event? Conversations beforehand help ensure that the whole family is enriched in congregational participation.

Not simply attending worship, but thoughtful participation in a congregation or other faith community will also strengthen your home as a sacred space for enriching, nurturing, and expressing faith.

Strengthening the home-church partnership

What is family ministry's role in an effective church-home connection? Too often parents feel ignored and church leaders feel abandoned in their separate endeavors to nurture the health and faith of families. At the beginning of this chapter, Amy yearned for a partnership between herself and the church. How can we help that happen?

*Six strategies for strengthening the
home-church partnership*

1. **Make the church a physically and emotionally safe place for children and families.**

   The responsibility entrusted to the church when children are put in our care must be taken seriously. Parents leave young children in the church nursery and church-sponsored child care assuming that the adult caregivers are trustworthy. We must see that they are. Children waiting for rides home from vacation Bible school, choir practice, or group meetings are vulnerable to invitations from drivers who may not be known by parents. Increasingly, congregations use background checks to ensure the trustworthiness of adults who are working with children and youth in churches. It has been an awkward and resisted action by many, but it has become necessary. Ensure the physical and emotional safety of children and families.

2. **Schedule congregational events so all families have opportunities to participate.**

   Certainly not every activity will be convenient for everyone in a church. Too often, however, our schedules take on patterns that continue to exclude the same people, over and over. Always having meetings or events at 7:30 P.M. on weeknights will always prohibit the participation of the same people: those who work at that time, those needing childcare, those who cannot drive at night, those without the stamina for evening activities.

3. **Cooperate more and compete less for the attention of families.**

Do we add to the conflict families experience between community and church activities? Some is inevitable, but if we want to strengthen our partnership between church and home, we must be sensitive to school calendars and community events. Some churches plan special events for children during the occasional schools-out days during the year. Both working parents and children needing childcare are grateful for well-designed and supervised activities that fit their schedule, and the church has another opportunity to engage children in quality activities. Some churches found that by adjusting the hours available for childcare, families with difficult work schedules were served.

4. **Become an advocate for families and children.**

In every community there are concerns and problems for families, such as safety, medical care, child care, education, after-school activities, and nutrition. The gospel calls the church to address injustice, to give special attention to the weak and oppressed, to favor those on the fringes. What are the issues facing families in your community? Church staff and members can be encouraged to participate in discussion and take leadership roles in the activities, church buildings can be available for meetings, churches can educate their own members about the issues.

5. **Identify and provide resources for families.**

Every family constantly looks for trustworthy advice on programs, events, books, media, software, childcare, and other resources. Churches can look for creative and effective ways to help families make good selections from an overwhelming number of choices being marketed aggressively today. Churches can point to resources prepared by denominational and other faith-related publishers especially for families. Web-based resources for home use will become increasingly available, and the church can identify and use such ministry tools as *ReadyClickGrow* from Augsburg Fortress, Publishers.

6. **Communicate, communicate, communicate.**

The best church-home partnership is only as effective as its communication. The Internet will become an important tool in church-home communication, but never the only tool. Newsletters, information sheets, telephone calls, community-wide publicity, and word-of-mouth conversations all remain vital links of communication. Parents need timely and complete information about activities and issues concerning children. Children and youth need to be part of the loop of communication. Well-designed communication is necessary with adults who are bombarded already by information We know how to communicate effectively. We need to do it!

Conclusion

People come in families—all sorts of families. While individuals participate in the life of the church, everything that touches individuals also touches their families. In addition, everything that happens in a family also affects its individuals. Family ministry is the church's efforts to strengthen families as they seek to live faithfully. Family ministry works to help families live together faithfully as family members, to help families create homes that are sacred spaces, and to help strengthen the home-church partnership. Already, every church does family ministry, but we can be more effective by thinking through how to do it better and organizing ourselves for action. It is the church's delight and responsibility to help families grow in faith and live out their faith.

Notes

1. For a detailed look at child-rearing advice over the last 100 years, see Ann Hulbert, *Raising America* (New York: Knopf, 2003).

2. The concept of "natural and logical consequences" is attributed to Rudolf Dreikurs (1964) and has been developed further by many parent educators.

3. *Effective Christian Education: A Summary Report* (Minneapolis: Search Institute, 1990), p. 38.

4. For more information about these and related statistics, visit the Web site for the Center for the Prevention of Sexual and Domestic Violence at www.cpsdv.org.

CHAPTER 5

Growing Faithful Children in Media Cultures

Mary E. Hess

THE DOOR PUSHED OPENED, and all three kids shoved through. Marvin and Jude, at 7 and 10, ran up the stairs and toward their own rooms. Fina, 4 years old and just a little less willing to body block, followed behind. Diane sighed as she set down the two bags of groceries and tried to sort out through the pile of mail that had fallen from the mail slot onto the floor.

Let's see, bill, bill, bill, oh yes, a request to support environmental action, junk mail, junk mail, junk mail, and . . . another bill. Diane sighed again. There was never enough money to feel comfortable and this month was going to be tighter than most, given the run of ear infections they'd had last month. Why couldn't health insurance really insure? There was no real answer to that, and Diane grabbed the groceries and walked into the kitchen. If she got dinner simmering in the next half hour she might be able to grab half an hour's peace before Mark got home.

"Mooommmm!" came a voice screaming down the stairs. "Jude won't give me the Scooby DVD!" "But, Mom," came Jude's equally shrill voice, "Marvin watched it yesterday. It's my turn."

Diane trudged up the stairs in response, wondering why it was that a computer in every room, DVD capable, hadn't erased the fights the boys seemed intent on having every day after school.

As she passed Fina's room she saw her hunkered down in front of her own TV. Why a 4-year-old would find a show about a high school spy enjoyable was beyond her, but at least it had some redeeming qualities.

Ten minutes later the spaghetti was simmering, the kids were entranced in front of various screens, and Diane sipped at her coffee, half an ear to the radio mumbling gently beside her, and her eyes on the paper in front of her. People were being massacred again, and the government couldn't decide whether to do anything about it. Children's test scores were falling, and the city wasn't ready for another tax increase. At least the weather was looking up—rain was finally expected and a soaking rain, at that. Maybe the corn could recover after all.

Diane's heart ached. It seemed like there was no end to the pain in the world. She wondered what she could do about it. Nothing, likely. It was hard enough just keeping her own family fed and clothed, let alone getting off to school and work on time.

Yet there was just a wisp of a song floating through her head . . . what was it? The lyrics said that you've got to get yourself together and can't get out of it. "Don't say that later will be better." U2 had always been one of her favorite bands, and that lilting, haunted phrase from the song "Stuck in a Moment" reminded her that, growing up, her mom had always believed that God was active in the world. Maybe there really were signs of such activity. It was hard to know. She wondered whether going to church could make a difference. The kids hated being dragged out of bed on a Sunday morning, and Mark—with some legitimacy—thought the hypocrisy of the congregation was teaching them something they didn't need to learn. Still, maybe Bono was right, maybe "later WASN'T better" and it was time to be more open to hearing God's voice in the world. It was an open question and she let it sit in her heart as she rose to stir the pasta sauce.

C hildren's ministries are once again a hot topic in many communities of faith. We are beginning to recognize how important it is to reach out to young families, to draw children into our programs, and to support parents. Far too many of our attempts, however, are based on outdated assumptions about the ways that children's ministry should be structured. Children's ministry is not so much about ministry *to* children as it is about ministry *with* children. The primary religious educators of children are those with whom they spend the bulk of their time, and thus our focus in children's ministry ought to be on these adults. No amount of carefully designed programming will "solve" our problems with supporting children, because the challenges are adaptive, not technical. Finally, for better and worse, media culture is the primary context in which children's ministry takes place, and communities of faith must engage that culture fully, understanding children's ministry as a deliberate cultural intervention.

These are strong statements, and I do not expect you to accept them without sufficient argument. I will, however, focus in this chapter on ways that communities of faith can support learning with children. Others' chapters in this book explore the theology of such learning environments or deal with the specificity of learning directly within a congregational setting. In this chapter, I hope to provide both a theoretical and a pragmatic foundation for supporting such learning in the larger media contexts of which we are all a part. A shorthand way of describing my topic would be to say that I am interested in learning with children in, about, and through media culture.

To help you follow my argument, here it is in outline form. First, we live in challenging times, and focusing on media culture makes those challenges particularly clear. Educational theory can help us to engage these challenges constructively, pointing to our need to radically re-vision what we understand learning with children to be about—that is, that it is both a relational process, and about relationality. Supporting children requires us to attend to the practices we use to share our relationality. Supporting children's ministry requires that we work adaptively, not simply technically, or programmatically. In particular, we need to provide adequate amounts of *confirmation*, *contradiction*, and *continuity* around issues of relationality for children and the adults who nurture them. Finally, the story of the disciples on the road to Emmaus points to specific, pragmatic interventions we can work with in making such deep relationality vivid and embodied.

The challenges we face in media culture

There has perhaps never been a more vibrant or more challenging time to learn with children. Just three decades ago, when today's parents of children were themselves children, the world looked very different—at least in the United States. The World Wide Web, now fairly ubiquitous, was merely a gleam in a science-fiction author's imagination. Television was the favored mass medium, but generally only three channels held much interest for people. Movies were something you went to the local movie theater to watch together, and telephones came with long, spiral cords attached to them.

In some ways it might be reasonable to expect that our increased access to such technologies would create more leisure time and increased affluence, but the opposite is actually the case. Statisticians point out that those Americans who are employed (and our rates of unemployment have been rising rapidly since the year 2000) spent "142 hours more per year on the job in 1994 than they did in 1973."[1] Additionally, "While there has been a per capita rise in income in the U.S. since 1970 of 62%, there has also been a decrease in the quality of life as measured by the Index of Social Health—to the tune of 51%."[2] These are statistics that get at the material circumstances, but what is also true about this period of time is that there have been significant shifts demographically, with immigrants arriving from all corners of the globe, practicing many different faiths. These statistics only begin to hint at the enormous changes now taking place in the United States, changes that reach from the most intimate to the most far ranging.

At the same time as families living amidst this change struggle to cope, they are also being bombarded more than ever by advice on "proper" parenting. Where once they might have relied on neighborhood institutions such as church or local school, on the extended family networks that lived around them, if not in the same house, they now often find themselves struggling to hold together multiple spheres of activity without such supports. Families that exist on the margins economically often must accommodate the schedules of others—social workers, aid agencies—along with their advice. Families that live comfortably often shuttle their children between play groups, after-school programs, and other activities. Parents rush home from work or other commitments to cram food down their kids' throats before taking off for the next round of activities (whether additional jobs, or structured recreation). Each of these environments may offer its own range of advice, and have its own rules for how to participate and how to "play," and parents and children must negotiate among them all at once, finding their own compromises and making their own choices.

Woven into all of this blur are the daily practices of media—so commonplace that we often take them for granted. TV programs on during breakfast, the car radio on while commuting, after-school "screen time"—all of these are part of our shared environment. It is into this context that religious educators must enter, and it is in this context that we will be supportive and engaged with learning with children, or not.

I want to suggest some very pragmatic and constructive ways to enter into this context, but before getting to those suggestions I think it will help to review some basic educational theory. Many people speak of the challenges we face, but how we describe them will inevitably affect how we choose to address them.

Educational theory that guides our interventions

There are two basic frames for thinking about learning that I find useful no matter the context I'm working in. The first is oriented more toward internal learning processes, that is, processes at work within a learner, and the second toward more external elements, that is, teaching processes that contribute to shaping the learning that is taking place within any person.

First, researchers tell us that learning takes place on three levels within each person—the *cognitive*, the *affective*, and the *psychomotor*. You may perhaps be more familiar with the language of ideas, feelings, and actions.[3] Why is this important? An easy answer would be that understanding the multiple levels at which learning is taking place allows teachers to attend more carefully to structuring learning effectively. A deeper answer would encourage religious educators to recognize that far too often our learning environments attend to *cognitive* issues—specific creedal formulations, details of Bible stories, and so on—all the while ignoring *affective* and *psychomotor* elements of the learning taking place. If learning is always taking place in all three areas, then ignoring particular areas means that we are either assuming that someone or something else will attend to those areas, or we are deciding that they are not important.

If the only time children engage a Bible story is in worship, and that experience requires them to sit still and listen to someone far in front whom they may not even be able to see, it is possible that the children's experience of isolation and boredom will attach to the Bible story regardless of its actual content. Imagine, on the other hand, a Bible story that a child engages through song, dance, and an illustrated picture book, perhaps while sitting on the lap of a loved one. The feelings surrounding the experience of that story mean that its content is much more likely to sink in. To use educational terms, such learning can be integrated into and held by multiple brain pathways.

Pause for a moment and think about some of your most vivid learning experiences: What were the ideas? What were the feelings? What were you doing physically in that situation?

It is perhaps obvious, but nonetheless worth pointing out, that certain kinds of media hold children's attention better than others. It is not coincidence that some of the most successful children's videos tell a story, sing a song, invite identification with several characters, prompt dancing, and so on. What may not be so obvious is that the most successful of such media are also those with stories compelling enough, characters interesting enough, to spark children's improvisation with them. McDonald's might include a movie tie-in toy with its children's meals, but the only toys that really get used are those that children find amenable to including in their own story-making.

This example already spills over into the external environment where the story is encountered. If *cognitive*, *affective*, and *psychomotor* issues are internal, then it is the second set of frames—that of *explicit*, *implicit*, and *null* curricula—that help us to attend to how we shape these processes. A *curriculum*, by definition, is a structured approach to learning. Elliott Eisner identified these three curricula as operative in any environment, and invites us to recognize, again, the multiple ways that people learn.[4] Another way to speak of these three is of the intentional, incidental, and unacknowledged forms of our learning. Teachers set out intentionally to convey certain kinds of information, to support certain kinds of learning. Anyone who has ever been a learner, however, knows that while a teacher may have an explicit intention of teaching something, many other things get taught along the way incidentally. Then there are the things that get taught by not being taught, by being ignored or being taboo, those things that we learn are not to be spoken of, although no one explicitly tells us these rules. Again, pause for a moment and try to remember some times in your own religious educational history when teachers were explicitly teaching one thing, and you found yourself learning something else.

In many cases, religious educators are very clear about our explicit curriculum—we may speak in terms of "deepening discipleship," "sharing Christ," "giving people access to a tradition," or "attending to God's action in our midst," but we are often less aware of the incidental learning that is taking place within our learning contexts. All of the goals I've just noted, for instance, clearly include *cognitive*, *affective*, and *psychomotor* elements. It is clear that you cannot deepen discipleship if you ignore people's feelings and actions alongside of their beliefs. But how often do we pause and deliberately ponder how to engage people's feelings and actions in their beliefs? How often do we ask whether the materials we're working with in one setting support or contest our community's voiced mission in another?

Further, how often do we consider that the ways that what we are teaching, the kind of understanding we're striving toward, may in effect be counter to many of the prevailing practices around us? Here I'm not thinking only of the larger cultural spaces we inhabit, but even those most close to us within the walls of our community of faith.

How do we teach and learn while remaining aware of the multiple levels on which learning occurs? What does it mean to invite people into a space where they will be challenged to overturn their whole way of understanding themselves? What does it mean to do that with children, let alone their parents, in media culture?

Part of what we can learn from the scholarship on learning, from the frames I've just noted—the *cognitive*, *affective*, and *psychomotor* piece, as well as the *explicit*, *implicit*, and *null* curricula piece—is that the vast majority of learning takes place relationally. This is not a difficult claim to substantiate from people's experiences. Consider your own response to my earlier question about a vivid religious education memory. Your memory probably included a person who shared an important relationship with you (parent, teacher, neighbor), whose judgment of you, you both desired and respected.

This relational component to learning it is even more true when understood from a Christian perspective. As Parker Palmer so pointedly notes that "we know as we are known," and we are known most intimately by God.[5] Yet it is one thing to affirm that our learning is relational, and quite another to name that belief theologically, particularly given the ways that traditional theological categories are less well known in popular mediated contexts. We may affirm as Christians that we are known most intimately by God—but we rarely believe it, or at least, we rarely act as if we have this experience at the heart of our knowing.

This lack of experienced knowing shines through in the ways that our children learn from us, it is the *implicit* and *null* curriculum of much that we teach in our current cultural contexts. This challenge—that gap between what we affirm theologically and what we embody in our daily experiences— is the key challenge children's ministries must face directly. We affirm relationality as at the heart of Christian being and knowing—we are a trinitarian people [6]—but we rarely act upon that knowing, we rarely trust it. One of the big opportunities here, however, is to recognize that we have at least as much to learn from our children as they do from us.

One of the most visceral and intimate ways that we understand knowing and being known by God is through the way we know ourselves with our children, and the way that we know our children through our love for and with them.[7] It is not a coincidence that referring to God as "Father" has had such a long and sustained history. We ought also to affirm that relationship by referring to God as "Mother." But even apart from the theological implications of this shift, consider the underlying issue—that we learn so much about love in the relationships we have with children. Some of that knowing comes about in our recognition of the extent to which we will go to protect children, but if we are honest, it also comes from our recognition of the elemental nature of their love for us and for others. This is relational knowing at its most pure and its most intense.

There is an opportunity here, to learn from our children and with our children in deep relationality. Yet this opportunity also poses difficult challenges in media culture, for representations of relationality pervade our media, but they are, by and large, fairly narrow and limited representations. You cannot engage the mass media without encountering depictions of relationship, yet you can engage the media and still end up with only a very narrow and limited range of such depictions.

Turning to media culture

Media culture really is a *medium* in which meaning is made. Think of the definition of *medium* you learned in science classes: a substance in which something can be cultured or grown. Contrary to popular conception— a conception shared by many communities of faith—mass mediated popular culture is not simply a set of content that is enforced by sheer market presence on passive recipients. Rather, it is a meaning-making space where enormous amounts of material are provided for people to draw on. As noted earlier, effective learning engages *cognitive, affective,* and *psychomotor* elements. Mass mediated popular culture does this in a variety of ways, not the least of which is by fusing sound and image to representations of being.

Indeed, *media culture* is best understood as a dynamic medium in which meaning is produced, circulated, contested, and improvised with.[8] That means that learning is taking place all of the time, all around us. That means that our relationships are often our most potent teachers. That means that when media culture encourages us to "reason by means of sympathetic identification" we are engaging one of its most powerful tools. If we truly do "know as we are known," what does it mean "to know" as media culture represents ourselves to ourselves and to each other?

First, and foremost, it means to know affectively, experientially. Media representations can be enormously powerful, pulling us into their worlds and helping us to suspend our disbelief. Unfortunately, it is also often the case that the sheer ubiquity of a particular representation captures our attention, limiting the database of possibilities we perceive as we engage in meaning-making, and focusing our attention on the "content" of that representation, rather than on its construction.

In addition, most media engagement in the United States in mainstream, middle-class families is increasingly happening in isolation. Whereas three decades ago each family might have one television set (with a handful of channels), many families have more than one set—perhaps even more sets than they have actual family members. Increasingly families are even buying more than one computer. So viewing screens (television or computer) is more often done in isolation. Movie theaters have evolved from showing one or perhaps two movies at a time, to big cineplexes where more than a dozen movies may be showing. Even families that go to the movie theater together may not see the same film. This reality cuts down on two important elements of media engagement—being in the same place at the same time when viewing media—so that people laugh together, cry together, yell at the absurdities, and so on—and being able to have shared conversations about media elements, being able to draw on the same database of meaning-making raw materials.

In this case a very tangible *psychomotor* element of the learning—that is, viewing done in relatively passive physical positions, and in relative isolation—contributes to some of the more challenging aspects of media practice. Mass mediated popular culture thrives on stories of relationality. Indeed, in some way, every genre of mass mediated pop culture, indeed almost every single piece of pop culture you can point to is at heart a reflection of relationality, whether *right* relationality, *broken* relationality, or at least *strained* relationality. Sitcoms tell stories about families and workplaces. News programs reflect our understanding of reality and its connection to our own experiences. Reality shows purport to represent how *real* people in *real* situations are responding to their relationships, or the lack thereof. Children's cartoons model relationships—some imaginary and some realistic. Indeed, communities of faith have always recognized how powerful a storyteller popular culture is, how much this storyteller reflects us to ourselves, and that is part of the reason we have been so reluctant for it to take center stage in our sharing of stories.

We have spent a large amount of time engaging the *cognitive* and *affective elements* of meaning-making in mass mediated spheres—seeking to tell our own stories in these media (think about the vast Christian broadcasting empire) or to deconstruct the stories already there. In that very way, we missed a far more powerful element of the meaning-making taking place there that has to do with this element of the *psychomotor:* the physical ways that we learn with these media. Consider the ways that mass-mediated stories used to be engaged amidst relational patterns that augmented them, that provided an *implicit* and *null* curricula in support of relationality. Families watched their one television set together. In the decades before television— and still in many parts of the world—families gather together around radio.

In our current contexts, we increasingly engage media in isolation, or at least in segmented groups—teens with teens, young children watching children's television, adults watching adult programming, and so on. The inter-generational, deeply relational patterns of practice with which we began engaging these media have broken down, and we find ourselves increasingly in a position in which the databases we draw on to make sense of our stories, literally to write our stories, are also segmented—intended for specific audiences. One painful consequence of this "target audience segmentation" is that we no longer have shared databases to draw on as we make sense of the world around us, as we struggle to make sense of ourselves, let alone share our sense of our deep relationality.

This is true of age-related programming. Think about the ways that various generations are identified, and all of the targeted marketing thrown at them. It is also true in terms of ideological and religious divides. People who share a particular view of the world can listen to particular radio shows and not encounter other views. People from a particular religious perspective—no matter how narrowly understood—can stay within a database of meanings that supports their background.

Indeed, many people engage mass media solely as a "window on the world"—without recognizing the shape of that window. That "frame," that specific construction of meaning may well be a good, solid, appropriate one, but it is nevertheless a construction of meaning. All of us need to be aware of the limited and narrow nature of any such construction.

One way to think about this is to suggest that the *explicit* curriculum of TV news teaches that what you see on the news is reality. Similarly, that "all the news that's fit to print" can be found in a specific newspaper—or perhaps linked through a specific news Web site. Yet there is an *implicit* curriculum found in news reporting, and it can be interpreted in multiple ways. One could learn, for example, that the world is primarily a dangerous and violent place. Some media literacy educators argue that the central problem with the portrayal of violence on television is not that it causes violence, but rather that people come to believe that the world is primarily violent, and that nonviolent solutions to conflict are not ever feasible. Another conclusion people might come to is that people whose stories do not end up reported in the news are not sufficiently important to warrant understanding. Of course, these are only some of the possibilities because *incidental* learning is neither linear, easily controlled, or even predictable.

Children, to get to the point of this chapter, are rarely present in the news, and almost never produce it. See the chapter "Who Is the Child?

Whose Is the Child? A Theology of Children." Indeed, the few attempts to provide opportunities for children to produce and report news have always been relegated to tiny local cable or public stations, or to very rare exceptions on national broadcasts (such as Peter Jennings's town meetings with kids following September 11, 2001). Indeed, children's active presence in news construction is so rare that perhaps instead of noting these as examples of an *implicit* curriculum, it would be more appropriate to note that children's role in news is instead part of the *null* curriculum of our current cultural contexts.

On the other hand, children are frequently at least present in entertainment genres, if not at the heart of the drama. Indeed, some of the most immediately resonant story lines on any number of prime time dramas are so moving precisely because children's lives are endangered (think about the children being hauled into the emergency room on a hospital drama, or the child dying on a mini-series). Children frequently stand as symbols of the most vulnerable of human beings, and of those most deserving of protection and support.[9]

Yet in cold, crass terms, the sheer statistics on children in the United States are stunning. More and more children are sliding further into poverty, hunger, and homelessness. Our schools are increasingly stressed and unable to provide adequate instruction. Unemployment among teenagers is often higher than among any other group, and the few jobs that are available can feel demeaning. Why this enormous paradox? Why can we find so many examples in popular culture that proclaim our desire to help and protect children, yet at the same time find so few examples of ways to provide real, material aid to improve the circumstances in their lives?

I imagine there are numbers of possible answers to this question. I will not attempt to offer any here, although I think communities of faith ought to take the question very seriously. I suspect that our frameworks of understanding—particularly in terms of sinfulness and reconciliation—might have a lot to offer in response. Instead, I simply raise the question to point out that we are learning, in the midst of mass mediated popular culture, how to identify sympathetically with people experiencing any number of compelling problems, but rarely are we given any models to follow for responding in any way other than through vicarious emotional identification.

We are drawn to these media because we can play with our sympathetic identification, we can think through our affectivity with them. It is often truly enjoyable to do so. Yet it is also the case that because the range of images and activities embedded in these media is so narrow, we end up acting in ways that narrow our relationality, that misconstrue it in fundamental ways.

Let me make this theory more concrete with an example: television commercials for personal care products. Most of us at one time or another have worried about how we appear to other people. Such worries are a basic part of being human. We draw conclusions about people based on our visual associations with them. The problem with personal care product commercials is that they tend to provide a database to draw on that emphasizes the concern, worry, and competitive comparison of such judgments, and then hooks those feelings to a limited range of responses that encourage the purchase of specific products. Simply representing something like this visually would probably not, by itself, cause people to believe that purchasing a product could remedy such an anxiety. But when more and more public spaces consist of shopping malls and other locations, and when increasingly more of what we identify as *fun* is shopping, then the physical activity of purchasing products is tied to the process of being with one's friends, and thus the link is inscribed in multiple learning pathways.

Numerous authors and producers have called attention to the destructive elements of this process, particularly for the self-perception of children. Girls and boys who only see girls and boys represented within a narrow range of physical type tend to begin to assume that that type is somehow normative, and that if they do not conform to it they are lacking in some essential way. When they further see this representation continually linked to the purchase of specific products, they become caught up in a pattern of practice that is difficult to escape from. Anyone who has ever tried to change a habit will recognize how difficult it can be to step outside of familiar patterns of practice, particularly if some element of them is enjoyable.

Adaptive versus technical challenges

This is why the challenge that communities of faith face in mediated cultural contexts is so difficult, and why it is what Ronald Heifetz has termed an adaptive challenge, rather than simply a technical one. The distinction Heifetz is drawing gets at the center of the problems we face in this analysis. His classic example of the *adaptive versus technical* challenge comes from thinking about medical challenges. What a doctor needs to know to treat a broken bone, for instance, is quite different from what is involved in treating heart disease. Treating a broken bone is essentially a technical challenge, involving issues like realigning the broken bone in the proper position, applying the cast adequately, and so on. Whereas treating heart disease inevitably involves helping people to change elements of their lifestyles— to shift eating and exercise patterns, to handle stress differently, and so on.[10]

If the challenge of supporting children in a mediated cultural context was simply a technical one, then communities of faith could choose the most effective media literacy curriculum to apply. We could try to provide the best vacation Bible school program, the best Bible translation, and so on. But it is not a technical challenge we're dealing with, but rather an adaptive one. We need to find ways to intervene in daily family practices that interrupt the narrowness and limited meaning-construction of relationality that is embedded in popular media, while at the same time affirming, expanding, and supporting those practices that encourage a deep relationality, that encourage and nurture rich religious life. While turning off the TV might be helpful once in a while, we can not hope to encourage the kind of adaptive practice necessary by ignoring mass mediated popular culture. We have to engage media, contest the elements that are narrow and limiting, and encourage those that help us to stretch our imagination and to feel deeply our global relationality. We need, in short, to envision children's ministry in this cultural context as a deliberate cultural intervention.

For years now it has been a truism that people "return" to church when their children are born. The argument given for this observation is that people want their children to have "good values," and that church is the place they turn to accomplish this goal. Religious educators have become, de facto, the professionals who are then expected to instill these good values. There are numerous problems with such a prescription, but what if the diagnosis itself is wrong? What if one of the main reasons people return to church is not simply to support good values—although that could be a good and sufficient reason—but because parenting young children raises very difficult existential questions for which other parts of our culture simply don't provide adequate answers?

Human beings are remarkably resilient and resourceful creatures, and we are created for and in relationality. When the standard, default practices of a culture on the one hand evoke that relationality in a dozen different explicit ways in various media—particularly affectively—but then subtly, in both *implicit* and *null* ways, seek to break that relationality, or at least to severely strain it, then deep questions and hungers arise. Communities of faith need to take these hungers very seriously, and recognize that our traditions hold resources with which to address and nourish them. We also need to acknowledge that children are those most vulnerable to broken relationship, and also most able to model uncomplicated love. Indeed, children have a gift for identifying new metaphors for relationality—particularly with God—and for asking questions that can open adult eyes to relationship. Ministry with and for children is thus at the heart of faith formation in our contemporary context.

Robert Kegan points out that transformative education, education that takes seriously the challenges to our frames of mind presented in this culture, has a three-fold dynamic to it that is always spiraling onward—*confirmation*, *contradiction*, and *continuity*.[11] This dynamic requires that teachers begin the process of transformative learning by entering into the realities of the learners with whom they are journeying. This kind of *confirmation* can be as simple as listening carefully and fully to the stories of the learners they are engaging, and as complicated as finding ways to walk in daily practice with them. What it must entail, though, no matter the context, is a deep appreciation of and respect for, the meaning-making in which they are embedded. Such respect does not assume that there will be no contestation of such meaning-making—that teachers will not disagree or confront problematic beliefs—but it does assume that there is real meaning being made, and that that meaning has deep connections to the narratives of the people involved. Jesus, for instance, did not engage his disciples by speaking in language with unfamiliar metaphors, or about issues that they did not care about. At the same time, however, he did confront their beliefs—often acting in ways that they could not understand, and telling them stories with endings they could not predict.

When an adult and a child arrive in your learning context, you can not assume much about them, other than that they are in some kind of relationship and that something about your learning context appealed to them. You will learn over time what kind of relationship they share: Are they parent and child? Grandparent and child? Foster parent and child? Caretaker and child (in the case of a child with severe disabilities)? Neighbor and friend? From there, in what other relationships are they a part? Perhaps there are two parents: those parents might be married to each other, or perhaps you have a parent and a stepparent. Perhaps the parents are "effectively" married but both of the same gender and living as committed life partners. Perhaps the grandparent brings the child because the child lives with her or him, but perhaps the grandparent brings the child because the child's parents don't much care about religious education, let alone children's ministry more broadly construed. The key here, is that until and unless you spend time getting to know the adult and the child, you can not hope to provide a learning environment that is both sufficiently *confirming* and also challenging, to support learning.

Yet, at the same time as you are listening and hearing deeply, you are also already teaching. You are teaching—via the *implicit* and *null* curricula, via *affective* and *psychomotor* modes—that the community of faith is one of deep hospitality. One of the earliest and most important lessons that a community of faith offers God's people is that God loves. We teach that lesson in many ways, but far too often we teach the opposite lesson by refusing hospitality, by making assumptions about people that are inaccurate, by refusing to meet and accompany people in the places where they are.

A major part of the challenge we face with media culture is the narrowness of the range of representations of relationality available, and the limited nature of the actions in support of such relationality that are modeled. Churches need to become communities where a wide range of representations is shared, and where deeply relational patterns of practice are supported. We can only do that, however, if we know where our people are, if we have entered deeply into the meaning-making they are engaged in, if we have *confirmed* the reality where they are embedded.

The second element that Kegan speaks of is *contradiction*. This is an element in the learning process that arises in many ways. Teachers can introduce contradictions, but life also poses them unasked. I have already noted a number of ways that mass mediated popular culture on the one hand evokes our sympathetic identification with children, but then systematically excludes and impoverishes many of them, let alone encourages them in leadership. This is a major contradiction in our meaning frame.

People interested in supporting growing in faith in a mediated culture must help each other to sense and engage such contradictions. How to do so? The process of *confirmation* just noted, with its deep attention to listening, is a first step. What are the primary images and metaphors, for instance, that a family is using to describe their experiences? When children talk with excitement about something in their life, what is it they are talking about? When they make analogies, to what are they referring? This is part of the process of uncovering and *confirming* the reality that they are embedded in, but it is also part of discovering in what ways religious education might pose difficult contradictions to our meaning frames. If the images and stories children are using draw on biblical characters and biblical phrases, it may well be that engaging popular culture will seem a contradiction and thus be challenging. If the images and examples stem from popular Saturday morning cartoons or Disney movies, then a biblical imagination might at first seem strange or disorienting. To return to an earlier example, if the range of representation of relationship is primarily a mass mediated one, then the kind of "love of enemy" embodied in Christian gospel will not only seem far fetched, but deeply wrong. Living into an understanding of daily life that requires hospitality, that seeks to engage the stranger, that pours out love and power, rather than hoarding them—these are notions that deeply contradict the common representations of popular culture. [12]

There are many ways to engage contradictions, some of which I will detail later in this chapter, but there is one more element to discuss in Kegan's framework first, and that is *continuity*. Kegan refers to *continuity* as the many ways that it is possible to "tell the same story" yet from multiple perspectives. I may experience a particular event when I am 13, and tell a story about that event in one way. When I am 23, I may describe the same event, but tell a very different story. This is also true at 33, 43, 53, and so on. In each case the same event is being described, and I am the same person describing it, but my understanding and thus description of the event shifts as my meaning-making shifts over time, as the experience base I draw upon shifts, and so on. These are time-based shifts, but there are many other experiences that can reshape such stories—changing context is often the most obvious, whether that shift in context comes from geographic move, financial move, life phase change, and so on. The key issue that Kegan raises about *continuity*, however, is that without it, people living with profound contradictions in their meaning frame will often retreat to either deep relativism, or rigid boundaries. To use John Hull's terms, they respond with "ideological enclosures" or "premature ultimates." [13]

Heifetz has written about this issue in relation to adaptive challenges, arguing that we must keep such challenges on a "low simmer" that permits them to be faced and engaged, but that does not send people either into denial or fleeing into avoidance. [14] Here again it is *continuity* that provides the support to enable the challenge to be met.

Whatever the language you use to engage this challenge, the reality remains that *confirmation*, *contradiction*, and *continuity* requires that communities of faith take seriously the fundamental ways that people are already making sense of their lives in mass mediated contexts. Children in particular live more immersed in these environments than perhaps at any other time in our history.

When communities of faith choose to respond to this challenge by refusing to acknowledge either the ways that meaning-making is embedded in these contexts, or by rejecting such meaning-making as trivial or not religious, we can force people into ideological enclosure, into adopting a "premature ultimate." That may be a retreat into closed religious community (and we have more than enough fundamentalists among Christian community to recognize this risk), or that may, in contrast, be a flight to relativism and "secular" community, or religious meaning-making deliberately isolated from religious institutions.

To the extent that a community of faith seriously and respectfully engages these challenges, they teach important lessons about the vitality and essential relationality of church. To the extent that they do not, they teach far more destructive lessons about a lack of values and respect. It is, as mentioned earlier in this chapter, a question of how we intentionally engage the *implicit* and *null* curricula, not simply the *explicit* one.

What are we to do?

What does this mean pragmatically? We have to consciously and intentionally provide adequate support for families (however defined) in the religious development of their children. Children's ministry has to be about creating a learning environment with adequate and appropriate support for learning with children, indeed for learning from them, not simply for believing they have something to learn from us.

At a bedrock level, this learning is and has to be supported as relational. In addition, because learning is always happening on multiple levels, we have to be at once both more ambitious and more humble about what is possible. Learning happens all of the time, and so communities of faith need to imaginatively find ways to enter into daily life. This used to happen automatically—daily devotions, simple table prayers, songs to greet the day and to end it, all of these were family rituals that intimately bound religious meaning up with daily life. Now many of these cherished rituals no longer hold much meaning for people, and have fallen out of daily practice. This is the ambitious challenge.

Humility is important as well when we ponder the realities of busy families, stressed communities, and so on. An effective children's ministry in a particular community of faith may not have the obvious markers of religious education programming from the past. While vacation Bible school still provides important services for some families—cheap summer childcare springs to mind—it may not be the best or most clear evidence of effective children's ministry; similarly with Sunday school. Instead we need to ask ourselves questions like, What do the families among us need? and In what ways can we support parents, helping them to see themselves as the first and primary religious educator in their child's life?

If one of the most stable markers of family life for many families is the bedtime story (since even shared dinners are less and less common), then how can we, as a community of faith, enter into that practice? How can we provide, for instance, books with a strong biblical imagination? How can we enter that space with deep confirmation of the importance of that practice, and then with some resources that challenge the imagination by bringing religious themes to bear?

Many programs are emerging that begin to recognize and meet this challenge. Sunday school is being revisioned as churches turn to stepping stones ministries, for instance, or to intergenerational workshop rotation programs. Curriculum such as Jerome Berryman's *Godly Play* actively provides a way to construct an environment that relationally uses stories and rituals to engage children and families in religious meaning-making. Yet all of these are primarily church-based, internal ministry programs.

We have to understand that learning is a daily process, that it always has multiple levels of which we can most likely only attend to a few at any given time. That recognition can be daunting, but it can also be an opportunity to revision and reshape our ministries. In the process, we might well discover that children themselves are in fact ministering to us. A more general summary of these pragmatic considerations would go as follows:

- Supporting children by supporting families means supporting adult learning that prepares primary caregivers to become the first and most important religious educators of children.

- Such education must draw upon the best principles of learning, requiring adults to learn how to listen deeply as an essential element of any teaching they aspire to do.

- All learning has to be understood as experiential and relational.

- All intentional learning attends to the ideas, feelings, and actions of the people engaged with it.

- Communities of faith must ask families, particularly children themselves, to tell us what they need from us—and then we must act respectfully on that knowledge.

- Learning with children should include creative opportunities to focus on creating and constructing their stories in multiple and various media.

- Learning with children should recognize the crucial role that rich ritual plays in the development of religious identity.

Essentially, what we are working toward supporting can be summed up in what Daloz, Keen, Keen, and Park call *responsible imagination*. This team of scholars has identified several factors that people who have lived long lives of commitment to the public good have in common. Among these is one they have identified as a "responsible imagination." Because their study is so important, and their eloquence so rare in academic analysis, I will quote them at length:

> The people we studied appear to compose reality in a manner that can take into account calls to help, catalyze, dream, work hard, think hard, and love well. They practice an imagination that resists prejudice and its distancing tendencies on the one hand, and avoids messianic aspirations and their engulfing tendencies on the other. Their imaginations are active and open, continually seeking more adequate understandings of the whole self and the whole commons and the language with which to express them.

> Their practice of imagination is responsible in two particular ways. First, they try to respect the process of imagination in themselves and others. They pay attention to dissonance and contradiction, particularly those that reveal injustice and unrealized potential. They learn to pause, reflect, wonder, ask why, consider, wait. . . . They also learn to work over their insights and those of others so that they "connect up" in truthful and useful ways. They seek out trustworthy communities of confirmation and contradiction.

Second, they seek out sources of worthy images. Most have discovered that finding and being found by fitting images is not only a matter of having access to them but requires discretion and responsible hospitality—not only to what is attractive but also to what may be unfamiliar and initially unsettling . . . these people live in a manner that conveys . . . the power of a responsible imagination.[15]

This is the kind of response to challenge—an adaptive response—that needs to be at the heart of our children's ministries.

Emmaus journey

The best way I know of to conclude this discussion of the active engagement of our shared narratives in media culture, this kind of responsible imagination in the context of children's ministry, is to share a Bible story as a mnemonic for the pieces of the process.

Consider the last chapter of the Gospel of Luke. Two of the disciples are walking along the road to Emmaus, shortly after Jesus' resurrection, but before they, themselves, have encountered him. They are down at heart, discouraged, and deeply confused about where their paths might lead. Nothing in their world makes much sense, and it has all been turned upside down by Jesus' crucifixion. In this moment they walk along the road, a daily kind of walk that is emphasized for its banality in the gospel passage. During this walk they encounter a stranger who seems all the more strange because he does not seem to share their disillusionment or despair at the events of the past days. Further, he engages them in a deep conversation that lasts the rest of their walk that day, and that radically reinterprets their known grasp of their core sacred texts. Finally, bowing to the dictates of hospitality and probably their interest as well, they invite this stranger to join them for a meal at the end of the day. In the process of that meal the stranger "breaks bread" in a manner that sharply resonates with the ritual practice they had shared with Jesus. The Gospel of Luke states that "their eyes were opened, and they recognized him; and he vanished from their sight" (Luke 24:31). They remark to each other that they should have realized it was Jesus: "Were not our hearts burning within us?" (Luke 24:32).

There are numerous ways to interpret this passage, and entire liturgical theologies build from it, but the far simpler point I'd like to suggest here is that this passage marks three crucial elements we need to remember in supporting children in mass mediated culture. First, we need to remember that it is a daily engagement. Second, we need to remember to encounter strangers, to have the kind of responsible imagination that sees "from whom" we are estranged. Third, we need to embed this knowing in rituals that help us to learn, to rehearse and thus to reinscribe, the meanings we hold dear.

To return to the anecdote at the beginning of this chapter, Diane and her children are deeply enmeshed in daily engagement with media. Diane is beginning to sense that this engagement might estrange her children from each other, and at the same time has the potential to help her feel connected to hurting people around the world. How can we support her in confronting those aspects of her family's media practices that favor estrangement while at the same time maintaining those practices that have the possibility of bearing empathy? One key will be finding ways to do so that are fully consonant with her daily practices that become habits, rituals even, interwoven with her family's daily life.

These elements will allow us to respond in truly adaptive ways to the challenges we face, and promise to allow us to learn from our children, even as they learn from and with us. How could this work? Here are just a few suggestions to spark your own ideas.

Daily life

- Ensure that media engagement is never done in isolation—watch television together, ask religious questions of the characters you're watching (even if they aren't asked explicitly on the show).

- Share the task of choosing programs to watch with children, respect and engage their choices and expect them to do the same with yours (which might require some encouragement).

- Ensure that media engagement is never simply mass media—search out and enjoy alternative media, too. The rise of independent and foreign film-making has provided an especially broad mix of additional media in this category. [16]

- Provide opportunities for kids to raise questions and to initiate conversations—just giving them the room to do so will raise religious issues.

- Consider listening to recorded music during daily commutes and meal preparation, instead of live radio.

- Have children tell you stories that build on the stories they've seen in media. For example, if they love Scooby Doo, have them tell a new story starring Scooby Doo.

- Tell stories that put characters children love in religious situations. For example, young children might pretend that some of their toys ar meeting Jesus.

Engaging the stranger and that from which we are estranged

- Respectfully listen to and engage your children's media (even if they're teenagers and you feel revulsion at first).

- Let your own religious questions be audible.

- Search out stories of those who are marginalized in popular mass mediated culture.

- Deconstruct the news—and then reconstruct it, especially locally!

- Risk your own stories by listening to others (that is, embrace conversation rather than fear contact with other religious perspectives).

- Provide multiple opportunities for children to take the lead in serving others.

Incorporate media into your rituals, and create new rituals with your media

- Do a television fast for Lent (that is, put away the TV for the 40 days).

- Create original videos for worship contexts that challenge the community to engage the "stranger."

- Add music to a dinner prayer. This should include adding so-called "secular" recorded music that resonates with your prayer concerns.

- Make a point of muting TV commercials and use the time as an opportunity to ask questions about the shows you're watching.

- Learn how to make video recordings and have your kids interview each other and friends/neighbors about religious questions.

- Add videos with explicit religious themes to your typical video watching practices.

- Incorporate blessings into daily practices—bless a child as she or he is getting dressed.

These are moments on the journey to Emmaus. They are elements of a shared process of retrieval and revisioning. Such a process invites us to recognize the "burning within us" in ways that share our deep relationality, and that allow us to draw ever closer to the God who created us, redeems us, and continues to draw us near. Children are a precious element of this process, and we must walk with them on this road.

There is an opportunity for a vibrant community of faith to reach out to people like Diane and her family. Diane and Mark could be supported—*confirmed*—in the difficulty of their lives together, but also have their meaning-making *contradicted* or contested by a religious community. They could be invited to simplify their lives together with their children: reducing "screen time," for instance, or moving screens into one room to reduce their ubiquity so that children (who will find ways to fight with each other regardless of context) might learn to argue effectively—with adult coaching—over the choice of program to watch or game to play. At the same time, though, the family's intuitions of the way God is present can be strengthened and supported. (Think of the song that helps Diane bring to mind this presence.) In short, a community of faith could provide *continuity* with that presence. Family is all about relationality, it is the heart metaphor of our faith as well. In working with children, we need to keep that metaphor—in all of its depth and complexity—at the heart of our ministries. We need to truly walk to road to Emmaus and honor our hearts burning within us.

Notes

1. *All Consuming Passion: Waking Up from the American Dream*, 3rd. ed., pamphlet (Seattle: New Road Map Foundation and Northwest Environment Watch, 1998).

2. Ibid.

3. This theory is described well by Jane Vella in *Learning to Listen, Learning to Teach: The Power of Dialogue in Educating Adults* (San Francisco: Jossey-Bass, 1994). Maria Harris explores its implications in the context of religious education in *Fashion Me a People: Curriculum in the Church* (Louisville: Westminster/John Knox, 1989).

4. For a more complete development of this idea, see Elliott Eisner, *The Educational Imagination*, 3rd ed. (Upper Saddle River, N.J.: Prentice Hall, 2002).

5.   See, in particular, Parker Palmer, *To Know as We Are Known* (San Francisco: HarperSanFrancisco, 1993); and Palmer, *The Courage to Teach: Exploring the Inner Landscape of a Teacher's Life* (San Francisco: Jossey-Bass, 1998).

6.   Powerful articulations of the way in which a trinitarian theology imagines our relationality appears in Elizabeth Johnson, *She Who Is: The Mystery of God in Feminist Theological Discourse* (New York: Crossroads, 1992); and Catherine Mowry LaCugna, *God for Us: The Trinity and Christian Life* (San Francisco: HarperSanFrancisco, 1991).

7.   By *our* children, I am not referring solely to biological children but rather to all those with whom we are in relationship—potentially all the children of the world!

8.   For a more full exploration of this idea, see Stewart Hoover and Knut Lundby, *Rethinking Media, Religion, and Culture* (Thousand Oaks, Calif.: Sage Publications, 1997); Stewart Hoover and Lynn Schofield Clark, eds., *Practicing Religion in an Age of Media* (New York: Columbia University, 2002); and Jolyon Mitchell and Sophia Marriage, *Mediating Religion: Conversations in Media, Religion and Culture* (Edinburgh: T&T Clark/Continuum, 2003). See also Delwin Brown, et al, *Converging on Culture: Theologians in Dialogue with Cultural Analysis and Criticism* (New York: Oxford University, 2001) for its theological implications; and Mary Hess, "From trucks carrying messages to ritualized identities: Implications of the postmodern paradigm shift in media studies for religious educators," *Religious Education*, vol. 94, no. 3 (Summer 1999), for its religious education implications.

9.   For the most up-to-date statistics on children and adolescents in the United States, visit the Children's Defense Fund's Web site at www.childrensdefense.org.

10. Ronald Heifetz, *Leadership without Easy Answers* (Cambridge: Harvard University, 1994). See, in particular, pp. 73-84.

11. See, in particular, Robert Kegan, *The Evolving Self: Problem and Process in Human Development* (Cambridge: Harvard University, 1982); and Kegan, *In over Our Heads: The Mental Demands of Modern Life* (Cambridge: Harvard University, 1995).

12. For a deeper exploration of the role of "practices" in Christian life, see "Project on the Education and Formation of People of Faith" at Valparaiso University (www.practicingourfaith.com/whoweare.html).

13. See John Hull, *What Prevents Christian Adults from Learning?* (Philadelphia: Trinity International Press, 1991).

14. See Heifetz, *Leadership without Easy Answers*); and Heifetz, Ronald, and Marty Linsky. *Leadership on the Line: Staying Alive through the Dangers of Leading* (Cambridge: Harvard Business School Press, 2002).

15. Laurent Daloz, et al, *Common Fire: Leading Lives of Commitment in a Complex World* (Boston: Beacon, 1996), pp. 151-152.

16. Indeed, three recent films, *Bend It Like Beckham*, *Rabbit-Proof Fence*, and *Whale Rider*, are some of the most profound representations of relationality produced in the last decade.

CHAPTER 6

Growing Faithful Children in the World

Nelson T. Strobert

Two conversations

MARRIC IS AN ACTIVE 8-YEAR-OLD. One day he was talking with me and asked whether I spoke a different language. I said that I did. I asked him if he knew other people who spoke a different language. Marric said that his godfather spoke Spanish. He said that he would like to speak a different language. I asked him, "Why?" He said, "So that I could understand people better." He then started talking about his experience at church camp with his counselor who was from Africa (he didn't remember the specific country) and another counselor who was from England.

. . . . .

MARTEZ IS A TYPICAL 11-YEAR-OLD who has developed an interest in Africa. When I asked, "How did you become interested in Africa?" Martez responded, "It happened through exploring on the computer and then I had to do a report for school." When I asked him what he learned about the continent, he talked about the climate and tribal life. In fact, from his school research and out of his own exploring on the computer, he said, "I really would like to visit that continent."

From these two brief conversations, we see that these young people through the experience of family relations, church camping ministry, and school are growing to be citizens of the world. Both of these young people are part of a global village. They see and experience people who live in different places and who might speak differently than they do.

～　～

It is very difficult for adults, youth, and children to go through the day without knowing what is happening in the world. Through television, newspapers, and magazines, as well as the Internet, e-mail, and cell phones, North Americans know about the events taking place in our own neighborhoods and across the oceans almost at the very moment these events occur. Through satellite and cable TV we are able to know the trends, interests, and views of our international neighbors walking through the streets as well as their political leaders in office. With air transportation, we no longer have to travel to foreign ports to sample *haute cuisine*, because it is available at our local markets or favorite restaurants, where it arrives the very day we shop or sit down to dine.

Living in rural Pennsylvania, I find it amazing that we are able to have a substantial number of tropical fruits and vegetables, along with other international foods. I am able to enjoy the same foods I consumed when I served as a pastor on St. Croix in the U.S. Virgin Islands. These foods are available here because of the increasing Mexican-American and Afro-Caribbean people represented in the population. This is just an example of the variety of foods that are available in any number of small towns across the United States and in similar countries around the globe.

What are the connections between and among the media, technology, and transportation? The interplay of these three elements in our lives indicates that we are no longer in isolation from one another. The boundaries are fuzzy. We are connected in various aspects of our lives. We are part of a world that is getting ever so small as we gain knowledge about its constitutive parts. We are connected to the most remote areas of the globe. This connection is not restricted to the business traveler, affluent vacationer, or corporate executive. It is available to all people—children, youth, and adults. They are the people in the very pews with whom we share our time at worship, education, and Christian fellowship. This is all to say that we are part of the global village.

This global perspective is a part of our everyday living in general and part of our lives within the church in particular. For example, each of the 65 synods that comprise the Evangelical Lutheran Church in America has a companion synod relationship. Synods within the United States and the Caribbean are paired with one or more Lutheran synods around the globe. In the 16 years since the formation of the program, pastors, associates in ministry, diaconal ministers, and congregation members have visited their sister synods abroad. Members of the ELCA travel overseas to observe, serve, work, and experience the church in various contexts—and delegations from abroad come to the United States for the same. The issues of poverty and human rights are no longer relegated to local concerns because they become the concerns of sisters and brothers in Christ across the seas and oceans. Robert Robertson calls this development *globalization*.[1]

What does this have to do with religious education in general and ministry with children in particular? As baptized people of God and as part of the church catholic, we all must prepare children to live, work, and thrive as children of God in the context of the global village. With this being the case, a few questions demand our attention: How can we prepare children for this type of living? What do we mean by globalization? What are the foundations for such living? What are the concerns of globalization and how are they being addressed? What practical resources and examples exist for parents, schoolteachers, and Sunday school teachers to use to bring the global perspective to the classroom? This chapter attempts to respond to these questions.

What do we mean by globalization?

With so many discussions, lectures, and forums on the topic of globalization, it is necessary that we have a common understanding of what the word entails. Although the term *globalization* has been part of popular discourse for several decades, I dare say the definitions abound. It is helpful to take a look at some these definitions and descriptions.

In the book *Globalization and Culture*, John Tomlison states that globalization "lies at the heart of modern culture; cultural practices lie at the heart of globalization." He goes on to say that "the broad task of globalization theory is both to understand the sources of this condition of complex connectivity and to interpret its implications across the various spheres of social existence."[2]

Other experts offer different definitions, showing the magnitude of this topic. For Clive Dimmoch, globalization "in educational management implies the export of theory, policy, and practice from some systems, chiefly the Anglo-American world, and their import into others, particularly in Western and developing countries."[3] Here we see an economic view of the term. Roland Robertson, on the other hand, defines *globalization* "as simply the compression of the world. This notion of compression refers both to increasing sociocultural density and to rapidly expanding consciousness . . . it is simultaneously cultural, economic, and political."[4] Here the term incorporates a social science dimension.

Multicultural scholar and educator James Banks uses the term *global education*. He argues that global education "should have as major goals helping students develop an understanding of the interdependence among nations in the modern world, clarified attitudes toward other nations, and a reflective identification with the world community." Banks adds that it "is essential that we help students to develop clarified, reflective, and positive ethnic and national identifications. However, because we live in a global society where the solutions to the world's problems require the cooperation of all the nations of the world, it is also important for students to develop global identifications and the knowledge, attitudes, and skills needed to become effective and influential citizens in the world community."[5]

We can see from this overview that the word *globalization* carries a variety of perspectives, including economic, political, social, and technological views. For the purposes of religious education of children, I use the term to incorporate the connections that we have as people of God to help us understand and respond to the issues and needs of peoples throughout the world. Barbara Wilkerson summarizes this point by stating the following:

> What must emerge is a framework for religious education in a new millennium, one in which the task of Christian religious education will be to proclaim Christ in a world different from what it has ever been—a world where groups once distant and foreign are now near neighbors; a world of interdependent but distinct peoples, whose identities resist submersion and instinctively refuse to melt into a new culture, even while embracing aspects of it . . . the calling of the church in the twenty-first century will be to unify a global Christian community without attempting to homogenize it; to preserve the gift of particularity within a context of solidarity.[6]

Globalization in biblical and confessional contexts

Although *globalization* has been a popular buzz word since the 1980s, I dare say it has always been a part of the Christian story. The gospel is global in scope, and a global perspective has always been part of the Christian community's self-understanding of discipleship. We only need to cite a few biblical and confessional statements to see the breath of the term as expressed in our various denominations through the ages. Thus, preparing children to think globally is part and parcel of our helping them to live within the life of the congregation, in particular, and the life of the Christian, in general.

In the Gospel of Matthew, Jesus says the following after delivering the Sermon on the Mount:

> You are the light of the world. A city built on a hill cannot be hid. No one after lighting a lamp puts it under the bushel basket, but on the lampstand, and it gives light to all in the house. In the same way, let your light shine before others, so that they may see your good works and give glory to your Father in heaven (Matthew 5:14-16).

Here Matthew reminds us that as followers of Jesus we live in the world and have a responsibility to show who we are and to whom we belong from what we do as the people of God:

> Now the eleven disciples went to Galilee, to the mountain to which Jesus had directed them. When they saw him, they worshiped him; but some doubted. And Jesus came and said to them, "All authority in heaven and on earth has been given to me. Go therefore and make disciples of all nations, baptizing them in the name of the Father and of the Son and of the Holy Spirit, and teaching them to obey everything that I have commanded you. And remember, I am with you always, to the end of the age (Matthew 28:16-20).

The global dimension of the gospel and the Christian community in the commission go beyond the parochial reaches of our lives and make disciples of various individuals around the world. In the global venture, the Christian community baptizes and teaches. Through baptism, people are made children of God and are directed to live within the community and remember to whom they belong through baptism. But there is also a responsibility to teach. We teach so that our children will be able to tell the story of God's everlasting presence with us. As baptized people of God, we are reminded of the life, ministry, and death of Jesus. This Jesus died for all humankind, not only for the sins of those within the community of faith. This is supported by these words from 1 John:

> My little children, I am writing these things to you so that you may not sin. But if anyone does sin, we have an advocate with the Father, Jesus Christ the righteous; and he is the atoning sacrifice for our sins, and not for ours only but also for the sins of the whole world (1 John 2:1-2).

These biblical texts are certainly not exhaustive of the global images or descriptions; however, these texts are illustrative of the integral nature of the expanding worldview of the Christian community. However important the community is toward nurturing global interest, it is from within the family that children can be introduced, nurtured, and supported in developing a sense of the world that is greater than what they see around them. In fact, parents have a responsibility to open the worldview of their children. The Fourth Commandment directs children to honor their parents. In Martin Luther's understanding, this Commandment also means that parents and all in authority have a responsibility to care for the children with whom God has entrusted us. We have a responsibility to teach them to live in this world. In part of his explanation, Luther wrote:

> No one is willing to see that this is the command of the divine Majesty, who will solemnly call us to account and punish us for its neglect. Nor is it recognized how very necessary it is to devote serious attention to the young. For if we want capable and qualified people for both the civil and the spiritual realms, we really must spare no effort, time, and expense in teaching and educating our children to serve God and the world.[7]

Parents have a responsibility to take parenting seriously for they model and represent God in the lives of the children. Luther further stated:

> For God does not give you your children to play with, nor does he give you servants for you to use them like assessing for work. As you learn from me, so children and servants should learn from you parents and masters.[8]

Parents do not have children to be used or abused but to be taught how to live and flourish within the community and world. Adults need to assist children to live to serve, honor, and be faithful to God. That responsibility brings children out from themselves and involves them in the care of those in need. Parents teach and model the serving creature. Stephanie and Rod are the parents of 13-year-old Christine, who is an active soccer player. When Christine had the opportunity to go to Australia to participate in an international soccer camp and tournament, her parents really had to think about giving her permission. Their positive response came when they came to the realization that they had to prepare her to live in the world. It was important for them to trust the values they had attempted to nurture and provide her with during the past years. They had prepared her to live and be responsible in the world.

Globalization and denominational concerns

This role of care that moves beyond the local to the global sphere is taken up in contemporary denominational documents. An example of this perspective is in the ELCA's Social Statement "For Peace in God's World." From the very beginning, the global concern is raised:

> At the end of a tumultuous and violent century, we share with people everywhere hope for a more peaceful and just world. With this statement on international peace, we strive to strengthen our global perspective as individual Christians and as a church body, in spite of strong currents that push us to turn in on ourselves.[9]

As Christians in community, we are called to live outside of our individual desires and live to assist with peace and justice for all people in the global village in the midst of distrust and isolationism that can occur among our denominations as well as civil governments. The Statement includes the following as one of its objectives:

> To call upon the educational institutions of this church day schools, colleges and universities, seminaries, centers of continuing education, and camps to review their programs in light of this statement, so as to further the study of peace and global affairs.[10]

This concern is more than lip service. The Statement calls for an educational process that can assist the home in inculcating the global perspective.

All educational institutions, agencies, and programs of the church have a responsibility to emphasize this concern. One example of this done programmatically is in the world of departments or divisions for mission. Within the ELCA, that responsibility comes from the Division for Global Mission, which states as one of its educational goals for the 21st century:

> Expand the current global mission network to include ELCA congregations and members, ecumenical partners, ELCA seminaries and institutions of higher learning, global companion churches, global-mission resource staff, and other specific groups (children, youth, men, women, bishops, educational leaders, multicultural communities). [11]

One sees the concern throughout the human life span and in various institutions. What is also intriguing here is the concern for what can be done ecumenically. We cannot do it alone as individuals and we cannot do it alone within our denominations but with trust and assistance from ecumenical partners.

Globalization and child development

The contention in this chapter is that educational ministry, under the leadership of teachers and other adults, must intentionally assist children to live in a global context. Examining the definitions, the biblical tradition, and confessional and contemporary denominational documents, shows that there has been a clear understanding that children can be aware of, learn about, and be sensitive to global concerns. Although these areas of ministry support this, it is also important that the grass roots of the ecclesiastical education system be a place where global foundations can be studied and worked through.

Francis Buckley states that "Christians welcome this globalization as a sign of the basic unity of the human family, which has its origin and goal in the one God, and which the church tries to promote through its own teachings and hierarchical structures. The church is one; there is one flock and one shepherd, one Lord, one faith, one baptism." [12] Again, the child needs to see that the unity of the church that he or she experiences locally, is the unity that we strive for within the context of the global. Buckley further notes that "Christian education must prepare the present and future generations for life in this global community, highlighting the opportunities and dangers inherent in globalization. Critical social analysis alerts people to the causes and consequences of the various trends—and to the possibilities of shaping and directing them."[13]

The goal of Christian education is to assist people in their lives of faith. It is also important that students know that they can engage and be active in this globalization process of the church. But we may ask ourselves, "Can we really expect children to be excited about and interested in people and places located around the world?" and "Are children prepared developmentally to tackle something that often is troublesome for us?" The response to both questions is a resounding YES! While the scope of this chapter is not on developmental issues, they must be addressed. While my colleagues in other chapters in this book do more extensive work in this area, it is important to see the possibilities of preparing children in the church for global participation by a brief overview of pertinent developmental issues.

In the discussion of globalization as it relates to children, the assumption has been that they are in middle to late childhood. When we think and work in the area of global education or globalization, we see that children in this stage of development are beginning to view and experience the world very differently than they did in their previous stage of development. By ages 7 and 8, children are beginning to see the wide range of viewpoints held by others. They are able to understand or take on alternative perspectives rather than being restricted to their personal viewpoints. Mary J. Lickteig and Kathy Everts Danielson state that these might be the optimal period for young people to reflect on global issues:

> The middle childhood years (ages 7 to 12) may thus represent the critical period in the development of an international, intercultural, or global perspective in children, especially considering the existence of attitude flexibility that is later followed by attitude rigidity. This age seems to be characterized by rapid cognitive development, related especially to the area of perspective and role-taking ability, low rejection of groups, and high attitude flexibility. It is a time when children begin to perceive another person's point of view.[14]

We want to go beyond the cognitive dimension of growth and appeal to the affective and active part of the child with equal importance. Robert Selman outlines five levels of *social perspective taking*. This is defined as "the ability to comprehend the inner psychological characteristics of oneself and others, thereby anticipating what that person might think, feel, or do."[15]

It is helpful to briefly examine these levels that aid our understanding of children in the global context.

LEVEL O

Ages 3-6. Ego-centric viewpoints. Children at this level are not able to make distinctions between their viewpoints and the viewpoints of others.

LEVEL I

Ages 5-9. Differentiated and subjective perspective taking. Children at this level can differentiate physical from psychological characteristics of others but think that this comes from the others having different information.

LEVEL II

Ages 7-12. Self-reflective reciprocal perspective. Children at this level are beginning to think outside of themselves. They can take on the viewpoint of another person while still keeping hold of their own perspectives.

LEVEL III

Ages 10-15. Third-person, mutual perspective taking. Children and youth at this level can take on multiple or generalized perspectives of others. Selman states that children develop an "observable ego" at this level, allowing them to see themselves simultaneously as actor and object.

LEVEL IV

Ages 12-15. Societal-symbolic perspective taking. Children and youth at this level come to realize that although there is a shared social system, one will not always understand the other completely.[16]

Selman helps us to see the expanding world of the child. The child is able to go beyond his or her world to see the other and eventually a variety of perspectives from a larger number of people. We also see from this typology and that it is the student or child who is making the connections, that the child is active. Parents and teachers cannot do it for the young person. The child is active in social perspective taking. Parents and teachers can provide an environment that gives the child opportunities for encounters with those who have different perspectives and ways of looking at the world. Parents and teachers are thereby assisting the child to be a citizen of the world. In Christian global education, the parents and teachers are preparing the child for participation in the church catholic. This means that the child should grow in a community of faith that helps him or her identify with the community—the baptized people of God. Our very identity is incorporated into the body of Christ the Savior of the world. That identity is seeing one as a unique and at the same time united creature; realizing one's own ethno-cultural identity in a multicultural nation with its particularity, and at the same time knowing one's ethno-cultural identity as co-citizen in the world.

One cannot become a global person without accepting the fact that one is in a multicultural nation. This is supported by the work of the multicultural pioneer James Banks. He hypothesizes that to achieve the level of positive global identification, students must have positive cultural identification. In Banks's typology of cultural identity, the highest and last stage is six, globalism and global competency. At this stage a person is able to function with knowledge, skill, and commitment with a positive ethnic, national, and global identification.[17] This is only possible when students have opportunities to engage and interact with the cultural diversity that exists. This is the challenge not only in general education but in religious education as well. We are challenged in our Sunday schools, day schools, and after-school programs to assist participants in seeing themselves as part of the world community or the church in its global expression. What are the concerns with children today? What really can be done? What are the resources that are needed to promote this global perspective? It is really important that we start locally, that is, right from within the congregation.

The global issues concerning children

What are the issues with children and how might we assist in tackling these issues within our respective churches or with our ecumenical neighbors? I recently had some extra time while in New York City and decided to visit the United Nations building. I had not been on the site in several decades—

I was an elementary school student at the time. The tour was informative as we walked through the maze of the main building, looking at displays and sitting in the galleries of the rooms where international decisions are discussed and debated. I stopped in my tracks at one point on the tour when we were in a display area where items of destruction were displayed. The tour guide, pointing to the various land mines on display, indicated that these weapons are a major cause of death to children in war-torn areas of the world. Children are attracted to the bright colors that might be on the mines. But once the mines are bothered, they explode. This is only one area of concern when we think about children, and in some ways for those of us in North America, it all seems so remote on the TV screen—but these devices are real. These children are vulnerable, like so many children around the world. As U.N. Secretary-General Kofi Annan, states:

> A world fit for children is a just and peaceful world. It is one in which all children are given the love, care and nurturing they need to make a good start in life, where they can complete a basic education of good quality and, in adolescence, can develop their potential in a safe and supportive environment that will help them become caring and contributing citizens. This is the kind of world children deserve—and one that we as adults have an irrefutable obligation to create. [18]

These are the goals, but what is the reality for children? The Secretary-General identified four areas of priority that emerged from various U.N. summits and conventions:

- Promoting healthy lives.

- Providing high quality education.

- Protecting children from abuse, exploitation, and violence.

- Combating HIV/AIDS.

What do the children have to say? In an unprecedented moment in United Nations history, a Children's Forum preceded the U.N. Special Session on Children in May 2002. The forum included workshops and smaller sessions in addition to individual statements from children who came from around the world. They were able to converse with key government officials from prime ministers to heads of agencies. After the conclusion of the forum, the young people addressed members of the United Nations and gave their vision for a better world. Their key statements included the following:

- We see respect for the rights of the child.

- We see an end to exploitation, abuse, and violence.

- We see an end to war.

- We see the provision of health care.

- We see the protection of the environment.

- We see an end to the vicious cycle of poverty.

- We see the provision of education.

- We see the active participation of children.

- We pledge an equal partnership in this fight for children's rights.

- We are the children of the world. [19]

These young people have a vision for themselves and the world in general. Their list of visions is not lofty but realistic. It challenges all of us to be a part of the movement on behalf of children. Their visions also coincide with the hopes and dreams of the adult population. Furthermore, their visions can inform us in the Christian community about the issues that face us all or that we can address as a community of faith. These visions remind and call us to be stewards of our resources to combat poverty. The visions remind us to provide safe places for our young people, to be sensitive to the environment, and to be peacemakers in a world that is plagued by war. With such broad issues that are identified, one might wonder how we can address the above issues as well as other issues in the parish where we are located. Aren't the issues too much to tackle in our small congregation? If we are going to assist children in becoming sensitive to the global issues, then we dare not start envisioning from abroad. Rather, we must transform their thinking within the local context. within the congregation.

Suggestions for globalization in the classroom

My contention is that no matter where one is located in the United States, global connections can be identified. Consider everyone in your congregation, from those members who have served in the military overseas to those young people whose parents, grandparents, or great-grandparents immigrated to the United States. At Epiphany Lutheran Church in Brooklyn, New York, the congregation is composed predominately of people of color. At the coffee hour following the liturgy, one will hear English spoken by people who come from the Caribbean, the African continent, and the British Islands, as well as the southern and eastern United States.

While I was serving as pastor at Advent Lutheran Church in Cleveland, Ohio, a number of the elementary school students participated in international exchange programs. These students were in public, private, and parochial schools. This is all to say that global issues are not as remote and difficult to embrace in the local context as we might think upon preliminary reflection. There are many ways within the local congregation that students and teachers might be assisted in recognizing their place in the "complex connectivity" of globalization. Here below are some ideas for use in Christian education in the local parish.

1. Invite a member from the congregation who was born in another country to visit your class. Ask this guest speaker to describe his or her experiences as a child growing up in that country. The guest could bring in photographs or other items from his or her homeland. The teacher might prepare the class for the session by bringing in contemporary pictures of the country the week before or prior to the presentation.

2. Ask a student in the class who has come from another country to share what his or her life was like in that country. If the student was too young to remember, you might ask the student's parents or guardians to share the story if they feel comfortable speaking in front of the class.

3. During the change of seasons in the liturgical year, bring in videos, songs, or pictures that depict how the church holiday is celebrated in other parts of the world. This is an especially good activity for the seasons of Christmas, Epiphany, and Easter.

4. Sing hymns from around the world. In cooperation with the choir director, organist, or other member of the music staff, have students learn a hymn or carol from another country—perhaps in the language of that country. The students might be able to share this with the congregation.

5. Contact the global mission committee of your synod or denomination to see if you can match up your students with pen pals from another country.

6. Attend a church service of a congregation that is ethnically different from your own. This may require planning to prepare students to worship in a language they might not understand, but the experience will help them to see the common elements of worship as well as the diversity of the Christian church.

7. Contact the global mission committee of your synod or denomination to identify future events that would be open to children.

8. Attend a global mission event with students from your Sunday school class, if there is an event close to where you live. This will allow children in your Sunday school to meet other children and families who are involved with ministry in various parts of the world.

9. Learn about church leaders outside the United States. Through the help of the pastor, associate in ministry, diaconal minister, or other congregation members, have children read about and report on the life of church leaders from another country.

10. Invite active or retired missionaries to speak to your class. They can share photographs, slides, videos, books, and samples of clothing as they describe the ongoing work of the church abroad. Some active missionaries might be on home leave and available to speak to your class.

11. Invite an international student studying in your area or living with a family in the congregation to speak to your class about life in his or her country of birth.

12. Have a map of the world in a prominent location in the classroom. Point out the location of key cities, regions, seas, and mountains mentioned in your class readings.

13. Pray for the world in the life of the church. Look at the prayer emphases each month and highlight the global concerns that have been identified so that students can remember the people or issues in their Sunday school class prayers as well as their personal prayers.

FOR REFLECTION AND DISCUSSION

1. How would you define *globalization*?

2. Reflecting on your first encounter with an international guest, what issues do you remember from your conversations?

3. If you have traveled out of the United States, what were the highlights of your trips(s)? What were the difficulties with your trip(s)?

4. Read the visions that were listed by the young people at the U.N. Special Session on Children. What would you or your Sunday school class add to the list?

5. Identify a country that you would like to investigate. What five items or issues would you want your Sunday school students to know about that country?

6. Reflect on teaching in your congregation. In what ways has globalization been explored with your students? What might you do in the future to promote global issues in the Sunday school or day-school classes?

Notes

1. Roland Robertson, "Globalization and the Future of 'Traditional Religion,'" in *God and Globalization* (Harrisburg: Trinity Press International), p. 64.

2. John Tomlison, *Globalization and Culture* (Chicago: University of Chicago), pp. 1-2.

3. Clive Dimmock, "Globalization and Societal Culture: redefining schooling and school leadership in the twenty-first century," *Compare* 30 (October 2000), pp. 303ff.

4. Robertson, p. 54.

5. James A. Banks, *Cultural Diversity and Education* (Boston: Allyn and Bacon, 2001), pp. 57-58.

6. Barbara Wilkerson, "Goals of Multicultural Religious Education," *Multicultural Religious Education*, Barbara Wilkerson, ed. (Birmingham: Religious Education, 1997), p. 55.

7. Martin Luther, The Large Catechism.

8. Ibid.

9. "For Peace in God's World," a Social Statement of Evangelical Lutheran Church in America, September 1995.

10. Ibid.

11. Ibid.

12. Francis Buckley, "Future Trends in Religious Education," *Religious Education* 86 (Summer 1991), pp. 377-382.

13. Ibid.

14. Mary J. Lickteig and Kathy Everts Danielson, "Use children's books to link the cultures of the world," *Social Studies* 86 (March/April 1995), pp. 69-73.

15. Robert L. Selman, *The Promotion of Social Awareness* (New York: Russell Sage Foundation, 2003). Used by permission.

16. Ibid.

17. Banks, pp. 34, 60.

18. Kofi Annan, *We the Children* (New York: United Nations, 2001), p. 101.

19. *The State of the World's Children, 2003* (New York: Unicef, 2002), pp. 66-67.

PART III

Practices

CHAPTER 7

Building a Children's Ministry Program

Margaret A. Krych

"Mom, Talisha gets really cool books and CDs from her church library when she goes to her Kids Klub Wednesday afternoon after school. Why can't our church have a Kids Klub and a library? Why do I always have to go to boring old Sunday school? Can we change to her church?"

"Absolutely not. Anyway, I never heard of a congregation wasting money on a children's library. Their church must have more money than sense. You get all the Bible you need at Sunday school—one hour a week is plenty at your age."

"But Talisha asked me to go to their Kids' Camp in two weeks. It's Saturday and Sunday. Her mentor said it would be okay for me to go."

"Her what? Jane, I don't know what's wrong with that fancy church of hers but you are not going to camps and clubs and libraries and whatevers. There's only one thing children need, and that is Sunday school. And our congregation has it. Besides, you know you have to baby-sit your brother every weekend. Tell Talisha, 'No.'"

Developing a program that uses many settings

Well, why would a congregation have an after-school program, a children's library, a mentor program, and other opportunities for children's educational ministry? Many congregations wonder if a multi-faceted program is really necessary for children. Isn't a Sunday school sufficient? In some cases, one setting such as weekly classes, may be the beginning point of an overall program. In general, even in small congregations, it is desirable to use more than one channel or setting for educational ministry with children.

At the outset, however, a cautionary word is in order. A program, including the settings used, is not an end in itself. You are not attempting to make changes or additions just for the sake of change. Rather, you are seeking ways to help children hear the good news of the gospel. The question then becomes, How may the children's needs for educational ministry best be met in our congregation?

In seeking to meet educational needs, it is important to realize that hearing the good news of the gospel does not happen haphazardly or automatically. Some person or group, usually the Christian education committee, has to plan under the guidance of the Spirit for the children in your congregation to have opportunities to learn about the Scriptures and about the Lord of their life. In planning, they need to consider that more settings may enable more children to have such opportunities. Before looking at the range of opportunities that might be desirable, let us start where all planning begins—with objectives.

Planning with objectives

Careful planning of overall objectives pays off because a road map is then able to be formed that can guide the educational ministry of the congregation for a considerable period, usually a number of years. Such an overall plan enables the various aspects of education to fit together into a whole so that the parts complement each other rather than competing with each other or, worse, negating or contradicting each other.

In developing an overall program for children's education in the congregation, the first place to start is with the aim or goal of educational ministry for the whole congregation (that is, for all age levels).

You want what you do in Christian education to be consonant with what is happening in the rest of the congregation's ministry. So study the mission statement of the congregation. What is it about? Outreach? Worship? Service? Speaking God's word in everyday life? All of these? None of these? So ask, "Where would education fit in our congregational mission?" and "How can education support and undergird the mission so that the people of God are equipped for ministry?" For example, if the overall mission statement of the congregation is about outreach, there may be two kinds of education that would immediately come to mind: Education of members to do the outreach, and education of those who are brought into the congregation through outreach. If possible, think carefully through the theological basis that underlies your congregational mission statement. Your education program will be built upon a similar theological foundation. See the chapter "Theology of Christian Education for Children." It is important to set overall objectives that are consistent with the mission of the congregation so that the congregation and the educational program will all be moving in the same direction, not fighting with each other for resources and ideology.

Once the objectives for educational ministry in the congregation are formed, then you can move on to develop the objectives for educational ministry with children in your congregation. These should flow from your overall educational objective and should carry out at a particular age-level (preschool and elementary-age children) what you desire for learning in your parish. The objectives will function like signposts—they will remind you what road you are on and the direction that you are headed in children's learning. "You" here means more than you as an individual—it more likely means "you as a member of the Christian education committee along with the other members," although occasionally the task may have to be done by just one or two people.

Following development of objectives for children's educational ministry, you need to choose topics and settings for education that are consonant with the objectives. For example, if one of your objectives is to help children with diverse backgrounds get to know and appreciate each other, you will want a setting that enables them to interact easily. Independent study in a library is good for many things, but it is not good for getting to know other people. A Saturday morning program that includes games and outdoor fun with group cooperative learning activities may be an excellent setting that will support what you have in mind.

This brings us back to the issue of multiple congregational settings for education, with which this chapter began. Sometimes churches think that children do not need many settings. Children are less likely than adults to loudly demand variety, so the assumption is made that a weekly class (often a Sunday school program) will be all that is needed. In fact, however, as at other age levels, various objectives will call for different approaches to childhood learning. One setting is usually not enough, even in a small congregation. Children have different needs and learn in different ways. Families have different time schedules. Teachers and mentors have different ways that they prefer to work with children, and all of these points lead to a multifaceted approach to children's education in the congregation.

Training leaders and teachers

The Christian education committee is responsible for the overall educational program of the congregation, and therefore will decide which settings are to be used in your congregation. A small congregation with few leaders may use only a few settings. A congregation that has many leaders may use many settings, but do not equate small with few leaders and large with many. The number of teachers, mentors, and leaders for children's educational ministry has much more to do with careful and regular training of teachers and leaders, than with membership statistics. Similarly, the complexity and range of needs of the congregation will determine the number of settings rather than the number of people on the membership roll.

Because training leaders, teachers, and mentors is so critical to a quality educational program for children, consider at the outset how you will train those you recruit. Also, it is wise to recruit—to ask people chosen by the Christian education committee, as opposed to begging for volunteers. In this way, you will choose people who, in the eyes of those with congregational responsibility, have gifts for teaching and leading. Discerning the gifts in the congregation should be taken seriously—and sometimes the individual is not the best person to decide whether she has the gifts! The early church long ago discovered the wisdom of deliberately choosing people and setting them aside for particular tasks.

Further, it is wise initially to ask the people simply to train for a task, rather than asking them to commit to the task from the outset. Until they have completed the training, people often do not really know whether they will enjoy serving in a particular capacity or not. They may even turn down the invitation because they do not feel adequate to the task. Following training, they may accept the invitation joyfully, or they may discover that their gifts are really most useful in another one of the congregation's ministries.

Training can be done in a number of ways. Sometimes synods have opportunities that bring together people from many congregations; such events have the enrichment of meeting others from outside one's own parish and from a variety of congregational experiences. In other cases, you might use a series of local training sessions geared to the particular needs of the congregation. Sometimes an apprentice system can link an experienced teacher or mentor with a novice. If each person has at least some experience, then team-teaching can further expand the learning of each person. Sometimes independent preparation through reading or watching tapes or DVDs is the only option because of work schedule. In this situation, the trainee often appreciates the opportunity to reflect on learning with an experienced teacher or pastor. Some congregations regularly carry out year-long weekly training sessions to prepare people to teach. Some of these programs are actually two or three years in length. Whatever the length or plan, bear in mind that people working with children generally need an understanding of the Bible, theology, child development, teaching/mentoring methods, and the curricular resources available. Church history has wonderful stories for children, and is also a worthwhile addition.

After completing this training, the Christian education committee and the individuals concerned need to discern whether and in what way those individuals can now serve in the children's educational ministry of the congregation. It goes without saying that all people in this role should be checked to ensure that they have no history of inappropriate behaviors with children. Churches should place a high priority on protecting the safety of children at all times.

Possible settings

As the Christian education committee looks at topics and settings in light of the educational objectives, it is helpful to keep in mind a wide variety of possibilities for children's education in the congregation. What follows are some possible settings that have long histories and are still very viable and lively in congregations. They will work in most denominations.

Each of these 13 settings is actually a grouping of possibilities, within which there can be several kinds of programs and opportunities. You will also notice that whether a program is slotted into one or more of the settings depends on the particular way it is configured. For example, "cradle roll" might include items for the child to use on her own (independent learning), visits by a congregant to the child with reading of stories (one-on-one), and items mailed to the family for use in the home by all members (family setting). These settings are not meant to be inflexible and exclusive. Rather, they are meant to get your juices flowing so that you can creatively meet the needs of the children in your congregation.

1. Independent and individual learning

The independent/individual learning setting includes all situations in which the child learns by himself or herself, as opposed to learning that takes place in a group of children. The congregation may arrange for such independent learning in a number of ways.

"Cradle roll" ministry for the baptized infants through age 3 (or whenever Sunday school or some other formal learning opportunity is afforded in your congregation) typically would be part of independent learning, in the sense that the congregation may mail materials to the parents and child, some of which the child will use by herself.

In educational ministry with older children, this setting usually will include a library (often part of a library that serves all age levels), with books, magazines, CDs, and DVDs. If you can't develop your own congregational library, consider developing a shared library with another congregation.

If you don't have a library at present, begin in a small way and let the library grow over a number of years. To start with the expectation that the whole library will be completed within a year is usually not realistic. Moreover, excitement builds as people peek in periodically to "see if any new books have been added." Slow growth is kind to the annual congregational budget.

Many congregations begin very modestly, with a few shelves in a small room, and 20 or 30 books purchased in loving memory of a dear member—perhaps one who cared for children and read to them. Year by year, books, magazines, CDs, and DVDs are added. It is wise not to ask for donations, since some materials will inevitably be unsuitable. (It is difficult to accept the donation of Mr. A. and then reject the donation of Ms. B.) However, donations of money to purchase materials are always welcome! Have a small committee of two or three (perhaps the pastor or director of religious education plus one or two theological and biblically informed members) who can scan and select purchases. Never rely on publishers' advertising to decide what to buy. Advertising is aimed at what the potential buyers want to hear rather than being an objective description of the content of the product! When funds are limited, each purchase should be as useful for your purpose as possible.

You may use a simple card system for borrowing books. As the number of books grows, you will need a cataloguing system—use one that fits your purpose and is simple but workable. Large church libraries usually use a formal system, such as the Dewey decimal classification system, but smaller libraries can use less formal means of categorizing the books. Be sure to note on cards the age level for which the books are suited. Some helpful categories include: preschool, grades 1-3, older children, and younger teenagers. You might put each group on a different shelf for ease of location and borrowing. Some congregations with large libraries have the luxury of a computerized borrowing system and age-level categories that are called up by borrowers with a click of the mouse.

Whether or not you have your own church library, consider a way to recommend materials available in school and public libraries that children and parents can borrow. It is most desirable to have a tutor/mentor, parent, or older sibling check out the learning that take place through independent means. A mentor who is a church member might become a real friend of the child by checking out learning on a regular basis and also sitting occasionally with the child's family in worship or attending the child's baseball games.

Use of computer programs, and instruction via the Internet, also fall under the "independent learning" setting. Further discussion about the Internet appears later in this chapter, under the heading "11. Public media." Computer programs, of course, have proliferated over the past decade and may be purchased in many stores or created independently. If you do purchase computer programs, be sure to check them ahead of time for quality and for theological and biblical content before you put them in the hands of children and families.

2. Live-in events

Live-in events include all situations where the child stays away from home overnight, such as conferences, camps, and overnight sleep-ins. Live-in events can be excellent opportunities for learning but need to be used sparingly and carefully with children. Many children are not ready to stay overnight away from family members until they are around 10 years of age, even if they routinely stay in the homes of grandparents or other relatives at younger ages. If you have an overnight event with younger children, try to stay close to the church premises and be ready with transportation to take a distressed child home in the middle of the night.

Live-in events have the advantages of being novel (away from home) and fun, and also including social learning along with biblical content. However, because such events lend themselves to adventurous and exciting activities, children will tire and you must gear learning to what can reasonably be expected. The first hour-long session of content and craft activities will be at a different level than that six hours later when the children are tired and thirsty (and perhaps cranky). With a little ingenuity, you will be able to adapt many published resources designed for the weekly class channel and will find ways to use them in the learning time slots of live-in events. Some resources even come with directions for such adaptation.

3. Free-time classes or events

Free-time classes or events include all those slots that are longer than the usual weekly classes, and in time segments that are apart from the daily routine of school or the regular routine of Sunday morning church and weekly class. For children, free-time events would include after school programs on weekdays, learning events on Saturdays (all day for the oldest children or part of the day for younger children), opportunities on Sunday afternoons or, for older children, perhaps early Sunday evenings. They also include events that take several days or are related to particular seasons of the year, such as vacation Bible schools, and Advent workshops. Free-time opportunities usually are popular with learners because there is time to include social contacts, games, projects, crafts, and music.

At age 3, children may not be ready for free-time activities, since they usually last two to three hours. Most 4-year-olds can handle such a program, such as vacation Bible school, but some may find the time slots too long. By age 11 or 12, children can take an event of several hours duration, provided there is plenty of variety and lots of activity, preferably with some time outdoors.

4. Weekly classes

Weekly classes are the most commonly used settings for children in most congregations, and are usually 60 to 75 minutes in length. Such opportunities include Sunday school, weekday classes after school, Wednesday evening classes after a light supper, and so on. Such classes are used frequently for the good reason that they work well for children. Most 3-year-olds can handle an hour's learning, provided there is plenty of variety in the session—movement, singing, finger plays, a brief story, and plenty of activity centers with interesting and age-appropriate things to do (book center, housekeeping center, water play, sand play, painting, drawing, clay, and so on.) Wise teachers can help older children to make good use of those minutes of serious learning through pleasurable activities.

Weekly classes have the advantage of regular on-going relationships with other children and trusted teachers. Because there is time between the classes, there is opportunity for reflection and review between sessions, and then further review in class while there is still some memory of the previous week's lesson. Mid-course corrections can be made by teachers easily when it is apparent that objectives were not met the previous week. It is usually easier to recruit teachers for a weekly time slot.

However, weekly classes alone have limitations. Some children will not be able to attend because of other regularly scheduled family activities. Most of the time, it is not fair to blame the children for non-attendance under these circumstances—it is the parent who is responsible. Other children may attend only sporadically due to court decisions about visitation rights. And some children simply learn better in more prolonged settings or in one-on-one situations than in weekly classes.

In addition, some topics will take considerably longer than one hour for appropriate activities to be included in the session. Especially this is true of social learning, in which games and outdoor activities can be very beneficial. While weekly classes are popular and have tested well over time, we cannot equate a good children's educational program simply with a Sunday school program. The Sunday school in fact is one type of weekly class setting, and the weekly class setting is only one of the 13 settings listed here—which itself is by no mean an exhaustive list. Your congregation may come up with many more settings.

5. One-on-one learning

One-on-one learning can be carried out one child with another, or an adult with a child, or a relative with a child. Any combination of teacher-student, peer-student, parent-student, or pastor-student would come under this category. In the best one-on-one situations, each person is able to give to the other so that learning is not always one-way. This may be difficult with adult-child, in which the adult always knows, so much more than the child. However, if the child can give to the adult, so much the better. Nowadays most children know as much or more about computers than many adults, so one can imagine a situation in which the adult offers input on the Bible and the child shares ways that input can be expressed through overhead presentations or other means using the computer.

There are dangers in one-to-one learning. The bright child may always help the slower child in a way that makes the latter feel inferior. Or worse, the brighter child may become impatient with the slower child and put him or her down. Children are more prone to this tendency than adults because they often have not yet learned the social ways to be tactful and patient in the face of slower learning. In an adult-child situation, the adult may find it difficult to break the relationship when he or he is no longer really able to spend the time. An established end-point clearly expressed from the beginning is desirable, and the child should gradually be weaned from the one-on-one learning routine.

In any situation in which an adult or teenager is one-on-one with a child, needless to say, the older individual should take precautions to prevent anyone from drawing the wrong conclusions. For this reason, it is desirable that no adult should be alone with a child at any time. Have another adult in the room, if possible. Perhaps another person could also work one-on-one with another child in the same area. If the adult and child must be alone, then leave the door open. Be within view of the parents, if possible. In any event, do everything to ensure that neither the child nor anyone else can draw wrong inferences from the adult's behavior.

The pluses of one-on-one learning are many. Such learning can be geared to meet the individual needs of the child and build on the child's previous learning. The learning can be geared to the pace of the child and sped up or slowed down according to need. Of course, the child gets personal attention, a situation that most children thoroughly enjoy and some actually crave due to lack of attention in the home. In child-on-child situations, long-term friendships can be formed. Children learn to give and take, and to respect the understanding and insight of others.

6. The family

The family setting means that the home itself is the setting for learning. It does not mean that *family* is the topic to be studied (although occasionally that might happen). It means that parents and children work together in learning. In this context, *parents* includes those adults who live with the child and are primarily responsible for the child's upbringing, whether they are grandparents, guardians, or parent-figures in a group home.

The family setting was Martin Luther's suggestion for Christian education in his day—that the father is bishop and the mother bishopess in the household and that the parents have the responsibility to teach the catechism to the young.[1] Luther gave new emphasis to a tradition that went back for centuries when parents were expected to have a role in catechizing their children.

The family is a particularly valuable setting for working with children because the home remains the major influence on the child's values throughout the elementary years and on into high school. Because of the high emotional investment in the family, learning tends to be remembered, and reinforcement is almost automatically built in because family conversation can continue throughout the week.

Yet many families today find it difficult to have time together. Some families do not find it possible even to eat a meal together once a day. Others struggle to do so by juggling schedules with difficulty. Thus, even family devotions are no longer practiced routinely in many busy households. It takes a conscious on-going effort to find the time for families to study and pray together, but the rewards are great both for individual family members and the family unit as a whole.

A further point of difficulty is that many adults feel inadequate to talk about the faith to children or youth, due to a perceived lack of biblical and theological education on their own part. This in turn is often due to the lack of adult religious education opportunities in their congregations. For the family to function as a major educational setting for children, it is essential that parents have access to good adult education. Congregations that want to use the family channel need to provide quality religious instruction through adult groups and through a church library. Desirably, Christian education committees will examine the use of all of the settings described in this chapter in terms of opportunities of adult learning also. In addition, congregations need to be explicit about expectations of family engagement with the faith; give help where possible by providing devotional/study booklets; help families have access to denominational magazines; and provide local newsletters that include educational articles for adults and children so that the families have something to talk about together. Newsletters may also include family quizzes or games. A church Web site may include items for children and adults that encourage communication ("Ask one of your parents to help you with this next question.")

As children approach adolescence, they struggle to break free from their childhood dependence upon parents. One way they do this is to turn to peers for support in making decisions about such things as clothing, music, and language. Another way they try to separate from parents is to argue with them, fighting verbally for their "rights." Preadolescents and adolescents want to remain dependent, but they also crave independence. They want responsibility but often not the accountability that goes with it. Parents, likewise, veer between wanting the child to grow up and, at the same time, wanting the child to continue in a dependent relationship. In this time of ambivalent feelings and family tension, it can be a blessing to have something in common to talk about: the Christian faith and catechetical learning can be just such a common focus. While the family setting contributes to learning, learning itself may contribute to healthy relationships in the family.

7. Interest and service groups

Interest and service groups in the congregation provide many opportunities for excellent learning with children, such as acolyte training groups and children's service groups. Motivation for learning is usually high, because the child understands that the group carries out important functions in the life of the church and/or community. Children are eager to learn how to do their tasks well, and to see the way that their work fits into the overall ministry of the congregation. Of course, it is important that the objectives of such groups mesh with the overall service ministry of the congregation.

Congregations may provide intergenerational service ministry opportunities, with young and old being involved together. Education can take place through such ministries, but conceptual learning is more difficult due to the different stages of thinking that typify preschool (preoperational), elementary children (concrete-thinking), and adults (abstract thinking). However, practical learning about ways of serving is appropriate and can be satisfying to a wide span of age levels.

8. Worship services

Opportunities for worship and learning occur in the weekly assembly gathered around Word and Sacrament. The major objective in worship is not education—sitting in rows and facing the front with little opportunity to ask questions on the spot, is not an ideal arrangement for learning. Worship, in fact, is centered on the proclamation of the forgiveness of sins, and the Spirit's work of calling forth faith through the Word. We would worship even if we knew all there was to know about the liturgy and the texts for the day, because we always needs to remember who we are as sinful beings, and the work of Christ for our salvation. We need to hear again the words of absolution, and we need to respond with praise and thanksgiving to the gospel read, proclaimed, and acted visibly in the sacraments. Education, on the other hand, usually moves from one point to the next—once we thoroughly know the alphabet, we do not need to keep on learning it, but we move instead to the next item we need to learn. Thus, education functions differently from worship, even though education is also an opportunity to hear God's word. Additionally, education has broader objectives than worship—one can imagine an educational objective to learn the names of the 66 books of the Bible, but one can hardly imagine a worship service designed for that purpose. (Imagine the sermon!) Worship and education cannot be considered the same thing, and education is not the major focal point of the community gathered in assembly around Word and Sacrament.

That having been said, we need also to acknowledge that learning takes place in public worship. For children, two kinds of learning take place in the gathered assembly: *conceptual* and *social-emotional*. Younger children are much more likely to be engaged in the latter than the former, since the vast majority of cognitive concepts in the church service are designed for teenagers and adults, that is, people who have reached the adult way of thinking that we call *abstract thinking* or *formal operations*. Much of the conceptuality and even the phrases in liturgy come from the Bible, and the Bible was written by adults for adults. Therefore, it is not surprising that younger children struggle with conceptuality. However, there is a great deal of important social and emotional learning in the service as children sense God's presence and love and mercy, and experience the joy of belonging to God's people.[2]

The atmosphere itself can be a teacher. In public worship children respond to an atmosphere conducive to awe, wonder, praise, and adoration. Dignified movement, silence, music, architecture, furnishings, and rich liturgical phrases all contribute to a sense of mystery and wonder.[3]

The communal experience can be teacher. Children learn in the assembly what it means to be part of the people of God who gather to pray and sing and hear God's word. They may learn by rote parts of the liturgy so they can join in the phrases of the Apostles' Creed and prayers. Singing, reciting psalms, and joining in with an enthusiastic "amen" at appropriate points, help children experience what it means to be part of the people of God. Further, as children gaze around at other worshipers, they learn to appreciate the people of God as an inclusive body with differences of many kinds, all of whose members share in the good news of God in Jesus Christ. They also learn in worship that the "people of God" includes all ages, and that children can participate in the same way the adults do—a rare experience in the life of children in today's society.

Conceptually, older children can appreciate more of the meaning of the phrases and biblical passages. If the preacher is attuned to children, they may hear in the sermon illustrations relevant to the daily experience of children as well as youth and adults. If Bibles are available in the pews, children can follow the readings and reinforce the understanding that the Bible is a book they can read.

In worship, children learn about baptism and communion. They see the acted visible expression of God's promise as they gather around the font to watch a child being baptized or kneel at the table with God's people.

Whatever the age of the children, it is important that they sit where they can see. A young child who prefers to wander might better be situated near an exit. For the most part, however, children are much better behaved when seated by an aisle or near the front where they can see everything.

No matter how much learning may occur in the worship service, it is never appropriate to cancel weekly classes and assume that children can learn all they need to know about Jesus and the Scriptures by attending public worship. Education of children is much better done in a setting where children can move and engage in age-appropriate activities that reinforce learning, and where children can ask questions as they arise, and can reflect on the material through individual review.

Thus children need to attend both worship and education in other settings. The ill-advised practice in some congregations is to schedule worship at the same time as the major opportunity for education. This forces a terrible choice between learning and worship. Moreover, such a practice usually implies that learning is for children and worship is for adults— an implication that is detrimental for both children and adults.

9. Community groups on the congregation's premises or under the auspices of the congregation

Congregations often host community groups, either free or by rental agreements. Sometimes the relationship to the congregation is little more than tangential. At other times the group may be inextricably woven into the fabric of the congregation or may be sponsored by the congregation. Scouts and 4-H groups would be typical examples of community groups that might meet on the congregation's premises.

In some cases, such community groups are autonomous and do not incorporate Christian education. But sometimes they may welcome the input of the congregation or the pastor and intentionally include Christian learning in the program. A scout badge called "God and Country," for example, can be an excellent learning opportunity. The Christian education committee needs to walk a fine line between being intrusive and being helpful when it comes to learning opportunities in such community groups.

10. Church-sponsored schools

Many congregations sponsor preschools that have a Christian education component in the curriculum. Some congregations also have a kindergarten program or an elementary school. The opportunity for serious ongoing Christian education taught by trained and qualified teachers in such programs is a gift to the children and the church.

In addition, whether or not the congregation sponsors a preschool or school, Christian education committees need to pay attention to what is happening in the public school system in the community. While proselytizing is prohibited, some schools have character education or courses on world religions, or other programs that support or enhance the learning the church may provide. Parents or community members may occasionally be invited to give input, or the church may simply want to be aware of the curriculum so that the congregation can expand on what is being taught in the schools to their baptized members.

The Christian education committee is also called to be vigilant in expressing congregational concern for quality public education for children in the community—not just in the religious realm but in all subject areas. This may mean encouraging members or parents to be present at school board meetings and to take an active role in ensuring acceptable local funding and community support for schools.

Martin Luther was vocal in his support of what many would now call "secular subjects." He called on council members of his day to establish schools that would teach not only the gospel and languages but also reading, history, mathematics, singing, music, and the arts, so that society and temporal government would be served.[4] For more information on this topic, see the section on "Two Kingdoms" in the chapter "Theology of Christian Education for Children." In today's society, it is still important for congregations to hold the community accountable and to vigorously support the quality of education in schools so that children will receive the best education possible to serve society throughout their lives.

11. Public media

The setting of public media has many aspects, from columns for children in local newspapers to children's magazines, TV and radio programs, and Web sites. The Christian education committee's work can be divided into two aspects: producing the congregation's own media programs, and reflecting on those that are produced elsewhere. See the chapter "Growing Faithful Children in Media Cultures."

Some congregations have the resources to produce local public media such as television or radio programs. These usually are geared toward adults, but there is no reason at all that they cannot include children's programming. However, it takes time, funding, and expertise to do this well, and it is obviously desirable to have high quality when producing for the public.

All congregations, however, can reflect carefully on commercial and other programming and make recommendations to their members about its use. Television and the Internet are big influences on children's lives that the church dare not ignore. See the chapter "Growing Faithful Children in Media Cultures." Possibilities for educational ministry include producing family or group study guides to go along with forthcoming programs; issuing sheets that list good quality programming for children; arranging for group viewing and discussion of particularly pertinent programs either for children or for their parents; lobbying for good quality programming by writing to companies that sponsor children's programming; and so on. Sometimes the congregation may do a service for members by noting Web sites or programs that families with children would do well to avoid.

12. Children's choirs, bands, and other music programs

Music is a very important part of learning for children, and indeed for all ages. Music is a powerful learning tool because it is holistic: it engages both sides of the brain—the logical/cognitive side and the creative/emotional side. Music has been part of all human societies and has been recognized as a teaching medium for thousands of years. Music has always been part of the church's life and worship, and it should be a vital part of any congregation's educational ministry.

Sometimes we think of learning in choirs as limited to memorizing notes and words to perform pieces in public, especially anthems in worship. But the educational possibilities of choirs are in fact much greater than learning words and notes. The music, whether for choirs or bands or other musical ensembles, usually has a story behind it that enhances the understanding of the piece and the way it will be interpreted. So, by all means, help children to study that story. Sometimes an interesting anecdote from the life of the composer can make the meaning of the piece come alive for children. Or the children can learn about the biblical text or story on which the lyrics are based. Or perhaps they can learn the way the piece has been sung or played, or where it has been performed, may be engaging. Learning how the psalms were sung in Hebrew and early church worship can enhance the singing of psalms. Watching a video on ancient instruments can help children imagine worship long ago.

Young children can develop a sense of rhythm by making and using instruments from cardboard and scraps of wood or by using a variety of play instruments. Movement to music—running, skipping, dancing, creeping, walking—also helps develop a sense of rhythm, and allows for release of energy. Older children can learn social skills, discipline, cooperation, give and take, and the joy of creative community, as they play in ensembles and bands. Much of the value of the choir or instrumental group will actually be in the practices themselves, quite apart from the performing of the pieces in a public setting.

Children as well as adults learn a great deal of their theology from hymns and Christian songs. They may also learn questionable theology when songs are chosen because of the swingy tune rather than the quality of the words. To minimize misunderstandings that must later be unlearned, choose the words carefully. It is worth giving up the swingy tune if the result is a better understanding of Jesus and his good news for the child.

When children's choirs sing in public worship, they should sing words that are meaningful to the children, and the difficulty of music should appropriately be geared to the age level of the children. Too often, children are forced to sing words they do not understand or attempt music that is too difficult for them simply because that's what the congregation expects. It is absolutely appropriate for congregations to expect that adult choirs will sing music that is suitable for adults. But it is not appropriate to expect that children will do so: this turns the contribution of the children into a performance to please adults, rather than what it ought to be—a genuine offering of worship on the part of the children which, in turn, leads the congregation in worship.

13. Local printed and electronic media

The very way that your congregation communicates regularly with its members provides great opportunities for learning for all ages, including children. The advantage of local media is that items can be designed to meet the needs of your particular congregation. Children recognize references to familiar people and events mentioned on your church Web site and in your newsletter, for example.

Never underestimate the influence of the newsletter. When a family puts the educational pages of the newsletter on the refrigerator, family members see the pages every time they go to the refrigerator for an entire month until the next issue is published. Multiply the number of times per day your own family members go to the refrigerator by the number of days in a given month to get some idea of the reinforcement of the educational ideas in the newsletter. Such intense reinforcement warrants very careful choice of topics and thoughtful writing for every issue of the newsletter.

It is wise to have a section of the newsletter devoted to children. Through word games and puzzles, biblical learning can be reviewed. A monthly quiz (with answers and winners given the following month) can generate hours of learning to come up with the answers. Children can write stories and poems for the newsletter. Seeing their work "in print" gives them recognition and of course they will also delight in further appreciative comments from congregation members whom they meet at church.

Web sites are the milieu of today's children. Perhaps part of your church's Web site can be devoted to children. You might have one Web page for preschoolers and another for elementary children. The children will be thrilled to see photos of their class or a note on their group's learning activities. Children are natural evangelists. They will share with their school friends what is happening via the Web site, so it is worthwhile to make the site exciting and interesting for children, and include worthwhile learning items that are updated regularly.

How do you begin an overall program?

Having looked at these 13 settings for learning in the congregation, you may now be overwhelmed. Where does one begin? Isn't it too much to expect a congregation to do all this? Well, the general rule is: begin small and grow. First, in light of your objectives for educational ministry, assess what is happening now in the congregation—and rejoice! Go through the settings one by one and note what is being done in your congregation at present. Type up your notes and observations. You will probably find that much more is being done for children than you ever knew! In doing this exercise, many congregations are amazed at the learning that is already taking place in their congregation.

In the assessment, decide what needs changing or even eliminating in light of your objectives. Perhaps some programs have been allowed to continue longer than they ought and are no longer really fulfilling the needs for which they were originally designed. Often, change or adaptation is all that is needed to make them a vital and functioning part of your church's ministry again.

Plan for changes and additions to fill gaps that you see. Perhaps there is a setting that is not being used but seems really to be needed: make that your focus for the next few months. Then get on with some long-range planning. For example, you could plan for one year, five years, and 10 years. Or, if you prefer, one-year, three-year, and five-year plans if there is a good deal of change in the community or context that makes long-range planning difficult. Such plans are not straight-jackets that limit your freedom, but rather broad guides so that you have a clear idea of where your energies and time will be spent instead of trying immediately to do everything you may want to do. Slow and careful implementation usually results in good long-term results.

One congregation uses the 13 settings as the basis for reports at the monthly Christian education committee meetings. Each committee member is responsible for reporting on one or more channels or settings. This prevents any particular program from dominating the agenda of any meeting. Some reports are long. Some are very short, especially for any settings that are in limited use, but the fact that they are mentioned keeps them before the committee. Someday these settings may be used more than they are now. By adopting the settings as the basis for reports, this congregation soon realized that independent learning was largely underused and so they started a library. Then someone noted that the baptized infants were not contacted for three years until they were old enough for Sunday school. So educational materials for parents and and children from birth to age 3 were purchased, and a cradle-roll visitation team was established to bring the materials to each family. Soon the person responsible for reporting on the family channel noted that families did not have sufficient resources for learning at home, so plans were made to fill this need. As a result, the planning and implementation continue at the present time.

Keeping the program going

Once the program is initiated, someone (typically the Christian education committee) must make sure that it continues to fulfill the objectives, that aspects that cease to be helpful are replaced, and that the program expands to meet new needs. If your congregation has no Christian education committee, form one. The job of the committee is not to do the work of the Sunday school or other specific program—for that you need a small committee that focuses solely on the work of that program. Rather, the Christian education committee has as its task the formation and continuance of the total program. It fills gaps, prevents overlaps, relates to other congregational committees (especially, property, worship, music, and evangelism), approves teachers and curricula, and has general oversight of the well-being of the congregation's educational ministry. It should devote about equal time to the learning of children, youth, and adults.

The Christian education committee is responsible for evaluation and change. Evaluation always is a function of the objectives. What are you trying to do? Are you accomplishing what you set out to do? If you are not totally meeting the objectives, then what might be done differently so the objectives will be achieved or achieved more adequately? Sometimes a minor correction is all that is needed; sometimes a replacement or new program will be necessary. Regular evaluation is needed to make minor adjustments before things get out of hand and problems become larger and more difficult to deal with.

The Christian education committee will continue to revisit the question of the settings to use and the way that they may be used more effectively. It will make recommendations for change and adaptation to meet changing needs in the congregation. Make change slowly, and always for the purpose of more adequately meeting the objectives. Never change for the sake of change. Especially in a volunteer organization such as the church, where people can leave if and whenever they wish, change should be made only when it is clear that the objectives are not being met—and then in a way that the need for the change to better serve the learning interests of the children can be clearly communicated. If parents and children are enjoying the program, then it is likely meeting a need. Don't throw out the baby with the bath water. But an exception to this general rule must be made if people are enjoying things that are not consonant with the gospel. If a program is failing to communicate the gospel then by all means discontinue it. However, someone's feeling that "I just think we should have a change of pace" is not a good enough reason for change that disrupts children and their families.

The fact that change comes slowly in the church is actually a good thing. Groups that change quickly—more than 10% of their membership or program at a time—quickly die or become so new they are not recognizable. The church has already lasted for 2,000 years. This means it is by nature "conservative," that is, conserving of tradition and the way things are done. A group that conserves its ways of doing things and changes slowly and thoughtfully (one might also say, often painfully) will tend to last for decades—and in this case, millennia. It may be comforting to bear this in mind next time change meets with resistance or seems painfully slow.

For Reflection and Discussion

- Which settings or channels are we currently using for children's educational ministry in our congregation? Are the programs serving the congregation's educational ministry objectives?

- What other settings could be used that are not used currently? Which of these might most appropriately serve the educational objectives of the congregation? How?

- Choose just one of these settings as a starting point. What would it take to begin such a program for children in your congregation in terms of planning, leadership, teaching, funding, and space?

Notes

1. Martin Luther, Large Catechism, Preface 4, and Fifth Part: "The Sacrament of the Altar," in Robert Kolb and Timothy J. Wengert, eds., *The Book of Concord* (Minneapolis: Augsburg Fortress, 2000), pp. 383, 476. See also Charles P. Arand, *That I May Be His Own: An Overview of Luther's Catechism* (St. Louis: Concordia, 2000), pp. 95-96.

2. See Margaret A. Krych, "Children and Worship," *Introduction to Sundays and Season*, 2000, Dennis Bushkovsky, ed. (Minneapolis: Augsburg Fortress, 2000), pp. 11-15.

3. Ibid., p. 12. Further ideas in this section on worship are reflective of this article also.

4. Luther, "To the Councilmen of All Cities in Germany that They Establish and Maintain Christian Schools," in Timothy Lull, ed., *Martin Luther's Basic Theological Writings* (Minneapolis: Augsburg Fortress, 1989), pp. 704-735.

CHAPTER 8

Let the Little Children Come: Teaching the Bible with Children

Carol R. Jacobson

I FIRST BECAME ACQUAINTED with the dangers and delights of teaching the Bible with children as a first-grade vacation Bible school teacher years ago. I had a dozen or so children in my class, and our task for the week was to learn about the life of Jesus. The first part of the week went very well. Using our prepared curriculum, we learned stories about Jesus from the Bible. My first-graders loved to listen to and interact with these narratives. We celebrated Jesus' birthday and learned about how we celebrated birthdays in our families. We found out that Jesus healed sick children, then talked together about being sick and about how happy we are when we feel better. We discovered that even Jesus got separated from his parents, then shared stories about how scary it is to be lost and feel alone. Together, we discovered that Jesus was a special person and a real friend to the children he met. And we learned that Jesus was our friend too—someone who loved us, cared for us, and was always with us, even when we felt lost and alone.

It wasn't until Thursday's class session that I began to worry. That day, the story of Jesus' life turned toward his passion and death.

Should I tell the Bible stories of Jesus' imprisonment, torture, and death to 6-year-olds? How could I help them understand what was happening to their friend Jesus at the end of his life without frightening them or breaking their hearts? Had I set the children up for emotional trauma? As the curriculum suggested, I told the story of Jesus' entry into Jerusalem, and we imagined it like a parade. We made musical instruments and special hats, then gave Jesus a "Welcome to Jerusalem" parade around the church grounds.

As I approached the end of Thursday's session, it was time to tell my students the next part of the passion story. I had to find some way of telling them that Jesus was arrested, tortured, and executed. I swallowed my fears and began. I said that some of the important people in Jerusalem were jealous because Jesus got a parade and they didn't get one. They were so jealous in fact that they arrested Jesus and took him to jail! My plan was to ask the children whether or not they were ever jealous of someone, but one boy, no doubt concerned for Jesus' fate, blurted out, "They aren't going to kill him, are they?" Now what? What should I say? "Yes," was the correct answer, of course, but what would happen to the boys and girls if I did?

Fortunately, before I could say anything at all, another child turned to the boy who had asked the question and said, "Don't worry, I've heard this story before. He raises from the dead. It's really cool!" As I breathed a big sigh of relief, the children began to ask me if that was really true. I happily assured them that it really was—and to cheer for their friend Jesus, who had risen from the dead. We put on our parade hats again, picked up our instruments, and gave Jesus another parade—an Easter parade! We didn't talk about Jesus' imprisonment, torture, or death at all. That wasn't what was important to these children. Instead, we celebrated the good news of Easter together—our friend Jesus is raised from the dead. It's really cool!

"I've heard this story before"

"Don't worry," said the boy, "I've heard this story before." What a delightful response that was for all of us in class that day. It wasn't until years later that I wondered just where that young student had heard the story before. In church? In Sunday school? On a mother's or father's lap? Where had this student heard the story about Jesus' death and resurrection before? Who had told the story? A pastor? A parent? A teacher? A friend?

Whatever the source, it is apparent that this child's previous encounter with the Bible story of Jesus was an important and meaningful one for him. The child remembered the story, and even better, wanted to tell it to someone who hadn't heard it before. This is good news for all of us who are involved in teaching the Bible with children. As faithful Christian adults, we value the Bible and the good news of God's love for us that we encounter there. We want our children to know and value the Bible, as we ourselves have come to know it and to value it. We want our children to hear the stories of God's love for them and for all creation—stories that we ourselves have come to regard as the very vehicle of God's self-giving to us. But we wonder, "Are children, especially young children, capable of understanding Bible stories? Are they ready for the complexities and questions they will encounter in the biblical narratives? Can children engage the Bible in ways that don't just confuse them at best, or cause them harm at worst?" [1]

These are significant questions—questions to be addressed in this chapter. Before doing so, however, we must ask two additional questions that can offer us some help in addressing just how the Bible can be used with children in appropriate and life-giving ways. These two questions are:

- What does it mean to understand the Bible?
- What do we wish to accomplish in engaging children with the Bible?

How we respond to these two questions will influence our subsequent discussion of whether and how it can be appropriate to teach Bible stories with children.

What does it mean to understand the Bible?

Behind much of the concern about whether or not it is appropriate to teach children Bible stories lies the recognition that the Bible is a complex and theologically challenging book. The Bible contains a variety of literary genres and theological points of view. So we rightly ask, can children, especially younger children, really understand all that is going on in the Bible? Most likely they cannot, we surmise, and so we may hesitate to share Bible stories with them until they can handle them. However, this way of thinking hides an assumption that is worth examining. When we conclude that children are not capable of understanding the Bible, what we assume is that to understand the Bible is to be able to grasp and handle its contents cognitively. But is this really the heart of what it means to understand the Bible—to be able to intellectually assess its theological claims and apply its mandates for Christian living?

As important as these are, I would argue that to understand the Bible is to encounter it on many levels, not limited to the cognitive level alone. To understand the Bible is something more than the ability to know and articulate what the Bible says. To understand the Bible is more than knowing something about what kind of book it is. To understand the Bible is to interact with the Bible, in the same way that to know and understand a person is to interact with that person. To understand the Bible is to open ourselves up to it—its stories of God's deep love for us and its perspectives on how we are to live with one another. To know the Bible is to let it become a part of what we think about and feel as we try to make sense of our lives.

If knowing the Bible primarily involves opening up ourselves and our lives to an ongoing relationship with the stories and teachings in it, then it seems possible to think that children are indeed capable of understanding the Bible in some significant ways. Children can engage and experience the Bible. Children can think about the Bible, and understand that it is God's book and the church's book—one that contains many kinds of stories about God's love for them and for the whole world. Children can feel things about the Bible and its stories. Remember that one boy in the opening story was worried that something bad would happen to Jesus, while another was so excited to tell the happy ending to the story—that Jesus is raised from the dead. Children can wonder about the Bible and can enjoy imagining what Jesus, Mary, or Moses did when they were children.

Moreover, children are often skilled interpreters of Bible stories from their own perspectives as children. In addition to the young biblical interpreter in our opening story, consider the Sunday school class description on the following page.

We present the Good Shepherd to children according to the method we usually use, that is to say, with the greatest respect for the text, without adding anything other than what is found there. . . . The points on which we linger, for it is these that most enchant the children, are above all the personal love and protective presence of the Good Shepherd: He calls each one of His sheep by name; He knows each intimately even if there are many sheep; He calls his sheep and gradually they become accustomed to the voice of their Good Shepherd and they listen to Him. . . .

An aspect that is not immediately clear to the children is that we are the sheep; *we should take great care not to explain this*. We would deprive the children of the joy of the discovery. . . .

[For example] a child (five years old) brought his finished drawing to the catechist and she asked him: "Why did you put two children in the middle of the sheep?" The child responded: "Because as I was drawing I understood that we are the sheep." The child had not caught the significance of the image of the sheep while the catechist was speaking to him but only afterward during his own personal meditation.[2]

Somehow, as this young child was thinking about the story of the Good Shepherd and drawing his picture, he had come to understand something important about this Bible story. He had recognized that the story of the Good Shepherd was a story about him, about how much he was loved, just as the sheep were. He had even understood that he was one of the Good Shepherd's sheep and belonged in the sheepfold with all the other sheep. And so, he drew himself and even someone else into the picture. Moreover, in recounting this story for us, Cavalletti points out that the child did not come to this understanding by having the teacher tell him the correct meaning of the story. Rather, he interpreted the meaning of the story for himself as he thought, wondered, and gave expression to the story in his own drawing.

Once we as teachers are convinced that children are capable of understanding the Bible in ways that are both significant and useful to them, it becomes possible to put aside many of our worries about the difficulties they might have in understanding biblical materials and to plunge into the adventure of experiencing the Bible with them. After all, "in their engagements with the Bible, children do and can learn to do what all Christians are to do. They make their interpretations and construct their understandings. They can learn to tell their stories of their engagements with the Bible, of the God who meets them there, and of themselves as God's people."[3]

What do we wish to accomplish in teaching the Bible with children? Recognizing that children can and do interpret biblical narratives in ways that are significant for them, it becomes imperative to provide opportunities for them to experience and interact with the Bible and its contents. Before we turn our attention to the ways that such opportunities can be effectively created, however, it is worth pausing to remind ourselves of all that we, as teachers, hope to accomplish in teaching the Bible with children. Simply stated, what we hope for is that children will come to know the Bible. This means both that children should be offered opportunities to interact directly with the Bible and its contents, as well as that they should be encouraged to ask their questions and offer their interpretations. This overall goal of assisting children to know the Bible contains within it several important elements.

First, we wish to present the content of the Bible stories themselves in engaging ways. Children need to know who God, Jesus, Mary, Moses, and Ruth are and about what they did.[4] Children also need to know that in the Bible we hear many stories about God's love for them and for the whole world. Unless children actually hear the stories of God's people and God's actions directly, "there is no Bible for them to think, feel, and wonder about."[5] Perhaps this seems self-evident, but such a basic assertion points us to the second thing teachers wish to accomplish.

In addition to teaching the content of Bible stories, teachers also wish to show children that they can do more than just listen to the stories, but can think, feel, and ask questions about them as well. As we have already said, to know the Bible is something more than accumulating facts about the Bible. To know the Bible is to be in a relationship with what is contained within it. To know the Bible is to engage it, to ask questions of it, and to make interpretations of its contents. Children need to learn from their biblical teachers how to engage in this interpretive, interactive task. Children must see their teachers engaging the stories for themselves—wondering about them, thinking about them, feeling about them. Children must be encouraged to try this activity for themselves with the teacher.

Moreover, in teaching the Bible with children, we wish to communicate to children just who they will "meet" in Bible stories. Not only will they meet many interesting people and hear many stories about God's people, but in their encounters with the Bible children will meet the God who loves and cares for them today. Simply put, "the same God who meets adults in their encounters with the Bible is the same God who meets children in their encounters with the Bible." [6] Perhaps this is the most compelling reason for teaching the Bible with children: God desires to meet children in this experience. Sometimes we can forget that God wishes to meet and dwell in the lives of the children in our congregations, even while they are still children— even though children may not be able to articulate these divine workings and holy encounters in the language adults would use. Nevertheless, it remains true that it is God who meets children through the Bible and their encounters with it.

Lastly, in thinking about what teachers wish to accomplish, it is helpful to remember that teaching Bible to children is important both for the present and the future. Think again about the young boy in our opening illustration who knew the end of Jesus' story, or about the boy who figured out that he was one of the Good Shepherd's sheep. It is clear that the Bible story each of these children were learning about meant something significant to each of them in their present experience. For one, the story of Jesus' resurrection meant joy. For the other, the story of the Good Shepherd meant love and belonging. These understandings will go with these two young boys into their *future* interpretations of both the Bible and of life. Indeed, as children continue to grow and develop *cognitively* and *affectively*, they will incorporate their present thoughts and feelings about biblical narratives into a further interpretation—one that can represent growth and can itself continue to grow and deepen. It should be pointed out that as children develop cognitively and emotionally, their initial interpretations of the Bible and its contents can either cohere or contradict with their later interpretations, sometimes both. This means that children often will need to "unlearn" their previous understanding of a Bible story when that understanding no longer makes sense to them. This does not mean, however, that the child was "wrong" in his or her previous interpretation. Rather, "learning, unlearning, and relearning" is integral to the development of a maturing Christian faith.

The role of the teacher

From all that has been said so far, one could conclude that I think teaching the Bible with children involves an "anything goes" approach. If children are the ones who should ask their own questions and make their own interpretations, then how can teachers correct children who have clearly misinterpreted a Bible story's meaning? Doesn't what I have said so far imply that children are to be left alone to make their own interpretations of the Bible and its contents and that we, as their teachers, should only smile approvingly at what they have said? Certainly not. Children's interpretations, such as "God was mean to make all those people die in the sea" or "Jesus was a magician,"[7] present real challenges for teachers and important learning opportunities for children.

On the one hand, teachers must resist the temptation to rush into a child's interpretive process too quickly to provide the "right" answer about God's character or Jesus' divinity. After all, by initially concluding that God is mean or that Jesus is a magician, a child is only trying to make sense of the story he or she has heard. Rushing in to provide the "right" answer for children is often motivated by the desire to protect them from thinking the "wrong" thing about God or the Bible. However, it incorrectly presupposes that what the teacher says (the "right" answer") will easily replace what the child has thought (the "wrong" answer). More often, what happens when teachers rush to correct children is that children "simply learn to keep those understandings private, while complying with adults' demands, and they go 'underground.'"[8] However, on the other hand, the conclusion that God is mean or that Jesus is a magician cannot go unaddressed by the teacher or the rest of the class. Here the teacher must take an active part in helping children in the process of learning together about the meaning of the story.

This can best be done, I think, by intentionally striking up a conversation. For example, when a child concludes that God is mean, it is time for the teacher to begin a conversation. The conversation might begin with some questions of clarification, such as, "Tell me why you think that God is mean" or "Is God only mean in this story, or is God nice in this story too?" The teacher might ask the child, and any other children present, to tell about when God is nice in this story. Do the children know any other stories about God where God is nice? What stories do they know? Of course, if the children cannot think of any stories to tell, the teacher must continue by saying something like, "I can think of a story where God is very nice and loving. Let me tell it to you." Here, the teacher could tell the story of how God made the world, or perhaps the story of God's sending Jesus to be born at Christmas.

In this way a teacher is able to challenge a child's initial interpretation— God is mean—without simply labeling this first interpretation as either wrong or bad. After telling a story about God's love, a teacher might then ask the children some additional questions. For example: "Does your mom or dad ever get angry with you?" or "Do you think they still love you, even if they get angry?" (It is important to assure children who are not sure about this and that their parents do love them, even if they get angry.) Allowing children to relate God's anger and love to a parent's anger and love may help them to understand that God can be angry, but God still loves us, even as our parents do.

Of course, striking up a conversation to help children articulate and refine their interpretations of biblical content does not always fix a child's questions or concerns. It does, however, teach children that it is possible and desirable to talk together about Bible stories and what they mean. It also helps children learn that not everyone will understand a Bible story the same way that they do. Having conversation together can sometimes call forth the children's new thoughts and additional questions. Providing this kind of conversation between teachers and children and between the children themselves is an essential part of a Bible teacher's role.

In addition, teachers have the responsibility of providing activities and experiences that will encourage and help children interact with the Bible and its contents. A more detailed discussion about how to select and carry out such activities follows below. More than merely a craft project to keep children occupied, these activities and experiences will assist children in thinking and feeling about the Bible story. Recall that the young boy who heard the story of the Good Shepherd came to the conclusion that he was one of the sheep only as he drew his picture of what the story was about. Keys to providing activities and experiences to help children engage the Bible story are freedom, variety, acceptance, and appropriateness.

Most Sunday school curricula suggest one activity per session for all children. While this can be appropriate, I prefer to provide children with a variety of supplies—crayons, paper, clay, glue, scissors, stickers, magazines, and the like—so the children may decide for themselves how and what they will use to respond to a Bible story. Allowing children to select which materials to work with in responding to a Bible story gives them some freedom to engage the activities that appeal to them in that moment. In this way, children are invited to think and wonder some more about the story they have just heard.

However, freedom to choose should not be equated with a lack of direction or with chaos in the classroom. Some children will be able to choose materials and get to work. Others, however, may not know what they wish to do or may become frustrated in trying something. Teachers must be ready to assist these children in deciding and perhaps even to work with them on their chosen activity. Additionally, sometimes it is appropriate or desirable for children and their teachers to work together on a single activity—acting out the story together, for example, or making a large collage together. Working together on a project can foster a sense of community in the class and children often delight in seeing the finished product—something they helped to make. Whether individual or communal activities seem most appropriate to experiencing the Bible story, the products of these activities belong to the children. Here I mean to suggest something more than that they should be allowed to take their products home at the end of class.

Recognizing that children of different ages will engage in activities with differing capacities, teachers do best when they interact with a child's finished product, asking the child to share with them about what it is and what it means. This is a more appropriate response than attempts to control a child's product in some way. I once observed a public elementary school teacher who invited her class to make big, red, shiny apples out of construction paper. She had carefully cut out the apple shapes, leaves, and stems for the children to use. When the children had finished making their apples, the teacher appropriately invited them to show them to one another. One child had chosen to glue the stem and leaves for the apple in a place other than the top. The teacher "corrected" the child's work by removing the leaves and stems the child had affixed, showing her instead where they "belonged."

As I watched the child, it became clear that she was no longer interested at all in either apples or her apple. Instead, she was embarrassed in front of her classmates and disheartened. Her apple no longer belonged to her. Instead of "fixing" the girl's apple, the teacher might have said, "I like your apple very much, but I see that it is different from the way most apples look. Why did you make your apple this way?" In this way, the teacher would have respected the child's apple as her own, avoided embarrassing the child in front of her peers, and perhaps even encouraged her developing skills as an artist. I have always wondered if that child had a reason for making her apple the way she did.

Lastly, teachers have the delightful privilege—and sometimes challenging responsibility—of loving children and welcoming them as fellow learners about the Bible and its stories of God's love and care. While this may seem like an obvious point, the importance of a teacher's genuine love for the children with whom he or she works cannot be overestimated. In learning Bible stories, teachers and children embark on a common journey and an amazing adventure. Trust, courage, curiosity, and love on the part of both children and teachers make the journey possible and make the adventure rewarding. Teachers can help trust, courage, curiosity, and love to flourish in the lives of children by being trustworthy, courageous, curious, and loving themselves. Thus, the role of the teacher is to strive for an environment "marked by a deep respect for and acceptance of children as children, as human beings, and as God's people. We are to greet and honor them as members, along with us, in the household of faith and as companions on the pilgrim way.[9]

Teaching the Bible to children under age 6

Before turning our attention to some suggestions for teaching the Bible with children under age 6, I want to return to the questions and concerns raised at the beginning of this chapter. There we asked, "Are children, especially young children, capable of understanding Bible stories? Are they ready for the complexities and questions they will encounter in the biblical narratives? Can children engage the Bible in ways that don't just confuse them at best, or cause them harm at worst?" Children are indeed capable of understanding the Bible in ways that are both significant and useful to them. Once we as teachers are convinced of this, and when we as teachers understand the nature of our roles in helping children to experience Bible stories, I believe it becomes possible to put aside many of our worries and to plunge ahead into the adventure of experiencing the Bible with them.

How can teachers of young children plan and execute age-appropriate activities and teaching times for children under age 6? Some preliminary discussion of this can be found above, particularly in the section "The role of the teacher." What follows here is a more detailed discussion about what to expect developmentally from children this age, as well as additional suggestions for engaging children in the activity of learning Bible stories. I will conclude this section with one possible format for organizing the study of a Bible story in a one-hour Sunday school class format.

As most scholars are quick to point out, children under age 6 have not yet developed the capacities to think either logically or abstractly. See the chapter

"The Child Grew: Understanding Children's Development." At this age, children move easily and unselfconsciously from one experience to another, and have no interest in logical consistency. Thus, they have almost no ability to relate one situation with another or one conclusion with another. Upon hearing one Bible story, a child under age 6 might conclude that God is nice, but upon hearing a different Bible story might conclude that God is not nice. This represents no contradiction for the younger child, nor will a teacher's pointing out the contradiction make any sense to the child.

Children at this age truly enjoy being told stories, but cannot reflect abstractly about a story's larger meaning. Although young children can recall a few details from a particular story, they will not yet be able to repeat the story in its sequential entirety. Let us illustrate our discussion here, using the miracle story of the feeding of 5,000 people. We might expect a 4- or 5-year-old to recall that some people were hungry, they sat on the ground, and Jesus fed them. Fragments of the story have been used and no causal relationships have been suggested. We may ask questions. Why did Jesus feed the people? Because they were hungry. How did Jesus do that? He just did. Given the opportunity to explore and muse, to talk about and ask questions of the story, the children may move beyond the terse "just are" responses. "Jesus is like my mommy. She puts the potatoes on the table. I eat them. They're good." A child may wish to relate a story of going to a restaurant, of a picnic, or of foods he or she likes.[10]

It is worth noticing some important things happening in this illustration. First, the children have enjoyed hearing a story about hungry people being fed by Jesus and can remember some of the details. In addition, they have been able to relate the people's experiences with hunger and being fed to their own experiences at home, on a picnic, or at a restaurant. However, they are not yet able to develop an interpretation of the story that goes beyond the details. That is, they do not draw any conclusions about who Jesus must be to feed so many people with just a few loaves of bread and some fish.

In truth, who Jesus must be in order to feed 5,000 people is not what intrigues children of this age about the story. Rather, what interests them is that Jesus feeds the hungry people, just the way their mom or dad feeds them when they are hungry. That is why in response to the teacher's questions, young children may want to tell their own story about eating. When this happens, teachers can sometimes feel as though they have failed in their teaching task, because young children seem to suddenly begin talking about something other than the Bible story. However, to draw such a conclusion of failure is incorrect. The young child who wants to tell his or her own story about being hungry or about eating is really experiencing the story on the level appropriate to his or her age and developmental stage. The teaching of the Bible story has been a success! The child has done the interpretive work of relating the feeding of the 5,000 in the Bible to his or her own experience of dinnertime or a picnic. Of course, when the child hears this story again at an older age, different questions will be asked and different interpretations will be made. For now, however, we can conclude that the children in our illustration have both heard and understood the story in ways that are meaningful and significant to them.

Children at this age use their imaginations as well, but their imaginations are bound by the concrete, physical world they know. Children under age 6 love to pretend and will do so using the physical world as their referent. Thus, when children at this age describe God, for example, they will do so in anthropomorphic terms. God will have physical characteristics—hair, eyes, nose, hands, and feet—and most likely will be thought to be like an important adult in the child's life—perhaps a parent, pastor, or teacher. It is not necessary, for teachers to worry about children's conceptions of God being anthropocentric at this age. After all, young children really have no other way of imagining who God is or what God might look like. To tell a young child that God is invisible or that God is a spirit will only confuse the child. Later, as children develop *cognitively* and *affectively*, their anthropomorphic understanding of what God looks like can be challenged and encouraged to grow by a sensitive teacher. For now, however, thinking of God as being like their parent, pastor, or another important figure in their lives means simply that children are using what they know (what adults look like) to make sense of what they are being asked to imagine (what God looks like).

When it comes to teaching Bible stories to young children, teachers can tap into the enthusiasm for hearing stories at this age by remembering a few simple things. Because children at this age love to imagine, why not try asking them to close their eyes and imagine pictures in their mind that go with the story as you tell it. When you have finished the story, ask children if they want to tell you about the pictures they imagined.

As another technique, try moving around as you tell the story. Don't be afraid to show emotion on your face, to change the sound of your voice to indicate surprise, or to clap your hands when you are happy. If there is a parade or a journey in the story, invite the children to come along with you. Move around the classroom as you go on your journey together.

After telling the story, it is time to have some conversation about it. It is helpful to have several questions prepared in advance, remembering, of course, that children of this age cannot think logically or abstractly. Rather than focusing on "getting the details correct" in the conversation time, teachers should concentrate their efforts on evoking from the children what they heard, liked, or had questions about in the story. It is not necessary, or even desirable for the teacher to "answer" these questions. More important is that young children have the chance to ask them and to offer their interpretations of what the story means to them.

After conversation starts to disintegrate, it is time to invite young children into an activity that allows them to further consider the story while doing something with their bodies. You can encourage children to draw a picture or make something with clay. They could also reenact the story if they would like. For example, in teaching the feeding of 5,000 people, a teacher could bring out a loaf of bread or the day's snack. Then ask if anyone would like to pretend that they are Jesus and feed their friends here at Sunday school. This may involve acting out the story several times so that every child who wants to can have the opportunity to distribute bread. If the children are shy about doing such an activity, the teacher should take the first turn at pretending to be Jesus. He or she can ask all the children to sit down, just as Jesus did in the story. Once the teacher has reenacted the story, other young children may be willing to give it a try.

At first, this may sound like a lot to accomplish in 45 minutes or an hour. Can all that has been suggested be done? I think so. In my work with children this age, I have followed a class format like the one described below.

Gathering time

Welcome the children as they enter the classroom and invite them to wait with you for everyone else to arrive. Show them where they can sit (perhaps a circle on the floor) and sit with them. Tell the children that you are glad to see them and look forward to being with them today. When most of the children have arrived, invite them to get ready for the story by asking them to be quiet and to say a prayer with you. This prayer should be simple, perhaps something like, "Dear God, thank you for our Sunday school class and for everyone who is here today. Amen."

Story time

Tell the children you have a wonderful story to share with them. You can invite the children to close their eyes and imagine pictures while they listen. If you prefer, you can gather their attention by moving around as you tell the story. As you tell the story, pause occasionally to invite them into the storytelling process. You might ask questions like, "What do you think will happen next?" or "I wonder if . . ."

Conversation time

Thank the children for listening to the story. Let them know that now is the time for them to talk about the story with you and with one another. As a transition from sitting to the coming activity, you might invite the children to gather at another location in the classroom. It is often effective to ask, "I wonder . . ." kinds of questions to get them talking about the story. For example: "I wonder how the people felt when Jesus gave them something to eat?" or "I wonder if you can think of a time when you were hungry?" Perhaps while the children are getting ready to use crayons and paper, begin to ask some additional questions about what happened in the story. If the children are interested in acting out the story, some conversation can occur while everyone is getting ready for the activity. Remember to allow every child an opportunity to respond to a question you have asked and to respect a child's right to pass.

Activity time

While the children are involved in the activity/activities for the day, further conversation about what children are doing or making naturally occurs. Be sure to allow plenty of time to help each child complete the activity to the best of her or his own abilities.

Leaving time

When the time for class to end approaches, invite the children to gather again in a circle on the floor and sit with them. Thank them for their participation in today's Sunday school and tell them how much you enjoyed seeing them. Invite them to come back whenever they want to. Then ask them to say a short prayer with you, something like, "Dear God, thank you for loving us and being with us all the time. Amen."

The above class structure is only one suggestion, of course. Each teacher should adapt this structure to best suit the needs of the children who are present. It is less important to get everything done than it is to be actively involved with the children as they hear the Bible story and interact with it. Such active involvement in and with these young children will help them experience Bible stories in ways appropriate to their age and their natural curiosity for listening to a good story.

Teaching the Bible to children ages 6 to 9

When children reach the age of 5 or 6, *cognitive* and *affective* changes begin to occur that directly impact the ways that they will experience and interact with Bible stories.[11] Children in these middle years often "appear to be more restrained in their use of imagination, fantasy, metaphoric language, and pretend play. They are not as inventive as they once were and not as enthusiastic about participating in certain activities."[11]

What is happening here? Children from ages 6 to 9 undergo a process of growth and development that results in both a shift of focus in what interests them, and a growing awareness of their own new cognitive abilities. Such changes can be exciting, and often a little frightening to the children. Children in these middle years have a wider range of experiences upon which to draw and to reflect. They have entered school and they find themselves asking more and different kinds of questions about what they experience. They become interested in collecting information and gathering facts about almost everything, including the Bible and its contents. Where once they did not have the interest or ability to repeat the details of a biblical narrative, children in these middle years are capable or remembering and repeating stories sequentially and enjoy doing so.

In addition, for the first time perhaps, the question "Is it true?" fascinates them. Moreover, they become increasingly aware of "the rules"—parental rules, teacher's rules, and God's rules—and how to apply them to their lives. Events, stories, and actions are either clearly "right" or "wrong." Children who experience the Bible and its narratives at this age will interpret them in these kinds of concrete and literal ways. They will want to know if the stories they hear about and read about in the Bible are "true" or if they are "just stories." Such questions present both wonderful opportunities and clear challenges for their teachers.

Children ages 6 and 9 have entered a new stage of development in their own interpretive abilities. Teachers can help children in these middle years to develop their abilities by thinking and wondering along with them both about the details presented in Bible stories and about what Bible stories can mean for them. Each of these activities is essential, and each requires a different kind of conversational atmosphere. Questions such as "How many books are there in the Bible?" or "What did God create on the first day?" stimulate children's newly found capacities and interests for learning and recalling the information they are gathering about the Bible and its contents. Questions such as "Why do you think Jesus welcomed the children when the disciples did not?" or "What do you think this story is about?" encourage children to move beyond thinking about information alone toward attempts to articulate the meanings contained in the Bible story itself.

Many of the questions that children of this age will ask their teachers about the Bible and its contents cannot be answered with factual information. For example, I once had a third-grader ask me how Noah kept the animals from eating each other while they were on the ark. I must admit that until she asked her question I had never thought about it! I responded by admitting that the story doesn't tell us how Noah did that. Then I asked her, "What do you think? How *did* Noah keep all the animals from eating each other while they were on the ark?" She thought for a minute and then said, "I don't know. I guess God must have helped him do that." "Yes," I replied, "I'm sure God took care of everyone on the ark."

Perhaps my conversation with this third-grader is a good way to begin thinking about how teachers of children at this age can plan and execute age-appropriate ways to engage children in the activities of learning about and understanding Bible stories. In designing classroom experiences for these children, I suggest a more interactive style of storytelling. That is, instead of either asking children only to listen to the story as you tell it, or asking them to read it aloud, I have found that telling the story together works best. Remember that children this age have different levels of ability with regard to reading and it can be frustrating or intimidating to ask all the children to take turns reading.

For example, instead of reading a story and asking children for their thoughts about it—a format that becomes tiresome week after week—why not spend several class sessions writing a skit or play about the particular story the class is studying?[12] Such a multi-session project puts learning the details about the Bible story into an intriguing context for children this age—they are being asked to learn about the story for the purpose of writing a skit together about it. After finding the story in their Bibles and following along while the teacher reads it, children can be encouraged to begin planning their skit. Who are the characters in the story that should be in our skit? What is happening in the story? What happens at the beginning of the story? The middle? How does the story end? What kinds of props and other things will we need for our skit? How can we make them together here at Sunday school? What will the characters in our skit say? What will they do? As the class works together, they will also talk with one another about the story and how best to act it out. Teachers should take an active role in facilitating this process but should still allow children to make their own decisions about dialogue and plot whenever possible.

I once helped some second-graders prepare a skit about the Christmas story. In that skit, the child playing Mary decided that she should tell the angel Gabriel, "I can't have a baby if I don't have a husband! I'm not that kind of girl!" In this way children are learning and interacting in significant ways with biblical materials. Their skit is becoming their own interpretation of the Bible story and its meaning for them.

Once the details of dialogue and action for the skit have been agreed upon, children will want to perform the skit, first for themselves and for the teacher, and perhaps later for others. Children under age 6, who truly enjoy stories, make the perfect audience for the skit. Younger children will enjoy hearing the story and seeing older children as characters in the story. Children from 6 to 9 years of age will enjoy the development of their skit, the acting, and the response of their young audience.

Another way to stimulate interest and imagination with regard to Bible stories at this age is to ask children to imagine with the teacher what people in the story might have said or done that isn't in the story itself. For example, ask children to imagine what Noah and his family did on the ark during those 40 days of rain. What did they talk about, I wonder? What did they do when they weren't feeding the animals? How did they feel when they finally got off the ark? Such imaginative activity helps children venture beyond the "facts" of the story into the realm of interpreting the meaning of the story in ways that make sense to them.

The structure of a particular class session will be more flexible and diverse for children this age. It remains essential to welcome the children into the classroom, to give them opportunities to pray, and to engage the Bible and its contents. Just how these activities follow upon one another will depend in large part on the directions in which the class, the teacher, and the curriculum are moving. Children at this age should each have a Bible they can use at Sunday school. But they cannot be expected to remember to "bring them from home," so Bibles that stay in the classroom should be provided for them.

At the end of this chapter, I offer my suggestion for Bibles appropriate to this age group. I recommend purchasing and placing tabs in each child's Bible as well, to help children find the books of the Bible with ease. In addition to Bibles, children at this age will enjoy maps of Israel, drawings of the temple in Jerusalem, and other kinds of reference materials that help them visualize what they are learning about. The children will also take pleasure in the challenge of a Bible treasure hunt, where they are asked to find answers to particular questions by looking up specific verses in the Bible. For example, a question might read, "What gifts did the wise men bring to Jesus when he was born? For the answer, look at Matthew 2:11." With help and encouragement, children at this age can become skilled at looking things up in their Bibles and will enjoy doing so. Many curricula for this age group include such activities. I encourage their use—not as an end in themselves or as substitute for learning Bible stories—but as another tool that can help children at this age to engage the Bible and its contents in meaningful and enjoyable ways.

Teaching the Bible to children ages 9 to 12

As children continue to mature and to make their transition into adolescence, they once again enter into a new phase in the ongoing development of their *cognitive*, *affective*, and *social* abilities. Unfortunately, they often express a lack of interest in the Bible and its contents at this age as well. Children in the later years of childhood "often resist engagements with the Bible, complaining, 'That's the same old stuff. We've already done that. We know all that. Can't we do something else?' Their complaint describes an attitude or posture toward the Bible that can persist throughout adulthood." [13] Experiencing the Bible with children in ways that are significant for them during these years can appear to be an uphill battle, but it needn't be so. Certainly teachers cannot force preadolescents to be interested in the Bible and its contents. However, they can help to create both a challenging and a freeing environment in their classrooms—one that may encourage these older children to meet the Bible in ways they have not encountered it before.

Preadolescents begin to possess the capacity to move beyond the confines of the concrete world of cause and effect, right and wrong, when engaging in interpretive activities. They are interested in moving beyond the question "Is it true?" when encountering Bible stories. Indeed, the nature of what constitutes truth and what makes something true has taken on some significant new dimensions. *Cognitively,* children at this age are able to develop concepts that are somewhat abstract in nature. In addition, their *affective* experiences of love, friendship and the like take on a multi-dimensional shape and are recognized as existing in realms other than the immediate family. Moreover, preadolescents are developing a much more sophisticated understanding of time and historical sequence. Whereas this ability is largely absent in younger children, at this age children can understand the differences between 100 years ago, 1,000 years ago, last year, and next year.

All these newly emerging capacities have clear implications for teaching the Bible with children between the ages of 9 and 12. Their growing abilities to move beyond the confines of the concrete world of "experiences they have had" means that the function and use of metaphor and of the imagination can become intriguing once again. While children in the middle years tend to resist relating to these aspects of the biblical narratives, preadolescents are well equipped to grasp the purposes and the power of this kind of language in the biblical text. Children at this age should be invited to notice and identify the various kinds of literature contained within the Bible—poems, parables, songs, histories, Gospels, epistles, and visions. In this way the Bible can become for them a more complex and interesting text than they might have previously thought.

Similarly, preadolescents' growing capacities to articulate their own emotions and empathize with the emotions of others means that they are able to understand that people have different ways of understanding and responding to the same event or situation. At this age, children can begin to understand some of the emotional complexities contained in Bible stories. They can grasp, for example, the reality that some people responded with joy to what Jesus did and taught, while others were fearful or distrustful of his actions and his words. In addition, they possess an increased ability to articulate the emotional states experienced by those they meet in the biblical accounts. Preadolescents are able to understand at a deeper level the reluctance Jonah felt when God asked him to go to Nineveh and prophesy, or the fear and disbelief Mary experienced in learning she was pregnant. Thus, these older children not only relate to the Bible story at a more sophisticated *cognitive* and *affective* level. But through their engagement with the Bible and its contents, preadolescents can also come to understand their own *cognitive* and *affective* responses to the events and situations in their lives. Their own experiences of fear, reluctance, and joy are mirrored for them in biblical narratives.

Because children at this age are developing a more sophisticated understanding of time and the sequence of history, teachers should encourage them to begin to put the Bible accounts into their historical contexts. Because children at this age are able to distinguish between the time in history when Abraham lived, the time in history when Jesus lived, and the time in history when the apostle Paul lived, teachers can and should be more explicit about contextualizing the biblical narratives in this fashion. Whereas for younger children Bible stories tend to "stand alone" without any clear relationship to one another, these older children are capable of beginning to think of the Bible and its contents as the story of God's activities in the world over time.

To recognize that preadolescents have these new and exciting *cognitive*, *affective*, and *social* capabilities is not the same thing as asserting that they will always want to employ them in their study of the Bible. The application of their newly developing capacities to the study of the Bible will not occur naturally or spontaneously. Therefore, "a primary task of any teaching is to challenge and call the learners to use their abilities as fully as possible." [14] How can this best be done?

Teachers of preadolescents can challenge and encourage them to take notice of the fact that in the Bible, many stories are told more than once. In Genesis, for example, there are two accounts of God's creation of the world. In the Gospels, we find many stories from the life of Jesus told more than once, each from the perspective of the particular author. There are multiple accounts of the resurrection, the feeding of the 5,000, the Sermon on the Mount, and so forth. Children at this age should be encouraged to compare and contrast these accounts.

A teacher might begin a class session of this kind by telling the children that they will be having a visitor in class today. Ask them to watch and listen carefully to what the visitor has to say. Let the children know that you will be discussing what happened after the visitor leaves. The visitor could be any adult. The visitor should address the children briefly, perhaps sharing a story of something that happened to them during the preceding week. The story need not be complicated and should not be "heavy." When the visitor leaves, the children should be asked to write answers individually to questions like the following: What was our visitor wearing? What happened at the beginning of their story? How did his or her story end? What was the most interesting part of his or her story? Once everyone has had the chance to prepare answers individually, the class should share what they observed together, with the teacher listing their observations and thoughts on paper or a chalkboard. What will become apparent is that different children observed different kinds of details and remembered different parts of the content of the story. Such an activity provides a good context for the further activity of comparing and contrasting different biblical accounts of the same event.

Working together as a class or in small groups, children can then take a look at the two Genesis accounts of creation, or any other story told more than once in the Bible. Ask the children to identify what the similarities and differences are between the two accounts? The teacher can list the similarities and differences noticed by students on paper or a chalkboard. Once the children have developed their lists, teachers can offer their own observations about any similarity and difference that the students may not have noticed. Further conversation about these accounts could proceed, with the teacher asking questions such as these: "What do you think are the most important parts of each story? What do you think each story wants to tell us? Why do you think there are differences between the stories? Could you make one story out of these different stories? What do you think the stories want to tell us about the world and about you and me?"[15]

Even though preadolescents are certainly capable of engaging in an activity like this, it is worth remembering that they will respond to these kinds of questions in ways different from the ways adults might respond to them. They may not know why accounts differ or why some elements in each account remain the same. They may hesitate to share their thoughts about what the stories are trying to communicate to them about themselves or about the world. Here teachers once again must take an active role in helping children talk about their thoughts and feelings. Teachers should feel free to share their own thoughts about these questions, not as "the expert," but as someone who has also given time and attention to the questions being asked.

Another effective way of encouraging preadolescents to bring their developing *cognitive* and *affective* abilities to bear on their study of the Bible is to challenge them to take a closer look at the parables of Jesus. What follows here is one example of how to invite children of this age to encounter the parable of the laborers in the vineyard (Matthew 20:1-16).

Preadolescents are beginning to examine their own understandings of fairness, justice, and equality. That all the laborers in the vineyard received the same wage regardless of the number of hours worked tends to challenge and upset popular notions of fairness and justice. Let the children engage the story, and encourage them to tell and share their reactions to the parable. Use questions such as the following to further the discussion:

- Have you ever had a similar experience at home or school?

- How did you feel in that experience?

- How would you feel if you had been one of the people who had worked the long hours?

By paying attention to the children's responses, you can move to new questions about the parable. Here are some examples:

- Were those who had worked the most hours justified in their complaints?

- What promises were made to each group of workers going to the vineyard?

- Were those promises kept?

- Who determined what was "just"? Did that person have a right to make that determination?

- Does the parable suggest how God may regard and treat us?

The children may generate a large range of questions about and responses to the parable. They can converse and challenge each other as they work for new understandings. Adults can take part in the conversations, giving expression to their own understandings, setting forth their own questions of the parable, and offering their own responses.[16]

There are a number of good reasons to study parables at this age, as well as good reasons to study them together. First, parables resist simplistic interpretation and "one right answer." This is an effective way of encouraging preadolescents to use all their abilities to try to understand all that Jesus is trying to illustrate about God, the world, and human living with this parable.

Second, parables present an interesting way to renew the interest of many children this age that may think that they already know everything about what is in the Bible. Parables also introduce the children to the fact that Jesus was someone who taught about God and taught by means of telling parables like these. Jesus told parables to many different kinds of people in many different kinds of settings. It might be interesting to ask preadolescents why they think Jesus chose to teach us about God by using parables. Why didn't Jesus just tell people what to think? It is even interesting to show children that others in the Bible used parables to communicate about God and human living. See, for example, the conversation between Nathan and David in 2 Samuel 12. By studying several biblical parables together, children at this age are invited to ask different kinds of questions, hear things they have not heard before, and capture a vision of the meaning of the Bible and its contents that were not available to them before developmentally. In this way, older children can continue to develop their own interpretive skills. They can still be involved in learning new ways to experience the Bible as a book that has meaning and significance for them and for their lives.

Offering children opportunities to compare and contrast two or more accounts of the same Bible story or inviting them to study the parables in the Bible with you are only two suggestions for ways that effectively teach the Bible at this age. Certainly, other activities and experiences can and should be utilized. Before turning our attention to teaching the Bible with children in settings other than the Sunday school classroom, however, I want to mention an additional activity that may help preadolescents learn to make connections between the Bible and their own lives.

Children ages 9 to 12 have begun to observe that there is sometimes a connection or disconnection between what people say and what people do. In their encounters with Bible stories, older children have come to understand that people in the Bible not only talked about what they believed but that they acted on what they believed as well. I have found a real passion in older children for working together on a project that serves others outside their immediate peer group. Such a project need not be elaborate, costly, or overly time consuming. What I am suggesting is that preadolescents are ready to try putting into practice what they are learning in the Bible about God and God's gracious dealings with the world. Perhaps these children could prepare and mail Easter greeting cards to church members who are homebound. Perhaps as a class they could bake bread for communion. Ideas for age-appropriate projects will depend, of course, on the contexts, interests, and abilities of both teacher and students. However, the benefit of working together on such projects cannot be overestimated. Not only will children be challenged to put their faith into practice, but during the course of the planning and executing of the project, many rich conversations about what they are doing and why they are doing it can take place.

Far from being an uphill battle, teaching the Bible with preadolescents can be an exciting, life-giving endeavor for all who participate. Older children have an increasing range of experiences and abilities that can be brought to bear in their conversations about the Bible and its contents. From their teachers, these children need the time, freedom, and encouragement to test out what they are learning and to make their own interpretations about the significance of what they are learning for their own lives. Whatever methods and activities teachers use to foster this activity, they should always strive "to serve as channels through which the Bible may make its claims and promises, and evoke from the children their responses."[17]

Teaching the Bible to children in worship and at home

Although we are perhaps most accustomed to thinking of teaching the Bible with children within the context of the Sunday school classroom, children's experiences with the Bible are not and should not be confined to this arena alone. Indeed, much of what has already been said in this chapter about the role of teachers and learners in the classroom can be effectively applied to experiencing the Bible with children in the worship hour and at home. For many children, in fact, their initial experiences of the Bible and its contents will occur at home or in the worship service. What follows here, then, are a few suggestions for enriching a child's experience of the Bible in these settings.

Children's most direct access to the Bible during worship occurs in the reading of the lessons, psalm, and Gospel—often followed by a children's sermon. Children should be encouraged to listen to the readings from the Bible, as they are able. For younger children, an adult sitting in the pew can call attention to the readings by saying something like, "Now we are going to hear a story from the Bible. Would you like to sit on my lap while we listen?" Older children can be invited to listen to the readings as well, or even better, to look up these readings in their Bibles and follow along. Of course, adults sitting with children should be ready to help them find the appropriate passages, perhaps even marking them before worship begins. Those sitting with children during this part of the worship hour need not be anxious if a child's attention for this activity wanders a bit. The ability to keep attention to the readings will develop over time, especially if such attention is encouraged from an early age.

In many congregations the liturgy includes a children's sermon, often located after the reading of the day's Gospel. This can be a significant opportunity for children to think, wonder, and feel about Bible stories. People differ in their opinions concerning the value and appropriateness of a special sermon or message for children within the worship setting. However, when such a time focuses around the appointed readings and the good news of God's love and care contained within them, I believe the practice has value. Not only will children experience God's address to them, as adults do in the sermon, but children will be learning that an important part of the liturgy involves listening to God's word and responding to it. The purpose of a children's sermon should always be the proclamation of God's love and grace to the children gathered there, rather than on either entertainment of children (or adults) or simplistic moralizing with children. In the parish I attend, the children's sermon is truly for the children. Often we adults cannot hear well what is happening between the pastor and the children. I have sometimes thought this gives me the experience that children often have in worship, namely, to wait quietly while something I cannot grasp fully is occurring!

In addition, a children's sermon represents an important chance for children to interact with their pastor or other adult member of the congregation. These sermons often either begin or end with a brief prayer, and should not be overly complicated. It is helpful to remember that most children are not capable of recalling the sequential details in the Bible stories and should not be asked to do so "on demand." If the children's sermon focuses on one or another of the details from the readings, children should be reminded of these at the beginning of the sermon. In addition, abstract theological conceptions are too difficult for children to grasp or reflect upon in a children's sermon. The children's sermon is a proclamation event, that is, it is an event where children have the opportunity to hear God's gracious word of grace proclaimed to them in the context of the community's worship hour. As such, it can be a powerful and meaningful time of connection with the Bible for children.

Likewise, children will enjoy experiencing the Bible at home with members of their families. Dinnertime and bedtime represent two good opportunities for interacting with the Bible during the week. As I was growing up, my family would pause after dinner once or twice a week to read a Bible story together. (We sat at the dinner table and didn't clean up the dishes until afterward.) When I was very young, one of my parents would read the story. Then everyone around the table would have the chance to say something about the story they liked, and something about the story they didn't understand. As I grew older, I was invited to be a reader, and also to share my favorite part of the story and ask my questions. In this way, I remember learning as a young child that my parents, and not just our pastor, read the Bible and talked about God.

In many families, stories are read with children at bedtime. One of these bedtime stories can be a Bible story. Below I have suggested Bibles that are appropriate for children of all ages. Reading Bible stories together at home— snuggled in bed—allows children to hear and respond to the Bible in a familiar and comfortable setting. Here, children can experience the freedom and the time both to listen and to ask their questions with the members of their families. In this way, the Bible and its contents become an important part of the family and its life together. When children grow "too old" for bedtime stories, they can nevertheless be encouraged to interact with the Bible at home, perhaps in the way described in the previous paragraph.

"He raises from the dead. It's really cool!"

To provide engaging and life-giving opportunities for children to experience the Bible and its stories of God's love and grace is a fundamental duty and delight for all Christian people. In their encounters with the Bible, children will find much about which they will think, feel, and ponder as they grow into the practice of their own lives of faith. Along the way, children will need encouragement and assistance in making the Bible a central part of their world of experiences. In their interactions with the Bible, children will learn many things, and begin to understand themselves as a part of the ongoing story of the people of God. Most importantly, they will be invited over and over again to meet the God who loves them and to respond to God's love for them with wonder and with joy.

FOR REFLECTION AND DISCUSSION

- Who first taught you about the Bible and its message of God's love and grace? How old were you?

- What do you think it means to understand the Bible? How has your understanding of the Bible grown and developed over the years?

- In what ways do you interact with the Bible today? How does the Bible help you make sense of your life and your experiences?

- What criteria should be used to evaluate a specific educational curriculum for its usefulness in your classrooms and homes?

- How can children of differing ages learn about the Bible from one another? How can they learn about the Bible together? What kinds of settings are most profitable for their learning about the Bible together?

- How can teachers, parents, and congregation members form effective partnerships in teaching the Bible with children?

Notes

1. Christian educators have differed significantly in recent decades as to whether it is appropriate to teach Bible stories with children. For example, some have argued that the Bible is not a book for children but rather one for adults. They rightly observe that children do not have the intellectual, experiential, and emotional tools to understand the Bible as adults do. As one scholar has said, "The Bible is certainly an adult book. It was written for adults. . . . It was never intended by its writers as a quarry of stories for children. Neither did its writers intend odd verses to be taken out of context and used for moral instruction of the young" (Jean Holm, "What Shall We Tell the Children?" *Theology* 76, March 1973, p. 141). Other Christian educators have countered that although children are not able to understand the Bible as adults do, they nevertheless must have the opportunity to experience the Bible as children do. Children can think, feel, and wonder about the Bible and the stories they hear from the Bible. These educators believe that to withhold the Bible and its stories from children is to withhold stories that belong to them as young members of the community of faith. As A. Roger and Gertrude G. Gobbel write, "If we can honor and respect the differences of understanding and if we can encourage children to engage the Bible as they are able whenever and wherever they meet it, the concern for reserving the bulk of biblical material until adolescence fades in importance," *The Bible—A Child's Playground* (Philadelphia: Fortress, 1986), p. 9. While it is proper to be concerned for teaching the Bible appropriately to children, the fact remains that it is not possible to withhold the Bible from Christian children—they hear and wonder about Bible stories

both in church and at home. Therefore, I advocate teaching Bible stories with children and believe that children are capable of encountering these stories in ways that are meaningful and important to them.

2. Sofia Cavalletti, *The Religious Potential of the Child: The Description of an Experience with Children from Ages Three to Six*, trans. Patricia M. Coulter and Julie M. Coulter (New York: Paulist, 1979), pp. 65-68. Emphasis mine. Reprinted by permission of Citta Nuova Editrice, Rome, Italy.

3. Gobbel, A. Roger, and Gertrude G. Gobbel, *The Bible: A Child's Playground* (Philadelphia: Fortress, 1986), p. 48.

4. Children should hear the stories and their contents even before they are cognitively capable of repeating the story or its specific contents back to the teacher. Scholars generally agree that such cognitive ability is first present in children ages 6 to 8.

5. Gobbel and Gobbel, p. 48.

6. Ibid., p. 49.

7. Ibid., p. 71. These are quotes from children in a Sunday school class.

8. Ibid., p. 72.

9. Ibid., p. 70.

10. Ibid., p. 102.

11. Ibid., p. 117.

12. Of course, writing a skit every few weeks would become tedious as well. The key to interactive storytelling is to employ a variety of methods to engage children in the biblical narratives to be studied.

13. Gobbel and Gobbel, p. 136.

14. Ibid., p. 141.

15. Ibid., p. 144.

16. Ibid., p. 148.

17. Ibid., p. 156.

CHAPTER 9

Teaching to
Engage Children

Susan Wilds McArver

AND LET NO ONE think himself too wise for
such child's play. Christ, to train men, had to
become man himself. If we wish to train children,
we must become children with them. Would to
God such child's play were widely practiced. In a
short time we would have a wealth of Christian
people whose souls would be so enriched in
Scripture and in the knowledge of God.

— Martin Luther

"The German Mass and Order of Service"
Luther's Works, vol. 53, p. 67

My small class of elementary school children gathered in the church library to begin a new year of studying the Bible. We began with the story of Abraham and Sarah—and the three mysterious strangers who stopped by their tent one day.

We talked about times when we have been strangers ourselves, times when we were new in a school, a group, or a place. We read the story from a children's Bible storybook and talked about the type of life Abraham and Sarah might have led.

I then asked one of the children to look out of the window of the library. To the astonishment of the class, he exclaimed, "There's a tent pitched out there!" In a tiny space of green grass, tucked between the building and the back fence marking the property line, a backpacker's nylon dome tent stood, well-worn and faded, but completely staked out with its front flaps flung open wide.

The class rushed outside to see this marvelous apparition. Inside the tent were greater treasures: soft oriental carpets to sit on (carefully mimicked by colorful beach towels) and simple food and drink that Abraham and Sarah would have known— grapes, pita bread, cheese, and water.

As we sat in our tent munching on our snacks, we asked questions about the story: "I wonder how the strangers felt when they were offered hospitality by the elderly couple who lived in this tent. What sorts of things might Abraham and Sarah have done to refresh travelers at the end of a long journey? How do you think Sarah and Abraham felt when the strangers turned out to be angels of the Lord himself? What kind of hospitality do we offer when friends come to see us? What do we offer to strangers?"

We acted out the story, taking turns playing the roles of Abraham, Sarah, and the visitors. It was a memorable class.

Overview

Students, whether children, youth, or adults, learn best when they are most directly involved as active participants in their own learning. In one sentence, this statement summarizes volumes of research across the last several decades. As discussed in the chapter "The Child Grew: Understanding Children's Development," children go through a variety of developmental stages as they grow toward maturity, while still remaining unique individuals as well. Common to all of the research into developmental stages, however, is the finding that children of all ages absorb information most meaningfully when they are actively involved in the learning process—when heart, soul, body, and mind, are engaged in the task.

Building on previous chapters, this chapter addresses practical issues related to the art of teaching. The first part of this chapter explores six themes found in the writings of Martin Luther, which can stimulate our thinking as we work with children. The second part addresses practical approaches by recommending 10 core principles to keep in mind while preparing active, engaging learning activities for children, and then concludes with a number of useful pedagogical techniques.

Six themes in the writings of Martin Luther

Martin Luther is primarily remembered today as theologian and reformer, and rightly so. But Luther also was profoundly aware of the needs and characteristics of children and how they learn. See the discussion in the chapter "Who Is the Child? Whose Is the Child? A Theology of Children." Part of this awareness stemmed from the many complementary roles Luther played throughout his life. Not only was Luther a biblical professor and church reformer, he also was a pastor and a father. For Luther, none of these roles ever conflicted as he worked to share his textual insights into the meaning of the Scriptures with people of every age and stage of life.

Education proved to be very important from the earliest days of the Reformation. The Reformation was born in a university, and Luther realized quickly that a monumental educational effort stretching well beyond university walls would be needed to undo centuries of what he viewed as misguided teachings. He recognized that a new generation would need to be trained in Protestant teachings if the Reformation itself had any chance of ultimate success. He found it crucial therefore, that pastors, parents, and teachers expend their best efforts in this endeavor.

In addition, Luther's emphasis on the priesthood of all believers meant that the laity needed to be educated just as surely as did the clergy. Because of his emphasis on all work as vocation in the world, Luther became a strong advocate for universal access to education. In a radical move, Luther wrote that education should be reserved not just for the wealthy, not just for the pious, and not just for the boys.[1] The world needed preachers, surely, but no less did it need physicians, jurists, and government officials among others.[2] All religious considerations aside, wrote Luther, "in order to maintain its temporal estate outwardly the world must have good and capable men and women . . . this one consideration alone would be sufficient to justify the establishment everywhere of the very best schools for both boys and girls."[3]

Luther worked constantly to bridge the intersection between his texts, his students, his church, and his world during a time of enormous social, political, and religious transformation. His pedagogy often proved innovative and occasionally, it proved brilliant. He did not have the findings of modern developmental psychologists to inform his work, and frankly, if he had, he probably would have ignored them anyway. Instead, he would still have gone, as he always did, to the Scriptures. Additionally, he coupled his deep study of the Bible with his own acute observations of the world of his parishioners and his own family to produce pedagogy sensitive to the needs of those around him, pedagogy that would engage children on their own level.

Even though Luther lived in a time far different from our own, at least six of his pedagogical insights prove helpful to us as we approach our own teaching with children today. His themes can provide a framework for our own attempts to engage children in the faith and can suggest the methods most helpful for doing so. Teaching that engages children is:

1. Clear, rather than convoluted.

2. Concrete, rather than abstract.

3. Varied, rather than static.

4. Repetitive, rather than isolated.

5. Child-centered, rather than adult-centered.

6. Deeply spiritual, rather than entirely secular.

Examining each of these emphases in turn will provide insight into the ways we engage children in our teaching. First, Luther emphasized that teaching directed toward children—and adults as well—must be clear. Teaching that engages children is teaching children can understand. Luther had an extraordinary ability to put complex theological discussions into the language of ordinary people, including farmers, homemakers, barbers, and children.

Adults serving as teachers often become so accustomed to speaking with adults that they forget that children often have little understanding—or hold a misunderstanding—of words we take for granted. We may therefore unintentionally use vocabulary and syntax that is simply unintelligible to our children. In 1530, Luther warned against this tendency in an essay on the art of translating texts from one language into another. Translators, argued Luther, should not be bound by the literal original language, if in so doing they produced a translation impossible for modern readers to understand. Instead, he wrote, translators should consider the audience for whom they write—"the mother in the home, the children on the street, the common man in the marketplace. We must be guided by their language, the way they speak, and do our translating accordingly. That way they will understand it."[4]

Luther himself proved to be a gifted translator, not only of Latin into German, but also of the difficult into the understandable. Intimately involved in the lives of those around him, his theological expression took on a robustness and immediacy that conveyed the gospel in a way that could not be ignored. Ultimately, scholar Timothy Wengert attributes much of Luther's "pedagogic clarity and simplicity" to one simple source: Luther's own children. Luther, he observes, was one of the first theologians since the early church actually raising children of his own, and thus observing them on a daily basis. This experience, of listening to the simple questions of his children and having to respond to them in ways they could understand, argues Wengert, made a profound impact on Luther the theologian.[5]

Luther considered the work of translating the gospel into clear language crucial to the success of the Reformation. Therefore, although he found himself fighting popes, emperors, princes, infidels, and even other reformers, Luther took time to condense the entire evangelical understanding of the gospel into the Small Catechism, written in language easy enough for a child to understand.

This was not, of course, reducing the gospel to its lowest common denominator. Rather, it was distilling its essence. Luther was not the first to write a catechism; the medieval world was full of them. But as Wengert points out, Luther was "pedagogically light years ahead" of other writers of catechisms of his day. Many medieval catechisms were filled with actually hundreds of detailed questions that covered all of the finer points and details of biblical and systematic theology. Luther, in a single stroke, reduced this plethora of questions to one: *Was ist das?* Literally, "What is this?" or more familiarly, "What does this mean?" [6]

Our teaching, therefore, engages children when it is clear and speaks to children in their own language. We do not use the term *justification* with first-graders, although we may convey to them the truth that God loves them through our words and actions. Using words and experiences that children can understand without confusion and relating to children on their own level makes teaching more alive and meaningful to them.

Second, Luther emphasized the concrete, not the abstract. Teaching that engages children must be specific and pointed, not intangible and theoretical. Citing an ancient Roman writer, Luther reiterated the following belief:

> . . . the very best way to teach is to add an example or illustration to the word, for they help one both to understand more clearly and to remember more easily. Otherwise, if the discourse is heard without an example, no matter how suitable and excellent it may be, it does not move the heart as much, and is also not so clear and easily retained. [7]

Luther lived in a day when students still studied the natural world by merely studying what ancient scholars had said centuries before about nature. Luther rejected this approach and instead urged that children be allowed to study things firsthand—by observation and by experience. He recognized that concrete specifics prove more useful in teaching than vague generalities.

Children become more engaged in a subject when they are given tangible experiences and are not asked to deal with abstractions they are not developmentally able to comprehend. Children can simply read a biblical story about Abraham and Sarah, or they can sit in a tent in the backyard of the church while munching on goat cheese as they talk about Abraham and Sarah's pragmatic experience and relate it to their own.

Third, Luther demonstrated a fundamental understanding that people, whether old or young, vary in the ways they are able to learn and incorporate information. Teaching that engages children therefore utilizes different methods that appeal to different types of learners. Luther did not have the scientific knowledge we have today about the ways children and adults learn, but he recognized that not all learn in the same way. He understood that simply hearing words—even hearing God's word—was not always enough.

When Luther produced the Small Catechism, for example, even the earliest 16th-century copies included illustrations—not just one or two, but a picture for each Commandment and element of the catechism. This innovation, notes Timothy Wengert, meant that even people who were illiterate could still "read" their catechism in much the same way that they could "read" medieval sculpture and stained glass in ancient cathedrals.[8]

Luther and other reformers recognized that images could be powerful tools in the education and propaganda wars of their times. The Reformation movement made extensive use of engraved woodcuts as theological statement, political commentary, and pedagogical method. Illustrations served as an aid to what we today would call *visual learners*, those who process information more effectively visually rather than by hearing or reading texts.

In a similar way, music also served an important catechetical function for Luther. Realistically, he warned, "you should not assume that the young people will learn and retain this teaching from sermons alone. When these parts have been well learned, one may assign them also some psalms or hymns, based on these subjects, to supplement and confirm their knowledge."[9] Here, as in his discussions about teaching, Luther urged that hymns themselves be simple and clear. In a letter to his friend George Spalatin in 1523, Luther urged Spalatin to write new hymns in the language of the people: "I would like you to avoid new-fangled, fancied words and to use expressions simple and common enough for the people to understand, yet pure and fitting."[10] Luther certainly did not know of recent scientific findings about the importance of music for actually wiring connections in children's brains, but he did recognize that good, theologically sound hymnody could convey the gospel in way that sermons alone could not.

Based on his flexibility and multitude of approaches, one could almost say that Luther was instinctually aware, in at least a rudimentary way, of modern educational theories of developmental readiness, multiple intelligences, and varied learning styles. In our own teaching, we must remember that making use of different techniques and methods within the same lesson will appeal to the different types of learning styles found in our children and will thus make our teaching more effective. Good teachers will therefore offer a variety of activities on the same theme to appeal to all types of learners.

Fourth, Luther recognized that while young and old alike possess a variety of different learning styles, in an even more fundamental way, all children process information differently from adults. Teaching that engages children does not simply replicate the teaching styles that prove effective with adults.

The apostle Paul's observation that "When I was a child, I spoke like a child, I thought like a child, I reasoned like a child" may have informed Luther's approach to teaching children. Luther's busy household just as surely reinforced the apostle Paul's reasoning that differences exist between children and adults, and Luther learned to adapt his teaching to different ages: "Now since the young must always be hopping and skipping, or at least doing something that they enjoy, and since one cannot very well forbid this—nor would it be wise to forbid them everything—why then should we not set up such schools for them and introduce them to such studies?" [11]

Teaching that engages children, in other words, does not involve merely lecturing to children sitting in their seats. Cognitively, children are not yet able to absorb all of the information we would try to convey to them by lecture. Rather, children learn most effectively when they are engaged in activities targeted toward their age group. Educational scholars often cite as a general rule of thumb that students retain only approximately 20% of what they hear; 40% to 50% of what they both hear and see; and up to 80% of what they hear, see, and do. Clearly, then, teaching which is primarily experiential will have the greatest probability of making an impact on the lives of children.

Teaching that is experiential involves all of the senses—sight, hearing, touch, smell, and taste. As children develop, their abilities change, but this reality remains constant throughout childhood. Games, activities, crafts, and dramas all draw children into stories and help them receive and process information effectively.

Fifth, Luther recognized that teaching that makes an impact on children is repetitive. Teaching that engages children recognizes that children need to hear a story, a text, or a concept often for it to make a lasting impression.

Any parent who has ever endured the constant playing and replaying of a favorite video or set of songs knows that children learn by hearing and seeing—over and over again. "Memory work" falls in and out of favor as a technique for teaching children, but Luther believed that repetition was more than just rote memorization. Luther pointed out that neither adults nor children can read a text once and get the full benefit from it. The purpose of careful attention to this principle, according to Luther, was simple: "The reason we take such care to preach on the catechism frequently is to impress it upon our young people, not in a lofty and learned manner but briefly and very simply, so that it may penetrate deeply into their minds and remain fixed in their memories." [12] Repetition, therefore, served an important function, far beyond transmitting knowledge from one person to another. For Luther, repetition was an aid toward deeper spiritual understanding.

Luther had no patience with adult theologians who felt that because they had read a text before, they had no need to study it again:

> Many regard the catechism as a simple, trifling teaching, which they can absorb and master at one reading and then toss the book into a corner as if they are ashamed to read it again . . . But this I say for myself: I am also a doctor and a preacher, just as learned and experienced as all of them who are so high and mighty. Nevertheless, each morning, and whenever else I have time, I do as a child who is being taught the catechism and I read and recite word for word the Lord's Prayer, the Ten Commandments, the Creed, the Psalms, etc. I must still read and study the catechism daily, and yet I cannot master it as I wish, but must remain a child and pupil of the catechism—and I also do so gladly. [13]

Stories, texts, prayers, and liturgy become part of us when we constantly repeat them, when we explore them at different ages and stages of our lives. It is not enough for children to hear the story of the good Samaritan once and never again. Children need to hear these stories constantly, to learn them and take them into their hearts, growing ever more deeply into the meanings of these ancient stories for their lives today.

Finally, teaching that engages children is deeply spiritual. Teaching that engages children is the beginning of a process in a larger journey of a lifetime. It is a process designed to nurture children's faith as they grow, mature, and develop.

For Luther, all Christian education was directed toward the goal of helping the Christian live out his or her vocation in the world. This growth along a spiritual path takes many forms. Even in such a fundamentally intellectual undertaking as reading the Catechism, Luther argued that something spiritual was taking place. "In such reading, conversation, and meditation the Holy Spirit is present and bestows ever new and greater light and devotion."[14]

Meditate on the words of a text, said Luther, "and take care that you do not grow weary or think that you have done enough when you have read, heard, and spoken them once or twice, and that you then have complete understanding. You will never be a particularly good theologian if you do that, for you will be like untimely fruit that falls to the ground before it is half-ripe."[15] Meditation, in other words, is more than hurriedly skimming a text in the shortest amount of time possible to draw out its essence. True reading "engages the heart"[16]; it is a deep, repeated, reflective absorption of the text that actually changes the meditator.[17]

In our own day, the work of Jerome Berryman[18] exemplifies the need to take children's spirituality seriously. While it is clear that different types of learning styles exist and must be addressed, teachers of children must take care not to keep students "active and busy" simply for the sake of keeping them active and busy. Children need times of quiet and reflection as well as activity, particularly in our contemporary society.

At the most basic level, prayer should become a regular part of the classroom experience. For the youngest children, simple, short prayers of thanksgiving for the people and world around them are the most appropriate. As children grow older, prayers growing out of concern for others become a natural expression of their growing maturity.

Leading children in prayer is actually the least we can do to develop a child's spirituality, not the most. Berryman speaks of the importance of developing a child's sense of wonder and of trust, of letting the story enter into children in quiet, reflective ways that work on children at a very deep level. Teachers nurture this spirituality by providing a safe, hospitable, and accepting space for questioning, for wondering, and for reflecting. Teachers who demonstrate care and acceptance of their students model the unconditional love and grace of God in powerful and long-lasting ways.

In sum, then, Luther's thought on the issue of pedagogy may point us in helpful directions as we consider our own teaching today. All six of Luther's general themes—clarity, concreteness, variety, repetition, child-centeredness, and spirituality—should be kept before teachers striving to engage children.

Ten core principles of active learning

The solid pedagogy embedded in the Lutheran tradition from its beginnings finds much resonance with contemporary theory and practice. Luther's emphasis on the importance of education proved enormously influential in the years following the Reformation and remains a part of the denomination's heritage to this day. The second part of this chapter focuses on specific, practical matters, beginning with 10 core principles to keep in mind when preparing to teach children and ending with a number of specific pedagogical techniques. Teaching that engages children is most successful when it follows these basic guidelines.

1. Know thy students

Teachers who wish to engage their students must first get to know them. Children come in all sizes, shapes, colors, and life experiences. To become an effective teacher, one must first know what to expect in a general way from particular age groups. It is important to know, for example, that younger children do not have the fine-motor skills necessary for certain types of activities or the abstract-thinking skills to process certain types of information. With this sort of knowledge, teachers are able to plan more effectively.

Beyond these fairly predictable stages of life and faith development, children are also individual children of God with their own unique gifts and needs. A good teacher will work hard to get to know each child as a particular person, not as a stage on a developmental chart.

Depending on the congregational setting, this may prove either to be easy or difficult. In smaller congregations, members may know not only each child, but also his or her parents and grandparents as well. In other situations, children may come from many different neighborhoods and schools, and even students in the same class might not know each other well. Particularly in these settings, teachers who wish to engage their students must invest time in each session to help them deepen their relationships with one another and to hold individual conversation with each student, even if they are brief, either inside or outside of the classroom. Through such conversations, teachers can begin to know their students' hopes, fears, joys, concerns, and passions. Short notes mailed home to students when they have missed several class sessions, achieved recognition at school or in the community, or celebrated a birthday, provide connections between teachers and students outside of the classroom.

2. Respect thy students

Part of knowing one's students also means learning to show students respect and consideration, to affirm their life experience and their culture. Allowing students the freedom to ask any question, listening to the ideas and feelings they express, and encouraging them to cooperate with each other, shows respect for each student as a unique child of God. Sometimes this may even mean temporarily derailing the lesson plan, but modeling respectful language and behavior for members of the class inspires the same reciprocal attitude in students.

Children today can feel especially vulnerable to forces beyond their control, and many deeply need to feel the acceptance of the grace of God. Modeling the love of God and accepting students unconditionally is perhaps one of the most important ways teachers communicate God's grace.

3. Know thyself

Like their students, teachers also come in all sizes, shapes, colors, and life experiences. Teaching that engages students is ultimately a matter of finding methods that work well for one's individual teaching and learning style. A method that succeeds for one teacher may fail miserably for another. Some teachers, for example, are comfortable leading and participating in dramas or role-play exercises. For other teachers, such activities would prove torturous and uncomfortable, and thus ineffective in engaging students.

Teachers should also feel comfortable responding to some questions from the children with the simple, genuine, and heartfelt response, "I don't know." If the question has an answer, volunteer to seek out the answer or help them to do so. If the question is fascinating but unanswerable ("How much does God weigh?"), be willing to explain that some questions, in fact, have no answers that we can comprehend.

4. Know thy place

It is crucial to create a warm, friendly environment for teaching. An attractive physical climate in the classroom can make the difference between creating a class the children are eager to attend and one in which they have no desire to participate. Teachers should ask if children entering into the room would feel welcomed by what they see and experience, both from the physical environment and from the hospitality of the teacher.

Although ideally every church classroom would be bright and roomy, with inviting and child-sized furnishings, many churches cannot offer such an environment because of physical and economic limitations. At a minimum, however, an inviting classroom for children should include a special area for storytelling (an area rug, carpet squares, or floor pillows) and child-sized tables and chairs. Even the most difficult space can be personalized by placing children's artwork on display for all to see. Bulletins boards for such work are ideal, but even classroom doors and hallway walls can easily become areas where student art can flourish. Paint and bright curtains are inexpensive additions that can enlighten even the gloomiest space.

In some congregations, a general supply closet serves all of the classrooms, while in others, each classroom needs to be outfitted with basic supplies. In either case, teachers and students alike need to know where items are easily accessible. Shelves containing books, toys, and basic supplies stored in simple containers (shoeboxes, egg cartons, plastic containers), clearly marked, make it easy for children and teachers to find what they need.

5. Know thy subject

The Boy Scouts are right—be prepared. For teachers this means never, ever walking into a classroom unprepared. This can prove a struggle for many of today's congregational teachers. Most volunteer teachers today lead incredibly busy lives, juggling jobs, families, and other responsibilities. Time is a luxury many simply do not have. Yet our students deserve our best. If teaching that engages children has as its end purpose to shape them in the life of faith, it will take more than a cursory reading of a prepared lesson plan five minutes before walking into a classroom to accomplish this.

Teaching that engages is teaching that is well-grounded. Reading the curriculum carefully several days in advance allows the teacher to be thinking about lesson themes as the week goes along. Teachers should pay particular attention to the overviews and background information of a lesson, listing their own questions and anticipating questions that their students may have. If one needs additional information about a story, theme, or concept, resources exist to provide these.

Many congregations sponsor monthly or quarterly meetings with their teachers to share not just information about details of the educational program, but to discuss the themes of coming lessons. In this way, leaders (whether a pastor, a director of Christian education, or an invited guest) can engage the teachers themselves in learning, enriching them and providing needed background and thematic emphases for their own teaching.

6. Prepare ye the way

Good teaching does not just happen—it must be planned. When preparing a lesson, teachers should always keep these questions before them: "What is the main concept I wish the students to learn in this lesson? How should they be changed by what we do here today?" Setting specific objectives in writing ("By the end of this session, students will be able to . . .") helps keep teaching focused. Whatever the concept or theme determined, it should always be in the forefront of all subsequent planning. Many teachers find a template for preparing a lesson helpful. If the lesson calls for an activity, whether it is a craft, game, or project, teachers should try it out first, and make sure they have all the materials needed before class time. Be sure ahead of time that any technological equipment planned for use (whether a VCR, computer, or digital camera) will work. Such preparation boosts one's confidence and makes one a better teacher.

7. Humble thyself

Remember—a little child shall lead them. It is difficult sometimes to remember exactly what it was like to be a child. Adults tend to forget that all adults look big, powerful, and old to 5-year-olds. We need to see again through a child's eyes—and at a child's level. Sit down with them, not above them. Take care in selecting words that children can understand, not words only adults know.

8. Use different methods to appeal to different types of learners

As Luther knew, children (and adults, for that matter) process information in different ways. Because children learn in different ways, teachers should utilize multiple methods that include all of the senses, each activity pointing toward the main point. The skillful teacher learns to incorporate a variety of activities in any given lesson.

Most teaching tends to be directed toward the *auditory learners*, who learn best by hearing information through lectures or stories, which may be told in a variety of ways. Although storytelling holds onto auditory learners, we forget that most children are not primarily auditory learners. *Visual learners*, in contrast, learn best through the use of images and other visual aids. They become engaged in a lesson when there is something to see, something on which they may focus their attention. Teachers engage *kinesthetic learners* most when they lead these children into actually doing something. Games, crafts, and other hands-on activities are most helpful to these children.[19]

Because any classroom will contain children who learn in different ways, it is important to offer more than one way to learn in each and every lesson. The child who is primarily an auditory learner, for example, may well be engrossed in the creative telling of a Bible story. A more kinesthetic learner, however, will also need a hands-on experience to make the story truly come alive. Activities for both of these learners should be offered.

Since the 1980s, scholars have begun to speak of an expanded theory of "multiple intelligences," emphasizing the wide variety of ways that people learn. Howard Gardner first proposed several intelligence styles, including those styles described above, in his 1983 book, *Frames of Mind*.[20] For more information about multiple intelligence, see the chapter "The Child Grew: Understanding Children's Development."

Multiple intelligence theory underlies the "rotation model" of teaching popular in some educational programs today. In the rotation model, children hear a biblical or other story, and then rotate to different activities based on the same story designed to appeal to the different ways they learn. A Bible story, for example, might begin with a creative telling of the story, and then children rotate to different centers that emphasize areas such as drawing, food, games, music, or science.

9. Expect the unexpected

Children are famous for getting off track, for asking impossible questions, for seeing things through new and different eyes. That indeed is their gift to all of us. We need by all means to be open to their wise truths. Therefore, teachers need to be flexible and willing to adapt as the class experience dictates. On the other hand, more prosaic events may derail a well-prepared lesson: the children may not have the hand-eye coordination to do the prepared craft, or the supplies that have "always been there" may have disappeared during the week. In such events, a "Plan B" proves invaluable.

10. Find joy in teaching

Smile. Be enthusiastic. Share your passion. Enjoy the story you are telling. Exude energy and enthusiasm, and always—always!—be ready to laugh. Love your students as children of God. Affirm them, support them, pray for them, pray with them, and let the Spirit guide you. Love each child that you teach—even (and especially) the challenging ones. Remember that the relationships built with children are as important, if not more so, than the lessons you are trying to teach them.

Methods for experiential learning

In her books *Exploring the Bible with Children* and *Experiencing the Bible with Children*, Dorothy Jean Furnish has emphasized the importance of "teaching the Bible experientially" to children rather than simply transmitting information to them. Acknowledging that the biblical world is very different from the contemporary one of children, she notes that children cannot be expected to pick up a Bible and understand it without preparation and guidance. She gives three guidelines for teaching the Bible to children. These guidelines can be applied to many other concepts as well.[21]

1. Teachers should help children *feel their way* into a text. This means helping them to understand the emotions and feelings of the people in the Bible story prepares them to hear the story itself. Activities that help children express emotions (such as singing, dancing, acting, and creating art projects) can help children relate to the feelings of the biblical characters. Furnish notes that *feeling into* the story is similar to preparing soil to receive seed.

2. Teachers should lead children to *meet with* the story in an engaging way. This means to hear it, perhaps for the first time, perhaps for the tenth time. Using puppets, pictures, videos, audiotapes, and creative storytelling all help children meet with the story in a very personal way. Good storytelling plants the seed in the prepared soil.

3. Teachers should help children to *respond out of* their encounter with the biblical text and do something based on the story they have heard. This response represents the harvest of the seed that has been planted in prepared ground. Children might respond, says Furnish, through feelings, thinking, acting, or deciding. After a story, a child may experience powerful emotions that can be expressed in movement or music. You could also use a questions-answers format and discussion to lead a child to creative writing of various types (songs, poems, or stories).

Furnish's guidelines can help teachers to engage children in the Bible story. Teachers can use a number of specific pedagogical methods as they prepare their lessons to follow these guidelines. Building on the themes developed in this chapter, teachers can choose among many different activities to actively engage students. The following list of suggested methods is not exhaustive, but is designed to stimulate one's thinking. Once one has the theme of the lesson identified, choosing more than one of the following methods can appeal to different types of learners.[22]

Arts/Crafts: These projects let children create artistic interpretations of a story or concept, to become involved in the theme of a lesson, and to express themselves creatively. Examples include the use of, but are not limited to:

- Paint, crayon, markers, chalk, colored pencils, sponges, glitter, yarn, cloth, glue, and other supplies.

- Murals, with each child creating a portion of the overall work.

- Collages, with children clipping pictures from magazines or newspapers to create either individual or collective works. Collages can be on any theme. For example, pictures of people helping each other, or pictures of people and objects for whom the children wish to pray.

- Mosaics, with children filling in an outline of a picture or symbol with smaller pieces of paper, fabric, or other material.

- Puppets of various types, from socks to paper bags.

- Masks created from construction paper or paper plates for storytelling.

- Mobiles to hang in the classroom or at home.

- Banners for use in worship or classroom space.

- Greeting cards for people who are sick or who have limited mobility.

- Quilt squares, with each child creating a design using fabric crayons or paint, that are then sewn together by the teacher to create a whole.

- Baking, such as bread to replicate the food of biblical characters, to use at communion, or to serve as gifts or snacks for others.

- Newspapers (older children) of events going on in Sunday school or the retelling of a Bible story from a modern perspective.

Field trips: Visits around the congregational buildings or neighborhood can be learning experiences that provide concrete example of points discussed in class.

- Visit the church sanctuary to study the symbols found there in stained-glass windows, the altar, baptismal font, paraments, banners, wreaths, Christmas trees, and other items. Then help children translate these symbols into crafts of their own.

- Visit the church office, child development center, a soup kitchen, and other locations in the neighborhood where the church is involved. This will demonstrate the "work" of the church.

- Depending on your surroundings, children can observe nature, the city, a farm or a neighborhood and talk about many different issues.

Games: A wide variety of games can help to review and reinforce a concept or story, and to build cooperation.

- Active games that build cooperation and team work (such as relays, charades, or flash cards) are always popular and can be found in many resources.

- Games that reinforce and review concepts include matching games or bingo.
- Jigsaw puzzles, crossword puzzles, and word searches are enjoyable to some students.

Multimedia: A variety of options is helpful in engaging children in lessons.

- Commercial video recordings on themes or stories.
- Audio or video recordings either made by the teacher or made by the students themselves. Teachers might choose to prerecord a narration or dialogue as a means to tell a story, or they might let children retell the story through audio or video tape. Older children might enjoy pretending to create a "newscast" of a Bible story, or filming classmates acting out a Bible story.
- Computer software. A number of excellent programs exist to illustrate "life in Bible times," to help with biblical literacy, or to provide children an opportunity to create artistic expressions of a theme or concept.
- Compact disks or cassette recordings of children's music, or other music.
- Photography. Children can use instant cameras for snapshots of a play or artistic creation to post on bulletin boards, digital cameras to provide pictures for a church Web site or to send via e-mail to congregation members.
- Maps, time lines, charts, and posters to clarify elements of a lesson.

Music: As Martin Luther knew, music can be an effective teaching tool.

- Singing songs about a story or concept helps students internalize details or even memorize the books of the Bible.
- Rhythm instruments (sticks, bells, drums, cymbals) allow students to express their feelings in a tangible way.
- Music can help people express their feelings and ideas as they listen, dance, or move in place.
- Music can create the right mood while working on crafts or other quiet activities.

Storytelling: Stories can be told and retold in a wide variety of ways by both teacher and students.

- Have children do simple body motions, dances, or finger plays to express elements of the story. They might use motion to show waves on the sea, walking through the wilderness, or the words of a psalm.

- Conduct creative drama or role play. Act out the story with simple props or costumes.

- Use a bag or box to draw out items at appropriate times in the story.

- Pantomime the story.

- Lead them in shadow play.

- Create a "magnet board"—a cookie sheet can provide a backdrop for paper characters with magnets affixed to them.

- Create sand pans—baking pans filled with sand make an excellent backdrop for characters attached to craft sticks, who are then placed in the sand as they emerge in the story.

- Use pictures or flannel board cut-outs. While some would hold that such "static" representations hold no appeal for children in a media-saturated age, a good storyteller can utilize these to great effect. It is important to keep the pictures or flannel board characters at the children's eye level.

Visitors: Members of your congregation, or other individuals outside of it, can bring special gifts to your children's classes.

- Arrange for members of the congregation to visit your classroom dressed as historical or biblical figures to tell a story, act one out, or respond to the children's questions.

- Members of your congregation can share a particular expertise, hobby, skill, or vocation with children in a lasting way.

Summary

Five centuries ago, Martin Luther looked out at the members of his parish and saw not just adults, but children in need of teaching in the faith. His efforts to deepen the faith of young children led him to think about the practical matters involved in such an endeavor. For the young and vulnerable in faith, whatever their age, Luther demonstrated care and sensitivity, compassion, and common sense. He taught in the vernacular. He cut to the chase. He appealed to the senses. Luther, in short, proved an excellent educator.

As we in our own settings also live through a time of transition and change, we do well to remember with Luther that children are a gift of God and deserving of our best education efforts. Children are endlessly inquisitive, energetic, and eager. By nature, they are easy to engage in a variety of ways. Teachers who work to engage them are both blessed and a blessing.

FOR REFLECTION AND DISCUSSION

1. Reflect on a memorable learning experience you had as a child. What caused this to be memorable for you? What happened in that instance that caused learning to crystallize?

2. Consider your present classroom setting and think of each child in it. How many of its members would you guess are auditory learners, visual leaders, or kinesthetic learners?

3. How do we use terminology and vocabulary in ways that may seem foreign to children? Give examples. Try to talk about a theological term (such as *justification, righteousness,* or *salvation*) using words that have only one syllable.

4. As an exercise, consider a familiar Bible story or parable. Using some of the examples above, what methodologies would help you convey this story to an auditory learner? To a visual learner? To a kinesthetic learner?

Notes

1. Norma Cook Everist, "Luther on Education: Implications for Today," *Currents in Theology and Mission*, 12:2 (April 1985), p. 77ff. Everist traces the development of Luther's advocacy of public education in her article.

2. Martin Luther, "A Sermon on Keeping Children in School," *Luther's Works*, vol. 46 (St. Louis: Concordia; Philadelphia: Fortress, 1955-1986), p. 252.

3. "To the Councilmen of All Cities in Germany that They Establish and Maintain Christian Schools" (1524), *Luther's Works*, vol. 45, p. 368, as cited in Everist, p. 79.

4. Luther, "On Translating: An Open Letter" (1530), *Luther's Works*, vol. 35, p. 189.

5. Timothy J. Wengert, "Forming the Faith Today through Luther's Catechisms," *Lutheran Quarterly*, New Series, xi, no. 4 (Winter 1997), p. 388.

6. Ibid., p. 388.

7. *Luther's Works*, vol., 34, p. 275. Luther attributes these ideas to Marcus Terentius Varro (116-27 B.C.).

8. Wengert, "Forming the Faith," p. 391.

9. From the "Preface to the Large Catechism," Robert Kolb and Timothy J. Wengert, eds., *The Book of Concord* (Minneapolis: Fortress, 2000), p. 386 as cited (Tappart edition of *The Book of Concord*) in Robyn Leaver, "Luther's Catechism Hymns: 'Lord Keep Us Steadfast in Your Word,'" *Lutheran Quarterly*, New Series, xi, no. 4 (Winter 1997), pp. 399-400.

10. *Luther's Works*, vol., 53, p. 221.

11. "To the Councilmen of All Cities in Germany that They Establish and Maintain Christian Schools," *Luther's Works*, vol., 45, p. 369.

12. "Preface to the Large Catechism," p. 386.

13. Ibid., p. 380.

14. Ibid., p. 381.

15. Preface to the Wittenberg edition of "Luther's German Writings," *Martin Luther's Basic Theological Writings*, Timothy F. Lull, ed. (Minneapolis, Fortress, 1989), p. 66.

16. Martha E. Stortz, "Prayer: A Four-Stranded Garland," in Taproot: *The Journal of Lutheran Theological Southern Seminary*, xii, 1996, p. 103.

17. James M. Kittleson, "Luther's Impact on the Universities—and the Reverse," *Concordia Theological Quarterly*, vol. 48, no. 1 (January 1984), p. 34.

18. Jerome Berryman, *Godly Play: An Imaginative Approach to Religious Education* (Minneapolis: Augsburg Fortress, 1995).

19. Debbie Trafton O'Neal summarizes these succinctly in *More than Glue and Glitter: A Classroom Guide for Volunteer Teachers* (Minneapolis: Augsburg, 1992), p. 61ff.

20. *Frames of Mind: The Theory of Multiple Intelligences*, 10th ed. (New York: Basic Books, 1993); and *Intelligence Reframed: Multiple Intelligences for the 21st Century* (New York: Basic Books, 2000).

21. The following discussion is taken from Dorothy Jean Furnish's works: *Exploring the Bible with Children*, 5th ed. (Nashville: Abingdon, 1981); and *Experiencing the Bible with Children*, rev. ed. (Nashville: Abingdon, 1990).

22. The following methods are compiled from a variety of sources, including O'Neal and Donald Griggs, *Basic Skills for Church Teachers* (Nashville: Abindgon, 1985).

CHAPTER 10

The Ministry of Children in Congregations

Nathan C. P. Frambach

IT WAS THE FIRST SESSION of our monthly "Life of St. Philip the Deacon" membership orientation process. The topic was grace, and we were just beginning. I asked the group, "How do you understand grace?"

Then we divided into pairs to respond to that question and to identify and share some "grace moments" with one another. There were 19 of us. Everyone had a partner except for Jay, who was 9 years old; so Jay and I began to talk. We chatted about school and sports and favorite foods—everything except the topic at hand.

Jay waited for an opening, and then said, rather brashly, "Hey, Mister Pastor, I thought we were supposed to be talking about grace."

I got the hint. "Okay, Jay. So tell me, how do you understand grace?"

Jay was ready. "My dad is like grace. He's so very nice to me and he doesn't always have to be. And every night he lays down beside me and reads me a story from the Bible."

Two people comprise the Krivo family, Richard and Jay. It sounds like there is ministry happening in that home on a daily basis. It's not exactly what comes to mind for many of us when we think of "youth ministry"—no guitars, no skating or mall scavenger hunts, not even pizza. But it is ministry, the ministry of faith formation.

I could only hope that the congregation was providing support, encouragement, and resources so that ministry could continue in the Krivo home, so that Richard could continue to be, in the words of Martin Luther, "the apostle, bishop and priest of his child."[1] Laying claim to the fundamental partnership between the home and the congregation lies at the heart of the renewal in ministry with the younger generations today.

Integrated, equipped, and empowered

Ministry with the young is the birthright of the baptized. This is an ecclesiological claim I am compelled to make up front and then unpack as this chapter unfolds. It is the privilege and responsibility of all adults—not just some, and not just the professionals—to love and care for young people.

A change is needed in the consciousness and imagination of many congregations so that every adult understands this birthright. Granted, not all adults have the gifts to communicate the Christian gospel to the young or to plan and lead programs. Yet every adult can acknowledge young people—speak to them, learn who they are, call them by name. Every adult can pray for young people and, furthermore, let them know that they have been prayed for. These are things that matter in the unfolding life of a child. Who can't afford to take three to five minutes a week to write a note to a child, letting them know that someone has prayed for them because they are known and loved? It is both a great challenge and privilege to hear and respond to God's call to attend to all of God's kids, particularly those to which one does not have to attend. Barbara Kingsolver offers a much-needed reminder in this regard:

Children are not commodities but an incipient world. They thrive best when their upbringing is the collective joy and responsibility of families, neighborhoods, communities, and nations. Children deprived—of love, money, attention, or moral guidance—grow up to have large and powerful needs. . . . We can see, if we care to look, that the way we treat children—all of them, not just our own, and especially those of great need—defines the shape of the world we'll wake up in tomorrow.[2]

Ministry with the young is also about adults loving and caring for those kids God has specifically entrusted to them—sons and daughters, godchildren and grandchildren, nieces and nephews. The primary and most effective locus of faith formation is the home. There is an expanding body of research on congregational ministry to support this contention.[3] This means a change in consciousness for many congregations as well. It is the high calling of all the adults in a home to teach and model the faith, and we need not make it too hard.

From the first morning our son, Garret Andrew, woke up in our home, Diane and I welcome each new day with him by making the sign of the cross on his forehead, saying, "Garret Andrew, you are a beloved child of God, and there isn't anything anyone can do to make that not so." Yes, it's a rather convoluted way of saying what the Scriptures announce toward the end of Romans 8, that nothing "will be able to separate us from the love of God in Christ Jesus our Lord." Nonetheless, it announces a reality we believe central to the Christian faith: what God has done in Christ for the sake of the whole creation and its peoples (cf. 2 Corinthians 5:17ff.) cannot be undone. Garrett is now 6 years old, and he can make the sign of the cross on his own forehead and on his parents' as well. Now we name each other and are reminded that we, along with each new day, belong to God. This emphasis on faith formation in the home liberates the congregation from being a *family* in the very modern, nuclear, and Westernized sense of the word. This allows *family*, regardless of the configuration, to be what happens in the home. Furthermore, it challenges the congregation to be God's gathering community that intentionally welcomes the stranger, announces the good news of God's love and mercy in Jesus Christ, and lives into God's vision of justice, reconciliation, and peace for the whole creation.

A critical confluence of partnerships is needed to tend the lives of children and youth. The central partnership is between the congregation and the home. How can congregations encourage, support, and provide resources for homes so that lively faith formation takes place there? Equally as important are the public partnerships between home, congregation, and community. The rich focus on asset-building research from Search Institute offers a usable, common language that can help forge and foster those critical partnerships.[4] Finally, it is the relationship between adults and children in faith communities that is paramount, and it is to that relationship that I will devote primary attention in this chapter.

Seen and heard

A saying has circulated for a long time now: "Children should be seen and not heard." Who knows where or when or even why it originated—or even whether or not it has any historical basis whatsoever. Regardless, I think it has become embedded, over time, like a rock in a streambed, in the consciousness of many adults, and even in many of our churches—although we certainly wouldn't want to admit it publicly or in polite company. Often we want to see a lot of kids running around our churches; we just don't want to hear them—both literally and figuratively. This sends a powerful message to kids, particularly when what so many kids want and need is to be heard. I still believe that one of the greatest gifts an adult can give to a child, teenager, or other adult, is one's full attention. In her poem "Fiery Spirit," read what 17-year-old Kate Erb had to say about being seen and heard:

> *The soul projects itself through eyes, I'm told,*
> *but mine springs out in piles of crazy hair,*
> *of spirals colored rust and brown and gold—*
> *my mind and mane an unruly pair.*
> *They are not ladylike, and brush the edge*
> *of etiquette—rebellious strands that pop*
> *from braids and buns to raise a wispy hedge*
> *like weeds sprung from an ancient statue's top,*
> *and small green questions that would break in time*
> *the stone of dogma's temple down to leas*
> *where mums and pansies thrive on crumbled lime*
> *and redheads charm the honey out of bees.*
> *So let the matrons point and gasp behind.*
> *I will comb my curls and speak my mind.* [5]

There are kids who want to be heard—indeed, who will be heard, must be heard—regardless of adult sensibilities or propriety. I would love to show you a clip from the wonderfully moving film *Simon Birch*, but since I can't I will do my best to describe it.

Simon Birch (Buena Vista, 1998, written and directed by Mark Steven Jackson) was suggested by John Irving's beloved 1989 novel, *A Prayer for Owen Meany*. The film is set in a New Hampshire town in the early 1960s, where lives Simon Birch—pint-sized, precocious, mischievous—who believes he has been put on earth as "God's instrument." His firm faith in his destiny enables Simon to endure the indifference of his parents, the mockery of adults, and the unmerciful teasing of the other children. Simon is quite outspoken at the church he attends, much to the dismay of his high-strung Sunday school teacher and Reverend Russell.

Among other things, *Simon Birch* exposes the ways that children are so often marginalized, their voices squelched. One scene from the movie in particular comes to mind. It takes place inside of the church during worship. Reverend Russell has just finished reading a Scripture lesson, to which the congregation has responded in a dull and somewhat rote manner. Simon then proceeds to speak his mind in response to some of the "announcements" that are shared. Reverend Russell, in response, publicly and privately chastises Simon (and Simon's friend Ben), concluding that "Simon Birch is NOT a *normal* person."

I dare say this scene from *Simon Birch* reflects the reality of many children. I fear that the old adage "Kids should be seen and not heard" has seeped into the ecclesiastical consciousness of many faith communities and become operative, perhaps more than many of us dare imagine. Of course congregations want kids around. The more the merrier, right?

In my small experience of relating to synods (judicatory bodies) in the ELCA, ministry with young people consistently floats to the top of most congregational lists of needs and desires. Yet the question becomes to what extent are children and young people—their voices, gifts, passion, curiosity, energy—heard, valued, and honored as fully participating members of the body of Christ? Congregations must resist the temptation to say, "Kids should be seen and not heard," and instead communicate the exact opposite to all of God's kids: "You will be seen and heard here, *really*."

Baptism

The biblical image of the body of Christ (Romans 12:4; 1 Corinthians 12:12-14; Ephesians 4:15-16) casts a vision for life and ministry in Christian communities that is naturally intergenerational and intentionally inclusive of all people. Congregations are intergenerational, local gatherings of the body of Christ. A congregation is created and called by God to provide a safe place wherein kids can come to voice as children of God, equipped and empowered for Christian leadership in God's world.

Children have a calling; children as well as adults are called to vocation. Although it is beyond the scope of this chapter to consider fully the relationship between the notion of *vocatio* and childhood, it is a relationship begging for theological exploration. It simply needs to be stated here that children are called by God to live and work in God's world in a variety of ways and through multiple relationships (home, school, friends). The calling of childhood is, alternatively, to play, question, wonder, worship, serve, learn, love, care, and, at times, to create chaos. One of the distinctive gifts that children and youth bring to life is "spice"—enthusiasm, zeal, impatience with the status quo, and occasionally a dose of chaos and disorder. This is what ministry in daily life looks like by way of the child.

The wellspring from which comes this calling of children to *vocatio*, to ministry in daily life, is baptism. "Baptism makes us priests before God and frees us to serve our neighbor in our particular arenas of life. *Vocatio . . .* had become in Luther's hands a word for the day-to-day world in which all Christians found themselves."[6] Baptism is the particular means through which God forges this purposeful relationship and grafts people into the body of Christ. Timothy Wengert has uncovered the profound importance of Luther's understanding of baptism in relationship to children and vocation. He asserts that baptism, for Luther, is the sacrament of justification by faith alone par excellence:

> Luther . . . realized that children came to Christ in Baptism. . . . In Baptism God links our destiny to that of Jesus Christ. In Baptism Christ himself baptizes and joins us to his death and resurrection, not just allegorically but, to use modern parlance, "for real." In Baptism God ordains all to the royal priesthood we share in Christ.[7]

Christian faith traditions that practice infant baptism as the primary means for welcome and initiation into the Christian community are called and challenged to consider more deeply the nature of that welcome and initiation. As Wengert states: "Baptism was no longer a stepping stone in the child's life, easily lost in the struggle against sin. Instead it had become the place where a child entered the realm of God's favor. . . . Baptism now remained a valid, irrevocable promise of God."[8] There is a purpose for welcome and initiation into the Christian community. Being grafted into the body of Christ through baptism into the death and resurrection of Jesus involves welcome and initiation into servant-living and mission-based ministry. Children, indeed, are members of the priesthood of all believers by virtue of their baptism into Christ, fully part of the body of Christ today:

> Probably nothing from the Christian faith better captures the essentially mutual relationship that should exist between individual Christians and the Christian community than the image of Church as body of Christ. As the historical Jesus was present in his physical body, St. Paul was convinced that the body of Christ continues in the world through the community-of-persons called Church. . . . But Paul's understanding of this body and how it functions places equal stress on the personal and communal. In the body of Christ, each individual is valued, cherished, needed, and has a unique function—a role that no one else can play. And yet each part needs the whole for its own functioning . . . So the well-being of the whole is crucial to the well-being of individual members, and vice versa.[9]

As members of the body of Christ, children, too, are called to ministry in the present moments of their lives. Theology such as this begs for local ecclesiologies that move beyond welcoming children passively, that is, primarily as those acted upon (as learners) to integrating, equipping, and empowering them actively as agents of the faith and bearers of the Christian gospel. Children need adults—parents, teachers, pastors, coaches, the whole people of God—who are present with them, available and accessible, serving as God-bearers.[10] Adults are called to accompany children and help kids discern and clarify their vocations and strengthen and deepen the ways they already "proclaim the praise of God" and bear God's "creative and redeeming Word to all the world."[11]

In an intergenerational matrix

> It is our view that the phenomenon of segregation by age and its conse-
> quences for human behavior and development pose problems of the greatest
> magnitude for the Western world, and especially for the United States. If the
> institutions of our society continue to remove parents, other adults and older
> youth from active participation in the lives of children, and if the resulting
> vacuum is filled by the age-segregated peer group, we can anticipate increased
> alienation, indifference, antagonism and violence on the part of the younger
> generation in all segments of our society. [12]

These words, written three decades ago, now sound like an eerie
prophecy. In many, many sectors of the Western world, the United States in
particular, hyper-paced lifestyles built on the increasingly pervasive values of
individualism, consumer choice, and mobility are pulling the generations
apart at the seams. As a result, generations, in families and communities,
experience fragmentation and are often isolated one from another. A host of
cultural analysts and observers are paying close attention to these dynamics.
In *A Tribe Apart,* Patricia Hersch has explored and narrated the effect of this
fragmentation in the lives of the younger generations as well as any in recent
times. At the heart of her analysis lies one reality—aloneness:

> A clear picture of adolescents, of even our own children, eludes us—not
> necessarily because they are rebelling, or avoiding or evading us. *It is because
> we aren't there.* Not just parents, but any adults. American society has left its
> children behind as the cost of progress in the workplace. This isn't about
> working parents, right or wrong, but an issue for society to set its priorities
> and pay attention to its young in the same way it pays attention to its
> income. . . . The most stunning change for adolescents today is their alone-
> ness. The adolescents of the nineties are more isolated and more
> unsupervised than other generations. . . . The aloneness of today's adoles-
> cents changes the essential nature of the journey. . . . Their dramatic
> separation from the adult world is rarely considered as a phenomenon in its
> own right, yet it may be the key to that life in the shadows. It creates a milieu
> for growing up that adults categorically cannot understand because their
> absence causes it. [13]

These last two sentences capture and summarize both the central curiosity
and essential thesis of *A Tribe Apart.* This "dramatic separation" of young
people from adults has far-reaching consequences:

It is a problem not just for families but for communities when the generations get so separated. The effects go beyond issues of rules and discipline to the idea exchanges between generations that do not occur, the conversations not held, the guidance and role modeling not taking place, the wisdom and traditions no longer filtering down inevitably. How can kids imitate and learn from adults if they never talk to them? How can they form the connections to trust adult wisdom if there is inadequate contact? How can they decide what to accept and reject from the previous generation when exposure is limited? The generational threads that used to weave their way into the fabric of growing up are missing.[14]

Neither are faith communities immune from the effects of this fragmentation, so often fueled by age segregation:

Most people experience the church on Sunday mornings as spectators to a traditionally prescribed worship form. There may be an educational opportunity for the young and more active adults, but there is generally very little conscious awareness of any need for intergenerational activity that enables people to experience "koinonia" wherein needs are shared, spiritual bonding occurs, people are energized, and "diakonia" is empowered. The norm is fragmentation in congregational life.[15]

It is difficult for people to love and care for one another, particularly the young, in the midst of age-segregation and isolation. The generations belong together; there is a desperate need for the lives of adults and children to be woven together in community. "T. S. Eliot posed the question succinctly: 'What life have you if you have not life together?' . . . we receive life, we foster life, and we pass life on within the context of fellow humans."[16] Human life is indeed a shared activity. Human life is not to be lived in isolation. God creates human beings for life together in community.

Christian spirituality, too, is a shared, communal activity. The doctrine of the Trinity affirms that the design for human community is grounded in the deeply reciprocal and communal nature of God. Theologian Justo González reflects on the deep relationality of God and the clear challenge this poses for the life of Christian communities:

If the Trinity is the doctrine of a God whose very life is a life of sharing, its clear consequence is that those who claim belief in such a God must live a similar life. . . . The doctrine of the Trinity, once cleared of the stale metaphysical language in which it has been couched, affirms belief in a God whose essence is sharing. . . . This love of God, however, is not only something we receive, or something we must praise. It is also something we must imitate, for if God is love, life without love is life without God; and if this is a sharing love, such as we see in the Trinity, then life without sharing is life without God; and if this sharing is such that in God the three persons are equal in power, then life without such power sharing is life without God.[17]

This sharp theological challenge issued by González has significant implications for the relationship between adults and children in congregations, particularly with regard to the sharing of power. The proverbial playing field is leveled in a community of the baptized, wherein the pattern and goal of life together is ordered and defined by the triune God: "Justification by faith alone implies that God is no rejecter of people. Baptism, as the sacrament of that justification par excellence, becomes the great equalizer of Christians. Even age no longer divides them."[18] The nature of this life together is such that life-sustaining fellowship, deeply reciprocal at its theological core, is an integral dimension of a Christian faith community:

> In the community of faith, personal identity is grounded in a Reality that transcends every individual, creating a basis for equality and freedom and the redress of wrongs committed. In Christian community, this equality and freedom is expressed in the access every individual has to God through the mediation of Christ. This mediation constitutes the people as a priesthood of believers, within which no privileged classes are recognized, but only redeemed sinners all standing under God's judgment and grace.[19]

Life with God, the life of faith, is deeply relational. Through our baptism into Christ, we are called into relationship with God and with others. This reality is made crystal clear as congregations prepare to welcome the newly baptized: "By water and the Holy Spirit we are made members of the Church which is the Body of Christ."[20] John Westerhoff reminds us that, at its inception, Sunday school was designed to foster this deep relationality between people of all ages as participants in Christian community:

> The function of the Sunday school, with its variety of programs, was to give people an opportunity to share life with other faithful selves, to experience the faith in community, to learn the Christian story and to engage in Christian actions. The key to these Sunday schools was not curriculum, teaching, learning strategies, or organization. Rather, it was people in community.[21]

In the final analysis, it is the quality of relationships between all of the members of a faith community that creates an environment where faith is nurtured.

Intergenerational ministry

A congregation is a rich, intergenerational matrix, and as such a natural crucible for such relationships between children and adults. A pressing question for faith communities is this: What best fosters genuine, mutual relationships within the body of Christ so that people of all ages can discover and exercise their God-given gifts for ministry? Intentional intergenerational ministry is a perspective, a way of thinking and acting together in community that integrates the generations rather than segregating them, thus seeking to pass on the faith from generation to generation. James Gambone defines intentional intergenerational ministry as the "determination to bring together all generations—past, present, and future—in the service and sacred conversation of the Body of Christ." [22] Most congregations are naturally intergenerational. However, thinking and acting in an intentionally intergenerational manner does not seem to come so naturally for manycongregations:

> Intentional intergenerational ministry means the entire church makes a commitment to involve as many generations in as many parts of church as possible. It requires a dramatic change in the church culture. It also means every church that takes up this ministry will work for the benefit of the most vulnerable of all generations. [23]

Although intentional intergenerational ministry seems to be the exception rather than the norm in many congregations, indeed often requiring a dramatic change in a congregation's culture, it is certainly not an alien notion within the Judeo-Christian heritage.

> The church has a long history of encouraging cross-generational relationships. The difference between the past and the present is that in previous times these relationships occurred more naturally. In an aging society, we need to make intergenerational relationships more formalized and much more intentional. By promoting intentional intergenerational ministry, the church will be in a position to increase opportunities for all kinds of transfers—spiritual and material—across the generations. [24]

In an intentional intergenerational ministry, adults must be willing to share their power, and younger people must be willing to take on and honor that responsibility. I heard preached once that "the first act of love is to listen." Intentional cross-generational ministry places a high priority on the faith community as a listening, nurturing environment wherein people of all ages are fully present to one another. A congregation I recently visited had attempted to implement a congregation-wide mentoring initiative between older adults and children and youth of all ages. As Mary, one of the leaders of this initiative, noted, "It was a valiant, well-intentioned effort, but it fell flat." The initiative was germinated and planned very intentionally and carefully, but it simply didn't take hold . . . at least as it was intended. There remained a vibrant constellation of relationships between adults and kids who were in fifth grade when the initiative began. It seemed as though fifth grade was the right time to focus on mentoring in that congregation.

Again, Mary put it well: "We took it as a cue from God. We listened. We paid attention. We jettisoned the overall initiative and held on to whatever was going on with our fifth-graders." Thus the inception of what eventually came to be called "Stories of Wonder, Stories of Wisdom." Fifth-graders and their older spiritual companions would gather every few weeks. They would eat yummy things served up best by grandmas and grandpas, play a game or two, giggle and laugh a lot, and eventually sit down and talk for a while —sharing their stories of wonder and wisdom. Mary summed it up best: "It was so simple. So spontaneous. So . . . God. Such a beautiful thing to be a part of."

After hearing this story during my visit, Robert Coles's final musings at the end of his book *The Spiritual Life of Children* immediately came to my mind:

> So it is that we connect with one another, move in and out of one another's lives, teach and heal and affirm one another, across space and time—all of us wanderers, explorers, adventurers, stragglers and ramblers, sometimes tramps or vagabonds, even fugitives, but now and then pilgrims: as children, as parents, as old ones about to take that final step, to enter that territory whose character none of us here ever knows. Yet how young we are when we start wondering about it all, the nature of the journey and the final destination.[25]

Hence the importance of creating regular occasions so that young and old can come together in a variety of ways and learn from one another, listening and talking, sharing prayer and praise, questions and struggles, life and faith stories. All of the senses are employed in attending to God's story—wonder and imagination, song and dance, puppets and paint and plenty of play. In this kind of an environment people of all ages are full and valued participants in the life of a faith community. Women and men, boys and girls come to voice together as the people of God, discovering and exercising their gifts for ministry. The baptized of all ages are integrated, equipped, and empowered to bear witness to the reign of God.

Apprenticeship into Christian leadership

A congregation is a rich, intergenerational matrix, and as such a natural crucible for such relationships between children and adults. A congregation is created and called by God to provide a safe place where kids can come as children of God, equipped and empowered for Christian leadership in God's world. Congregations are intergenerational, local gatherings of the body of Christ. However, the overarching purpose of ministry within such faith communities is to communicate the good news of God's reign in Jesus Christ to one another and to the world:

> The community of faith is thus a gathering of those responding to God's saving grace by devoting themselves to God's plan for the restoration of all creation . . . therefore, "the people called" is a people belonging to God. This sense of being God's possession constitutes its identity, its vocation, and its vision. . . . Life accordingly presents itself to the faithful as a summons to participate in God's purpose of redeeming all who remain in bondage, and of restoring a creation long ravaged by sin to a state where righteousness and peace prevail.[26]

As members of the body of Christ, children, too, are called to ministry in the present moment of their lives. For many congregations this entails moving beyond welcoming children passively, that is, primarily as those acted upon (as learners) to integrating, equipping, and empowering them actively as agents of the faith and bearers of the Christian gospel:

> God is an agent. God acts in history on behalf of [God's] coming community where justice, liberation, wholeness of life, unity, peace, and the well-being of all peoples are realized. That is the central affirmation to be made about God. It is the good news of what God has done in Jesus Christ.

... We are created by God in God's image. ... The human self, like God, is an agent. ... The self as actor is not an isolated individual. Our existence is dependent upon interactions with God and other persons. ... Our created corporate selfhood places us in an essential relationship with all others.[27]

This theological claim about human agency applies to all people, and children, of course, are fully people. When thinking about children it seems more natural to readily claim that God's creative gift is given to them, but all too often congregations seem reluctant to see the ways that the Holy Spirit may be at work through them as children. How can we ensure that the agency of children is honored? How can we cultivate children as agents of the faith?

The teaching and practice of Jesus in the four Gospels reveal a dynamic perspective of childhood grounded in the full participation of children in the reign of God. Judith Gundry-Volf has explored Jesus' perspective of children in the Gospels and suggests a number of ways that the significance of children is accented in Jesus' teaching and practice.

- **Children as recipients of the reign of God (Mark 10:13-16):** Jesus blesses the children who are brought to him and teaches that "it is to such as these that the kingdom of God belongs." Jesus does not point to what they might become but what they are now. Jesus has a particular concern for the lowly and powerless (in Matthew, note the use of the phrase "the least of these" and "little ones") and claims that they are the beneficiaries in the kingdom.

- **Children as models of entering the reign of God (Mark 10:15):** Jesus says, "whoever does not receive the kingdom of God as a little child will never enter it." Jesus points to children who are not required to be obedient to Jewish law and hence not under obligation to the law. Thus, entering the kingdom "as a child" means to enter dependent entirely upon God, trusting in God as opposed to a trust in any works of one's own doing.

- **Humble like a child (Matthew 18:1-5):** "Who is the greatest in the kingdom of heaven?" Jesus answered, "Whoever becomes humble like this child is the greatest in the kingdom of heaven. Whoever welcomes one such child in my name welcomes me." This warning is particularly for the greatest among Jesus' followers. Those who are "great" stand most in danger of thinking highly of themselves at the expense of others.

- **Serving children and being great (Mark 9:33-37):** "Whoever welcomes one such child in my name welcomes me." This is the language of hospitality, which implies serving children. Caring for children was a low-status activity. To be great in the kingdom, disciples have to love and serve children, specifically.

- **Welcoming children and welcoming Jesus:** To welcome a child in Jesus' name is to welcome Jesus. Welcoming children may also enable one to welcome Jesus, who became like a child.

- **Children and knowledge of Jesus (Matthew 21:14-16, children in the temple praising Jesus):** Children have true insights about who Christ is, and those insights come from God. The religious leaders who "know" the most don't "get it." Children who "know nothing" can also "know divine secrets" and believe in Jesus. Jesus does not commend the children for what they might become or what they might accomplish, but he commends them for who they already are—gifted children of God. [28]

The radical nature of Jesus' teaching and practice regarding children has profound implications for Christian life and practice in congregations today:

> In light of the traditional reception of the New Testament teaching, the most significant challenge before us is to recapture in our own particular contexts the radicalness of Jesus' teaching on children. Children are not only subordinate but sharers with adults in the life of faith; they are not only to be formed but to be imitated; they are not only ignorant but capable of receiving spiritual insight; they are not "just" children but representatives of Christ. What makes that challenge so difficult is that it would entail changing not only how adults relate to children but how we conceive of our social world. Jesus did not just teach how to make an adult world kinder and more just for children; he taught the arrival of a social world in part defined by and organized around children. He cast judgment on the adult world because it is not the child's world. He made being a disciple dependent on inhabiting this "small world." He invited the children to come to him *not* so that he might initiate them into the adult realm but so that they might receive what is *properly theirs*—the reign of God. [29]

Children are not valuable because of what they might become; they are valued and valuable for who they already are: children of God and recipients of the reign of God. The efforts of adults in the faith community should not be directed at turning children into valuable and useful Christians. Rather, it is incumbent on the adult community to find ways to honor and value the unique and authentic gifts that children bring and offer as children. Children and young people need to be nurtured as agents in all aspects of Christian life and practice within the body of Christ.

Agents of faith

To see children as agents of the faith means that the voices and gifts of children are honored and valued, and children are given meaningful and vital roles in the life and ministry of the congregation. It means that people of all ages engage in ministry together. Ministry in the body of Christ is with children, not to or for children. So what might this look like in the life of a congregation? Here are a few examples.

- Create and offer children's activity bags or bulletin inserts that will help children to make connections with what they actually see and hear in worship. In other words, draw children more deeply into the life of worship rather than distracting them from it.

- Instead of having them take sermon notes, invite confirmation students to engage in text study and sermon preparation with the pastor (even if it means springing for some pizza or a few sodas on occasion).

- Involve children and youth in pastoral care, accompanying pastoral leaders, when appropriate, to visit people who are sick and to share communion with homebound members.

- Recruit young people to create and/or manage a Web site for the congregation. This involves young people at the interface between church office, staff, congregational leaders, and communication. Provide opportunities for young people to teach adults in the congregation about the Web site.

- What other examples or ideas can you add to this short list?

Apprenticeship

If an intentionally intergenerational environment seems most conducive for nurturing the faith of young people, then an important question comes to the fore: How can children and youth best learn the faith, discover and exercise their gifts, and live into their calling as sons and daughters of God? I want to offer apprenticeship as a natural and appropriate way to equip and empower young leaders for Christian witness and mission, particularly (1) within an intentionally intergenerational environment and (2) in light of the agency of children in the body of Christ, full participants in the reign of God. In the life of congregations, apprenticeship is the wedding of mentoring and leadership development. In common usage, an apprentice is someone who is learning by practical experience under skilled workers a trade, art or calling. For our purposes here, I am less concerned with apprenticeship as the learning of a trade or an art and more interested in apprenticeship as a crucible within which one catches the faith and lives into one's identity as a child of God. Apprenticeship, at its core, is a deeply relational way of living into one's calling—little by little, day by day—as a full member of the body of Christ.

A few years ago I was traveling on the West Coast. It was Pentecost weekend, and I joined a California congregation for worship. In many ways the service began as garden-variety Lutheran worship—well-done, good music, and lots of red for the occasion. Then came the reading of the texts. Perhaps you can recall the texts set forth for Pentecost Sunday, the first of which is from Acts 2:1-21. It is a powerful and profound text, and none too easy to read, given that the crowd came from places such as Cappadocia, Phrygia, and Pamphylia. A young woman stepped up to the lectern. (I found out later that she was in fifth grade.) She carved up that text from Acts 2, and I mean that in the best sense of the phrase. For two or three minutes she owned that sanctuary. She read carefully, confidently, and deliberately. Her pacing was exquisite. There was passion and inflection in her voice. I was on the edge of my seat; to this day it is hard for me to hear that text read without hearing her voice.

Afterward, I quickly sought her out to thank her for such a fine reading. "How did you learn to read the lessons so well at such a young age?" I asked.

"Jim," she replied.

"Jim?" I responded, looking for more.

"I learned to read the lessons for worship by reading with Jim. He's a really good reader. We take turns reading and listening. Then, before we leave, we pray together."

At another congregation, Ellen and Joan practice and read the texts in worship together. So do Brian and his mother, Kathy. This is apprenticeship

—young people learning and living into their gifts and calling in relationship with others, a bit older perhaps but no less guided by the Spirit. It is within this relational crucible that mutual transformation occurs and people of all ages bloom as they are planted in God's world.

Let's imagine apprenticeship at work from another, quite different perspective. Many congregations have reached the place where young people who are able and willing can participate on the congregational council, with voice and vote. This is no small feat and is to be affirmed. It represents one way that power can be shared with the younger generations by integrating them into the primary decision-making body of a congregation. Yet how are young people prepared and equipped to serve in such a capacity? One way would be to give them their own copy of the council notebook and tell them to enjoy their reading. Most young people I know would file it with the rest of their notebooks—in their backpack—and end up with a heavier back-pack. What if, rather than equipping them with a notebook, we paired them up with another person, say, a council veteran. Someone a bit more seasoned, who has served on the council and knows the kind of things that are not likely to be in a notebook. This becomes their go-to person—for any questions or quandaries, this is the person to whom they can go. A young person is equipped for a particular calling within the congregation, and another generative relationship is fostered within the body of Christ.

Voices, gifts, silliness, chaos

The young people in our midst need to hear clearly that their voices and gifts and silliness—and even the chaos they often bring—are needed and wanted within the body of Christ. "If you are gifted, interested, willing, committed, there is nothing off limits in terms of your participation in this congregation." A message such as this is truly good news for kids. If, indeed, the first act of love is to listen, then children are hungry for times and spaces within which adults will be truly and fully present with them. Children of all ages need adults—parents, teachers, pastors, coaches, the whole people of God—who are present to and with them as people, pilgrims, and sojourners together. Adults are called as spiritual companions to accompany children and help the young discern their gifts, clarify their vocations, and strengthen and deepen the ways they already are proclaiming the praise of God and bearing God's creative and redeeming Word to all the world.[30]

A companion is literally one who shares bread with us as we walk alongside one another. Jesus was such a companion to those with whom he walked, as tired and confused as they were, on that dusty road from Jerusalem to Emmaus (Luke 24:13-35). The Risen One opens up a whole new world to those who are Christ followers, a world where people of all ages walk together along the Way. So often Jesus' first act of love for us is to listen. As we walk alongside one another, may we do the same, focusing on the other, the stranger, the child, the Christ in our midst.

For Reflection and Discussion

- In your opinion, how do adults in the congregation where you worship perceive children? How are children perceived in the larger community where you live?

- How are children perceived and portrayed throughout Scripture? What texts or stories come to mind? Specifically, how did Jesus seem to perceive, understand, and portray children?

- What is the relationship between adults and children in your congregation?

- In what ways are children and youth involved in public leadership in your congregation? What is considered off limits to kids . . . and why?

- How are children and youth "trained" to serve in a particular area of ministry in your congregation?

Imagine this. You walk into the church on Sunday morning. People of all ages are gathering in a fellowship hall. You see a melange of old furniture and plenty of blankets, cushions, and beanbag chairs covering the well-worn carpet. Two tables along one wall hold many kinds of supplies for learning. The room is oriented toward a front, where there is an altar prepared for Eucharist with a large cross that stands behind it, a couple of banners, a reading stand, a piano, a guitar on a stand, music stands, some sound equipment, and some chairs for those who will lead. People of all ages gather in small groups that are a combination of various home configurations. This is intentional—it is clearly stated in the worship packet you received upon entering the space, and the hosts at the door make a point to walk new guests to a small group. It is obvious that each group has a person serving in the role as leader or facilitator.

When you begin, this feels like worship. There is music as you gather. There is a worship leader, a pastor, two musicians, and a small "choir" that helps to lead the assembly's song. After singing a few hymns and songs, the worship leader continues with a greeting and invocation, a responsive litany, and a prayer for the day. A young person comes forward and reads the first lesson. He sits while the "choir" leads the responsive singing of a psalm; he then reads another Bible passage.

The pastor then invites all of the smaller children to come closer and sit toward the front while she reads the gospel and then proceeds to preach something like a children's sermon. However, a number of things stand out. It is longer than the typical children's sermon, and directed at everyone, not just the children, yet a number of times she involves some or even all of them to make a point. It is well done—she communicates clearly and simply, with great sensitivity to the diversity among those gathered, yet neither at the expense of content nor depth. At this point you have been in a form of worship for about 30 minutes.

After singing a song, the worship leader then indicates that for the next 30 minutes you will learn together in your small groups, facilitated by your small group leader. Immediately you look around your group—you and your partner, a retired couple, your group leader and her 10-year-old daughter, a teenage couple, and a single man about age 40—and wonder if this can work. By and large, it does. Your lesson involves the gospel text that was preached, questions and conversation, something like a craft activity for the purpose of evangelism, and prayer. You notice that the group leader has a puppet beside her that was never used and, upon asking, discover that it for smaller children if they are present. It's actually a pretty cool experience.

After about 35 minutes, the worship leader calls your attention back to the front of the worship/Christian education space. The prayers of the people are followed by the sharing of the peace, offering, and then a simple Eucharist led by the pastor. At the time of distribution, your group leader goes to the front and returns with a small tray, which holds a dozen empty miniature chalices, a larger pouring chalice, and a small bowl, containing the host. After the groups commune, there is a prayer, the benediction, and a closing hymn. You have been there for almost 90 minutes.

This case study could be used as the basis for discussion in a learning setting, a small group or a congregational council or committee meeting.

For Reflection and Discussion

- Is this worship or Christian education? What do you make of this?

- This is described as an "intergenerational" case study. What, specifically, makes it intergenerational?

- What do you see as the particular gifts or benefits of an experience such as this?

- Likewise, what do you see as challenges or obstacles to actually doing something like what is described here?

- Could something like this happen in your congregation? What imagination does this spark for possible ministry in your congregation?

Notes

1. The full reference is from *Luther's Works*, vol. 45, "The Estate of Marriage," (1522), (Philadelphia: Fortress, 1962), p. 46: "Most certainly father and mother are apostles, bishops, and priests to their children, for it is they who make them acquainted with the gospel."

2. Barbara Kingsolver, "Somebody's Baby," in *High Tide in Tucson* (New York: Harper Perennial, 1995), p. 103ff.

3. Cf. Marjorie Thompson, *Family: The Forming Center*, now a classic in the field; a variety of research that has emerged from Dr. Peter Benson and Search Institute in recent years; and the work by Dr. David Anderson of the Minneapolis-based Youth & Family Institute, specifically "The Child in Our Hands" initiative.

4. For more information on Search Institute's growing body of research on developmental assets and asset-building communities, visit www.search-institute.org.

5. "Fiery Spirit," by Kate Erb, in Mary Motley Kalergis, *Seen and Heard: Teenagers Speak about Their Lives* (New York: Stewart, Tabori, and Chang, 1998), p. 59.

6. Timothy J. Wengert, "Luther on Children: Baptism and the Fourth Commandment," *Dialog* 37:3 (Summer 1998), p. 187.

7. Ibid., pp. 188, 186.

8. Ibid., p. 189.

9. Thomas H. Groome, *Educating for Life: A Spiritual Vision for Every Teacher and Parent* (Allen, Tex.: Thomas More, 1998), pp. 181-82.

10. I find this metaphor, employed by Kenda Creasy Dean and Ron Foster, a beautifully descriptive and much-needed way of reframing the relationship between adults and kids in ministry. Cf., Dean and Foster, *The Godbearing Life: The Art of Soul Tending for Youth Ministry* (Upper Room, 1998).

11. Holy Baptism, *Lutheran Book of Worship*, p. 124.

12. Urie Bronfenbrenner, *Two Worlds of Childhood* (New York: Pocket Books, 1973), pp. 120-121.

13. Patricia Hersch, *A Tribe Apart* (New York: Fawcett Columbine, 1998), pp. 19-20, 23.

14. Ibid., p. 20.

15. Harold J. Hinrichs, "Intergenerational Living and Worship: The Caring Community," *New Directions in Religion and Aging* (*Journal of Religion & Aging*, vol. 3, nos. 1-2, Fall/Winter 1986), p. 183.

16. Paul D. Hanson, *The People Called: The Growth of Community in the Bible* (San Francisco: Harper & Row, 1986), p. 1. The full text of the Eliot quote reads: "What life have you if you have not life together? There is no life that is not in community, and no community not lived in praise of God."

17. Justo L. González, *Mañana: Christian Theology from a Hispanic Perspective* (Nashville: Abingdon, 1990), pp. 114-115.

18. Wengert, "Luther on Children," p. 186.

19. Hanson, *The People Called*, p. 501.

20. Holy Baptism, *Lutheran Book of Worship*, p. 121.

21. John Westerhoff, *Will Our Children Have Faith?* (New York: Seabury, 1976), p. 83.

22. James Gambone, *All Are Welcome: A Primer for Intentional Intergenerational Ministry and Dialogue* (Crystal Bay: Elder Eye, 1998), p. 63.

23. Ibid., p. vi.

24. Ibid., p. 3.

25. Robert Coles, *The Spiritual Life of Children* (Boston: Houghton Mifflin, 1990), p. 335.

26. Hanson, *The People Called*, pp. 514, 517.

27. Westerhoff, *Will Our Children Have Faith?* pp. 33, 35-36.

28. This is a summary of the essential points made by Judith Gundry-Volf in "To Such as These Belongs the Reign of God," *Theology Today*, 56:4 (January 2000), pp. 469-480.

29. Judith Gundry-Volf, "The Least and the Greatest: Children in the New Testament," *The Child in Christian Thought*, Marcia J. Bunge, ed. (Grand Rapids: Eerdmans, 2001), p. 60. Italics in original.

30. Holy Baptism, *Lutheran Book of Worship*, p. 124.

BIBLIOGRAPHY AND RECOMMENDED RESOURCES

Chapter 1: Theology of Christian Education for Children

Arand, Charles P. *That I May Be His Own: An Overview of Luther's Catechisms* (St. Louis: Concordia Academic Press, 2000). Arand's clear writing makes this a must for any teacher of the catechism. While you will not use the catechism itself with children (since its concepts are more suited to youth and adults), familiarity with the catechisms and their background is excellent preparation for teaching in ways that will prepare children for formal catechetical instruction in the early teenage years.

Conrad, Robert, et al. *Confirmation: Engaging Lutheran Foundations and Practices* (Minneapolis: Fortress Press, 1999). Because the Lutheran definition of confirmation includes all the educational and pastoral ministry of the church to the baptized (from the point of baptism on through young adulthood), many parts of this book are pertinent to educational ministry with children. People from many denominations have found value in this book.

Jenson, Robert W. *Systematic Theology*, vols. 1-2 (New York: Oxford University Press, 1997, 1999). Somewhat longer than Peters but much shorter than Tillich or Pannenberg, Jenson covers the major doctrines of the Christian faith.

Kolb, Robert, and Wengert, Timothy J., eds, *The Book of Concord* (Minneapolis: Fortress Press, 2000). The 16th-century confessions of the Lutheran Church, normative in part or whole for Lutheran churches today. The Evangelical Lutheran Church in America in its constitution accepts the Augsburg Confession and the other confessional writings in *The Book of Concord*.

Krych, Margaret A. *Teaching the Gospel Today: A Guide for Education in the Congregation* (Minneapolis: Augsburg, 1987). A theological look at Christian education with children, based on the theology of Paul Tillich.

Luther, Martin. "To the Councilmen of All Cities in Germany that They Establish and Maintain Christian Schools" (*Luther's Works*, vol. 45, pp. 339-378) and "A Sermon on Keeping Children in School" (*Luther's Works*, vol. 46, pp. 207-258). Also, Melanchthon's "Instructions for the Visitors of Parish Pastors in Electoral Saxony" (*Luther's Works*, vol. 40, pp. 269-320). These writings from the 16th century contain wonderful insights into the importance of education for children in both kingdoms.

Pannenberg, Wolfhart. *Systematic Theology*, vols. 1-3., trans. Geoffrey W. Bromiley (Grand Rapids: Eerdmans, 1991, 1994, 1998). Pannenberg has produced this *Systematic Theology*, which looks at all the great themes of the Christian faith from a contemporary Lutheran point of view. This book contains technical theological language suitable for advanced theological thinker.

Peters, Ted. *God—The World's Future*, 2nd ed. (Minneapolis: Fortress Press, 2000). This is a systematic theology that covers the major Christian doctrines and may help you think about various doctrines from which you may draw implications for church education. Easier reading than Pannenberg.

Tillich, Paul. *The Shaking of the Foundations* (New York: Charles Scribner's Sons, 1948). In Tillich's sermons we see in action the method of correlating human question with gospel answer. Easy reading for those who want to look at the correlation pattern but don't want the depth of his *Systematic Theology*.

_____. *Systematic Theology* (Chicago: University of Chicago Press, 1957). Tillich's three-volume *Systematic Theology* is a monumental work that translates the concepts of the Reformation into terms that are appropriate today. Volume 1 deals with revelation and God. Its introduction is a commentary on question-answer (law-gospel) methodology. Volume 2 expounds the heart of the Reformation faith, the doctrine of justification. Volume 3 deals with the Holy Spirit, church, and God's kingdom, especially in the sections on "The Spiritual Presence and the Ambiguities of Religion" and "The Spiritual Presence and the Ambiguities of Culture." Tillich also draws implications of the gospel for education in the church. Tillich writes further on church education in the article "Creative Love in Education," in *World Christian Education* 18:3, pp. 70, 75.

_____. *Theology of Culture* (New York: Oxford University Press, 1964). Particularly in chapters 11 and 15, Tillich addresses the religious education of children from a theological point of view.

Chapter 2: The Child Grew: Understanding Children's Development

Bruce, Barbara. *Seven Ways of Teaching the Bible to Children* (Nashville: Abingdon Press, 1996). A helpful resource for teachers in the church on how to incorporate the multiple intelligences into their classrooms. Because this was written before Howard Gardner identified the naturalist intelligence, that one is not included.

Elkind, David. *A Sympathetic Understanding of the Child: Birth to Sixteen*, 3rd ed. (Boston: Allyn and Bacon, 1994).

Erikson, Erik. *Childhood and Society* (New York: W. W. Norton, 1963). For people who would like to read more about Erikson's theory as it relates to children, this is the classic text.

Hull, John M. *God-talk with Youth Children: Notes for Parents and Teachers* (Philadelphia: Trinity Press International, 1991). A wonderful book about children as theologians.

Piaget, Jean, and Barbel Inhelder. *The Psychology of the Child* (New York: Basic Books, 1969). This is a basic introduction to Piaget's theory.

Chapter 3: Who Is the Child? Whose Is the Child? A Theology of Children

Billing, Einar. *Our Calling*, trans. Conrad Bergendoff (Rock Island: Augustana, 1958).

Bruce, Gustaf Marius. *Luther As an Educator* (Minneapolis: Augsburg, 1928).

Bunge, Marcia J., ed. *The Child in Christian Thought* (Grand Rapids: Eerdmans, 2001). A thorough review of how children were viewed by theologians and the church through Christian history.

Charlesworth, Marie Louis Charlesworth. *Ministering Children: A Tale* (New York: American Tract Society, ca. 1850s).

Painter, F. V. N. *Luther on Education* (Philadelphia: Lutheran Publication Society, 1889).

Chapter 4: Family Ministry

Benson, Peter L., and Carolyn H. Elkin. *Effective Christian Education: A National Study of Protestant Congregations—A Summer Report on Faith, Loyalty, and Congregational Life* (Minneapolis: Search Institute, 1990).

Garland, Diana R. *Family Ministry: A Comprehensive Guide* (Downers Grove, Ill.: InterVarsity Press, 1999).

Hulbert, Ann, *Raising America* (New York: Knopf, 2003).

Strommen, Merton P., and Richard A. Hardel. *Passing on the Faith: A Radical New Model for Youth and Family Ministry* (Winona, Minn.: St. Mary's Press, 2000).

Web resources

The Center for Family and Community Ministries of Baylor University works with the Center of Congregational and Family Ministries of Louisville Presbyterian Theological Seminary for research, resources, conferences, and networking in areas of family ministry. Visit cfcm@baylor.edu.

The Center for the Prevention of Sexual and Domestic Violence is a non-profit, inter-religious organization that acts as a resource to help religious leaders end abuse and serves as a bridge between the religious and secular communities in addressing issues of domestic violence and sexual abuse. Its Web site can be a valuable starting point for education, resources, and networking. Visit www.cpsdv.org.

Marriage Encounter is the most widely recognized program developed by Christians to strengthen couples in their marriages. Founded by members of the Catholic Church, this independent program has been embraced by many Protestant denominations throughout the world. Visit www.reststop.com/info/marriage/index.html.

Chapter 5: Growing Faithful Children in Media Cultures

Brown, Delwin, et al, eds. *Converging on Culture: Theologians in Dialogue with Cultural Analysis and Criticism* (New York: Oxford University Press, 2001).

Daloz, Laurent, et al. *Common Fire: Leading Lives of Commitment in a Complex World* (Boston: Beacon Press, 1996).

Eisner, Elliot. *The Educational Imagination: On the Design and Evaluation of School Programs* (Prentice Hall, 2001).

Harris, Maria. *Fashion Me a People: Curriculum in the Church* (Louisville: Westminster/ John Knox, 1989).

Heifetz, Ronald. *Leadership without Easy Answers* (Cambridge: Harvard University Press, 1994).

Heifetz, Ronald, and Marty Linsky. *Leadership on the Line: Staying Alive through the Dangers of Leading* (Cambridge: Harvard Business School Press, 2002).

Hess, Mary. "From trucks carrying messages to ritualized identities: Implications of the postmodern paradigm shift in media studies for religious educators," *Religious Education*, vol. 94, no. 3, Summer 1999.

Hoover, Stewart, and Clark, Lynn Schofield, eds. *Practicing Religion in an Age of Media* (New York: Columbia University Press, 2002).

Hoover, Stewart, and Knut Lundby. *Rethinking Media, Religion, and Culture* (Thousand Oaks, Calif: Sage Publications, 1997).

Hull, John. *What Prevents Christian Adults from Learning?* (Philadelphia: Trinity International Press, 1991).

Johnson, Elizabeth. *She Who Is: The Mystery of God in Feminist Theological Discourse* (New York: Crossroads, 1992).

Kegan, Robert. *The Evolving Self: Problem and Process in Human Development* (Cambridge: Harvard University Press, 1982).

_____. *In Over Our Heads: The Mental Demands of Modern Life* (Cambridge: Harvard University Press, 1995).

LaCugna, Catherine Mowry. *God for Us: The Trinity and Christian Life* (San Francisco: HarperSanFrancisco, 1991).

Mitchell, Jolyon, and Sophia Marriage. *Mediating Religion: Conversations in Media, Religion, and Culture* (Edinburgh: T&T Clark/Continuum, 2003).

Palmer, Parker. *To Know as We Are Known* (San Francisco: HarperSanFrancisco, 1993).

_____. *The Courage to Teach: Exploring the Inner Landscape of a Teacher's Life* (San Francisco: Jossey-Bass, 1998).

Vella, Jane. *Learning to Listen, Learning to Teach* (San Francisco: Jossey-Bass, 1997).

Web resources

www.awaytolive.com (music reviews)

www.luthersem.edu/mhess/film.html (film ideas)

www.mediafamily.org/index.shtml (media's influence on children)

www.medialit.org (media literacy)

www.mediatedspirit.com (mass media and entertainment)

www.newmediabible.org (Bible and society)

www.practicingourfaith.org (faith in daily life)

Chapter 6: Growing Faithful Children in the World

Annan, Kofi A. *We the Children: Meeting the Promises of the World Summit for Children* (New York: Unicef, 2001).

Global Mission in the Twenty-First Century (Chicago: Evangelical Lutheran Church in America, Division for Global Mission, n.d.).

Puthiyottil, Cherian, *Our Neighbors: An Introduction to Cultural Diversity and World Religions* (Minneapolis: Augsburg Fortress, 2001).

Stackhouse, Max L., Tim Dearborn, and Scott Paeth, eds., *The Local Church in a Global Era: Reflections for a New Century* (Grand Rapids: Eerdmans, 2000).

The State of the World's Children, 2003 (New York: Unicef, 2002).

Web resources

Division for Global Mission, ELCA: This site contains useful information about the division as well as information about the various Lutheran churches and agencies around the world where there is an ecclesial relationship. Visit www.elca.org/dgm.

Inter-cultural E-mail Classroom Connections (IECC): Three professors from St. Olaf College in Minnesota created this site. It promotes international understanding through the establishing of e-mail pen pals as well as other international exchange projects. Visit www.iecc.org.

Kidlink: This site assists children and youth in becoming more globally aware by connecting them with their peers throughout the world through electronic access. Visit www.kidlink.org.

Rafá Rafá: This site provides information about this simulation game that helps students understand different cultures. This site is the simulation for adolescents and adults that can be a good in-service experience for Sunday school and day school teachers. Visit www.simulationtrainingsystems.com/schools/rafa.html.

The United Nations Cyber School Bus: This site introduces students to the work of the United Nations, information on member nations, curriculum, and activities. Visit www.un.org/Pubs/CyberSchoolBus/index.asp.

World Wide Schools: This site assists elementary school students to have the opportunity to inquire about the world. This site might be particularly helpful to parochial school teachers. It is a program of the Peace Corps. Visit www.peacecorps.gov/wws.

Chapter 7: Building a Children's Ministry Program

Armstrong-Hansche, and Neil MacQueen. *Workshop Rotation: A New Model for Sunday School* (Louisville: Geneva Press, 2000).

Dumke, Miriam. *Entry Points for Nurturing Faith in the Home* (Chicago: Evangelical Lutheran Church in America, Division for Congregational Ministries, 1999).

Foltz, Nancy. *Handbook of Planning in Religious Education* (Birmingham: Religious Education Press, 1999).

Hendrick, Joan. *The Whole Child: Developmental Education for the Early Years*, 7th ed. (Prentice-Hall, 2001).

Krych, Margaret A. "Children and Worship," *Introduction to Sundays and Seasons*, ed. Dennis Bushkovsky (Minneapolis: Augsburg Fortress, 2000), pp. 11-15.

Monroe, Diane. *We've Never Done It That Way Before: A Guide for Assessing and Strengthening Your Sunday School Ministry* (Chicago: Evangelical Lutheran Church in America. Division for Congregational Ministries,1999).

Ratcliff, Donald. *Handbook of Children's Religious Education* (Birmingham: Religious Education Press, 1993).

Ratcliff, Donald, and Blake Neff. *Handbook of Family Religious Education* (Birmingham: Religious Education Press, 1995).

Chapter 8: Let the Little Children Come: Teaching the Bible with Children

Bibles

Adventure Bible (Zondervan). This complete Bible (New International Version) is suitable for children ages 9 to 12. In addition to the full text, there are pictures and activities that older children can engage effectively with the biblical contents.

Adventure Bible for Young Readers (Zondervan). This complete Bible (New International Version) is suitable for children ages 6 to 9. In addition to the full text, there are pictures and activities that young children can engage effectively with the biblical contents.

The Beginner's Bible (Zondervan).This is a good beginning Bible for children under age 6. Although it does not contain the full biblical text, its extensive selection of stories from both Old and New Testaments are told well and illustrated effectively.

Curriculum

Life Together: Revised Common Lectionary Resources for Christian Living (Minneapolis: Augsburg Fortress). This lectionary-based curriculum provides age-appropriate activities that assist children in Sunday school to study the Bible texts that are used in worship each week. In addition, this curriculum offers helpful suggestions for ways that connections can be made between experiencing the Bible story in worship, Sunday school, and daily living.

Reference books

Berryman, Jerome W. *Godly Play: An Imaginative Approach to Religious Education* (Minneapolis: Augsburg, 1991). Berryman offers practical advice for teaching Bible stories to children in ways that engage their imaginations, hearts, and bodies. Pages 29-41 are especially helpful because they provide a concrete description of a successful class session with children that focuses on the parable of the mustard seed.

Cavalletti, Sofia. *The Religious Potential of the Child: The Description of an Experience with Children from Ages Three to Six,* trans. Patricia M. Coulter and Julie M. Coulter (New York: Paulist Press, 1983). Cavalletti offers an insightful and theological perspective on teaching the Bible with children. Influenced by her work with Dr. Maria Montessori,

Cavalletti sets forth compelling and practical advice for teachers. Pictures of classrooms and activities, as well as many of the drawings young children produced are also included.

_____. *The Religious Potential of the Child 6 to 12 Years Old: A Description of an Experience,* trans. Rebekah Rojcewicz and Alan R. Perry (Chicago: Archdiocese of Chicago Liturgy Training Publications, 2002). Cavalletti describes her experiences and offers recommendations for teaching the Bible with older children in the classroom. Pictures of classrooms and activities, as well as many of the drawings young children, are included.

Fowler, James W. *Stages of Faith: The Psychology of Human Development and the Quest for Meaning* (San Francisco: Harper and Row, 1981). Fowler has done extensive research into the process of faith development from infancy to adulthood. Particularly helpful are his insights into human development (part II) and faith development (part IV). Sometimes his language is difficult for those not trained in psychology. A helpful summary of Fowler's insights regarding faith development in children can be found in *The Bible: A Child's Playground.*

Gobbel, A. Roger, and Gertrude G. Gobbel. *The Bible: A Child's Playground* (Philadelphia: Fortress Press, 1986). The Gobbels have presented a comprehensive, readable, and theologically grounded approach to both the why and the how of teaching the Bible with children. This would make a wonderful text for a congregational education committee, as it does its work of designing educational ministries for its children.

Kozol, Jonathan. *Ordinary Resurrections: Children in the Years of Hope* (New York: Crown Publishers, 2000). Although this is not a book specifically concerned with teaching the Bible with children, Kozol writes compellingly about his experiences of sharing the gospel message with children in an after-school program in the South Bronx operated by a local Episcopal parish. Readers will find stories about how to share the gospel with children as well as stories about how children bring hope to the author.

Chapter 9: Teaching to Engage Children

Furnish, Dorothy Jean. *Adventures with the Bible: A Sourcebook for Teachers of Children* (Nashville: Abingdon Press, 1995). A workbook for groups or individuals giving practical advice on how to implement the models Furnish discusses.

_____. *Experiencing the Bible with Children* (Nashville: Abingdon Press, 1990). An appendix entitled "We Lived the Story" gives a fascinating description of one congregation's year-long immersion in the story of Jesus from Advent to Pentecost.

Griggs, Donald L. *Basic Skills for Church Teachers* (Nashville: Abingdon Press, 1985). Offers practical tools for volunteer teachers.

Luetje, Carolyn, and Meg Marcrander. *Face to Face with God in Your Home: Guiding Children and Youth in Prayer* (Minneapolis: Augsburg Fortress, 1995). This excellent handbook discusses each age group from infants to adolescents and describes ways that parents and teachers can assist in their spiritual formation.

O'Neal, Debbie Trafton. *More than Glue and Glitter: A Classroom Guide for Volunteer Teachers* (Minneapolis: Augsburg Fortress, 1992). Contains many practical suggestions for teachers to use in their classrooms.

Chapter 10: The Ministry of Children in Congregations

Across the Generations: Incorporating All Ages in Ministry: The Why and How (Augsburg Fortress: Minneapolis, 2001).

Gambone, James V. *All Are Welcome: A Primer for Intentional Intergenerational Ministry and Dialogue* (Crystal Bay, Minn.: Elder Eye Press, 1998).

Hersch, Patricia. *A Tribe Apart: A Journey into the Heart of American Adolescence* (New York: Fawcett Columbine, 1998).

Strauss, William, and Neil How. *Generations: The History of America's Future, 1584 to 2069* (New York: William Morrow, 1991).

White, James W. *Intergenerational Religious Education; Models, Theory, and Prescription for Interage Life and Learning in the Faith Community* (Birmingham: Religious Education Press, 1988).

Web resource

Generational Inquiry Group: www.millennials.com

SUBJECT INDEX